D1196337

MATTHEW ARNOLD
IN HIS TIME AND OURS

Matthew Arnold in His Time and Ours:

Centenary Essays

Edited by

CLINTON MACHANN
and FORREST D. BURT

University Press of Virginia
Charlottesville

THE UNIVERSITY PRESS OF VIRGINIA
Copyright © 1988 by the Rector and Visitors
of the University of Virginia
First published 1988

Library of Congress Cataloging-in-Publication Data
Matthew Arnold in his time and ours : centenary essays / edited by
  Clinton Machann and Forrest D. Burt.
      p.   cm.
    Papers delivered at a symposium at Texas A & M University, Feb.
28–Mar. 1, 1985.
    Includes index.
    ISBN 0-8139-1173-7
    1. Arnold, Matthew, 1822–1888—Criticism and interpretation—
Congresses.   I. Machann, Clinton.   II. Burt, Forrest D.
PR4024.M376   1988
821'.8—dc19   87-25271
                                                                CIP

Printed in the United States of America

The editors dedicate this book to their wives, Ginny and Veva Nell.

Contents

Acknowledgments

Professor Roger L. Brooks, of Houston Baptist University, whose col-lection of Matthew Arnold's Unpublished, Unrecorded Letters and First and Successive Rare Editions of His Works was acquired by the Sterling C. Evans Library at Texas A&M University in 1983, has been an invaluable consultant throughout the course of the project which has led to this collection of critical essays. His lifelong dedica-tion to Arnold scholarship has served as a model for us.

The early advice and support of Professor Robert H. Super, who served as Distinguished Visiting Professor in the English Department at Texas A&M in 1984, and David J. DeLaura, of the University of Pennsylvania, were also crucial. Generous funding from the Presi-dent's Office, the College of Liberal Arts, and the Department of English, along with the help and cooperation of our department col-leagues, made possible the Matthew Arnold symposium at Texas A&M in the spring of 1985. Included among the participants in that symposium were the Arnold scholars represented in this volume. We are deeply grateful to all the administrators, colleagues, and friends who helped to make this project a success.

Preface

Among the major British Victorian literary figures, Matthew Arnold probably has the most ambiguous reputation today. In a 1973 summary of Arnold criticism for the Modern Language Association's *Victorian Prose: A Guide to Research*, David J. De-Laura referred to "the continuing insecurity of Arnold's reputation as a poet," and, in regard to Arnold's literary theory and criticism, he pointed out that "the value and even the meaning of almost every term or doctrine associated with his name . . . remain matters of controversy." One decade later, a major series of essays published in *Critical Inquiry* made it clear that Arnold's work remained as controversial as ever. In one essay, for example, Eugene Goodheart argues that Arnold's humanistic values are still central to English letters though for many scholars he represents "an abandoned path or a path to be abandoned." Subsequent notes on Arnold scholarship by Fraser Neiman in the *Arnoldian* (Spring 1984) and William B. Thesing in *Victorian Poetry* (Autumn 1985) do not suggest that recent criticism has resolved the Arnold controversy.

As the 1988 centenary of Arnold's death approaches, it becomes particularly appropriate to reevaluate his works and his overall influence on literature and culture in the English-speaking world. The essays in this volume, many of them by the foremost Arnoldians of our time, originated in papers delivered at a symposium devoted to Arnold studies at Texas A&M University in the spring of 1985. They address several, though by no means all, of the major issues in Arnold scholarship today. Although these essays will not clarify in a definitive way Arnold's ambiguous standing in English letters, they show very well why he has been and will continue to be discussed. Arnold clearly was representative of his time and is an essential figure in the study of the nineteenth century, but in important ways his struggles with the moral, intellectual, and aesthetic dilemmas of his day are akin to our own experience a century later.

Probably the most generative line of Arnold research in recent years has been directed toward understanding those elusive key words *culture* and *religion* and, in particular, the dynamic relationship between them. The essays by David J. DeLaura, Ruth apRoberts, and James C. Livingston represent the latest efforts of three important critics taking part in the monumental task of sorting out the complex of meanings involved. DeLaura, author of a landmark article on Arnold and Carlyle (*PMLA*, 1964) and the influential *Hebrew and Hellene in Victorian England* (1969), has in recent years turned to a careful study of Goethe's influence in nineteenth-century England. In "Matthew Arnold and Culture: The History and the Prehistory," he concentrates on English ambivalence toward the Goethean ideal of culture as self-development as it relates to Arnold's search for a general social ideal. Ruth apRoberts, author of the provocative 1983 book *Arnold and God*, in her essay "Arnold and Natural Supernaturalism" continues to explore Arnold's analysis of Christianity focusing on his essential secular concept of culture by locating an antecedent in Carlyle's treatment of Odin as Christ. The increasing emphasis on the centrality of religion in Arnold's works is reaffirmed by Livingston, who, however, differs from apRoberts in placing Arnold in the mainstream of liberal Christian theology. His essay "Matthew Arnold's Place in the Religious Thought of the Past Century" is partially based on his book *Arnold and Christianity* (1986). The dialogue between those scholars who, like apRoberts, argue for Arnold's interpretation of the Scriptures as metaphor and fiction and those who, like Livingston, see him as standing in the modern tradition of Christian humanism, will surely continue to increase the sophistication of the old "poetry versus religion" dichotomy as articulated by T. S. Eliot and others.

The essays by Sidney Coulling, Mary G. McBride, and

Laurence W. Mazzeno and Allan Lefcowitz shed new light on Arnold's views of America. Coulling, best known for his work on the critical reception of Arnold's works and ideas, describes Arnold's special affection for the American South and relates it to his characteristic sense of melancholy. In "Matthew Arnold and Andrew Carnegie: The Religion of Culture and the Gospel of Wealth," McBride examines the curious relationship between the two men. She is certainly correct in describing it as illustrating "one of the most interesting of the anomalies of Arnoldian influence on American civilization." Mazzeno and Lefcowitz's "Arnold and Bryce: The Problem of American Democracy and Culture" serves as a foil to the two previous essays with its view of Arnold as the elitist, antidemocratic critic of America and provocatively invites today's "Arnoldians" to search for internal contradictions in their own cultural values. It also introduces a new case of Arnold's influence, albeit in a negative sense.

The essays by Linda Ray Pratt and Patrick J. McCarthy cast new light on Arnold's poetics. Pratt addresses herself to the controversial topic of nascent modernism in Arnold's poetry. To what extent did Arnold anticipate modernist poetry? In her study, Pratt locates certain images in his work which "momentarily sustain a self-consciously created alternative to reality." Pratt's reading of "Tristram and Iseult" is particularly suggestive. In "Matthew Arnold, the Novel, and the World Without," McCarthy, the author of the important study *Matthew Arnold and the Three Classes* (1964), helps to explain the often-noted fact that Arnold failed to appreciate the novel as a major literary genre. His analysis of the Arnoldian protagonist draws on A. Dwight Culler's study of Arnold's private geography in *Imaginative Reason* (1966) and, once again, suggests the crucial opposition between Arnold's ideal of individual, solitary perfection and social reality, which figures in several other essays.

In their essays, Allan C. Dooley and John P. Farrell openly confront the most fundamentally controversial issue in Arnold studies, one which impinges on almost everything written about Arnold's prose today: Does Arnold's criticism have any validity in today's critical climate? Dooley unabashedly asserts the conservative position of literature as a criticism of life in the

Arnoldian sense and thus can argue for Arnold as an "anti-dote" for the "critical confusion" he sees all around him in academia. Farrell's essay "'What I Want the Reader to See': Action and Performance in Arnold's Prose" suggests an approach to reconciling Arnold's doubleness of individual and social vision that is treated in various ways in this collection. Farrell offers Arnold as a *homo duplex* who was "fundamentally concerned with the problem of connecting action in the world of practice with the inward drives of personal growth and self-culture." Performance analysis and Emile Durkheim's theories of "collective conscience" are employed in a fresh reading of key critical essays by Arnold. Every college instructor who teaches Arnold in the classroom should read the essays by Dooley and Farrell.

Leonard Orr and Saundra Segan Wheeler turn their attention to Arnold's relatively neglected lectures *On the Study of Celtic Literature*. Orr makes use of his background in Irish studies in "The Mid-Nineteenth-Century Irish Context of Arnold's Essay on Celtic Literature" and finds his views to be compatible with, though not influenced by, those of Irish Protestant intellectuals, as he sorts through the various Irish reactions to the lectures. Wheeler emphasizes Arnold's sense of the Celtic tradition as a source of creative energy and imaginative renewal.

The final two essays, by eminent Arnoldians, bring new clarity to the sometimes enigmatic personality of Arnold. Park Honan brings the personal viewpoint of Arnold's biographer to the significant Arnoldian influence on the twentieth-century critics T. S. Eliot and Lionel Trilling. For Honan, Arnold's wit, dandyism, jokes, and slang concealed an early "impressionable sentimentalism," and his disciplined reaction against emotionalism provided an important model for both Eliot and Trilling. On the other hand, Robert H. Super, the editor of Arnold's *Complete Prose Works* (1960–77), in "Sweetness and Lightness: Matthew Arnold's Comic Muse," calls attention to the playful wit and humor that run throughout Arnold's works, including the capacity for self-irony that is sometimes overlooked or underestimated by modern critics. Super's essay, originally delivered as a banquet address, seems appropriate for closing a collection written by and for those critics, and it may help us keep our work—and ourselves—in perspective.

The essays in this centenary collection together demonstrate that it is still profitable to argue about Arnold's works and their significance. Widespread agreement on the precise nature of Arnold's importance in either his own time or ours is unlikely in the near future, for in his evolution from lyric poet to biblical critic he dealt with different areas of human experience in different ways and, most important, shifted his relative emphasis upon central aesthetic, intellectual, and moral issues. In a synchronic sense, however, both his personality and his work were always charged with inner tensions.

The dialectical method that Lionel Trilling long ago noted in Arnold's approach to history can be identified with a deep-seated tendency in Arnold's personality as well as the critical habit of mind he advocated—and demonstrated—in much of his work. In his biography of Arnold, Honan refers to the "subtle, psychological dualism in his thinking [that] made him look for the healthy interaction between amoral and moral forces, between sex and love, beauty and piety, or Hellenism and Hebraism." This dualism at the heart of Arnold's thought and works helps to account for his elusiveness for modern scholars and critics, but it also helps to explain his continuing influence. Though some think that the Arnoldian heritage should be rejected altogether, many others continue to believe that Arnold anticipated our modern dilemmas and that he offers a quality of consciousness and versions of cultural memory and cultural development that still appeal to us.

Walter Houghton taught us to see the significance of the Victorians' realization that they were the first to think of their time in history as an age of transition, "an era of change *from* the past *to* the future." Arnold both affirmed the modern spirit and defended the passing order, constantly struggling to define adequate responses to their various claims upon society. His resistance to mere nostalgia and sentimentality, while insisting on the priority of human experience over abstract systems of thought, can still inspire humanists today in an age of continuing transitions.

In the Afterword, William B. Thesing comments on the essays as they relate to the general state of Arnoldian scholarship and probable lines of development in the future.

References to Arnold's prose are taken from *The Complete Prose Works of Matthew Arnold,* ed. Robert H. Super, 11 vols. (Ann Arbor: University of Michigan Press, 1960–77) and are identified in the text by the abbreviation *CPW* with volume and page numbers. References to Arnold's poetry are from *The Poems of Matthew Arnold,* ed. Kenneth Allott, 2d ed., ed. Miriam Allott (London: Longman, 1979). For the convenience of readers who have access to other editions, references are to line numbers.

MATTHEW ARNOLD
IN HIS TIME AND OURS

David J. DeLaura

ONE

Matthew Arnold and Culture: The History and the Prehistory

The use of the word *culture,* in the sense of *self-development,* as it emerged in England in the nineteenth century, deserves a natural history of its own. Culture, as a free-standing term, came into widespread use around 1850, long before the time, in the 1860s and 1870s, when the term became indissolubly associated with the writings of Matthew Arnold and Walter Pater. The more standard term, the equivalent of the German word *Bildung,* had been *self-development* or *self-cultivation*—and both had a strongly problematic ethical coloration. Above all, this nexus of terms became the center of a widespread dispute over the significance of the life and works of Goethe from the 1820s on. A surprising number of English figures, from the Tennyson generation on, were attracted to the Goethean "view of life," with a strong sense of the privileges of the "Artist": this "temptation of Art," as I think it should be called, was usually put aside, in career after career, but only after a struggle.[1]

English arguments about Goethe and self-development—and there was a great deal of discussion about Goethe (twenty-seven hundred pages have recently been collected)[2]—tended to repeat, though usually without any developed sense of the dynamics of Goethe's career, charges leveled in Germany after 1820: as one reviewer put it, Goethe's "want of heart, laxity in morals, [and] indifferentism in politics."[3] Of course Goethe had his defenders, some of them able, notably Thomas Carlyle, and we know that the generation of Matthew Arnold in the 1840s viewed *Wilhelm Meister* as a manifesto of liberation. Contrary to long-standing assumptions, however, Carlyle's almost hagiographical reading of Goethe's career—that in his works we see an "earnest," toilsome Goethe who suffers through blackness, denial, and despair, moving up finally to light and better vision—was challenged from a very early time, and even Goethe's other defenders stopped well short of such high-flown rhetoric. The uneasiness about Goethe's artistic self-development arose from scattered hints regarding his personality and creative life, repeated often and usually out of context. Particularly damaging was the famous letter to Carl Friedrich Zelter, in which Goethe announced: "The desire to raise my existence, the basis of which is already laid, as high as practicable in the air, absorbs every other desire, and scarcely ever quits me."[4] Or Goethe's much-cited remark to Johannes Falk: "Religion and politics are a troubled element for Art: I have always kept myself aloof from them as much as possible."[5]

The earlier standard usage of *culture* was prepositional, with a strong educational content: the culture *of* the mind, *of* the faculties, *of* the poet, and the like. Carlyle's chief innovation in his early essays was his frequent addition of adjectival modifiers—with a clear developmental force: human or universal culture; or moral, philosophical, or intellectual culture. Very rarely does the word *culture* stand alone: for example, in Carlyle, Goethe's "culture was too high" to be understood by his generation.[6] Only once does Carlyle reach for a high generalization, in the 1827 Richter essay, which looks back to the tradition of the Weimar Germans and anticipates John Stuart Mill and Matthew Arnold more fully. In this German context, which nevertheless carefully avoids mention of Goethe, we hear that "the first and last of all culture" is a "harmonious development of being": "the great law of culture is: Let each become all that he was created capable of being; expand, if possible, to his full growth; resisting all impediments, casting off all foreign . . . adhesions; and show himself at length in his own shape and stature."[7] (That is not, perhaps, a very characteristically Carlylean statement, but it is prophetic of later developments.) To this should be added the often-cited sentence in Coleridge's *On the Constitution of Church and State* (1830) on the need to ground a "progressive civilization" "in *cultivation, in the harmonious development of those qualities and faculties that characterise our *humanity.*"[8] (Raymond Williams in *Culture and Society* places an improbable amount of weight on that single sentence of Coleridge's;[9] but Carlyle comes three years earlier, in 1827, and the German context is, I think, far more "explanatory.")

And so it is not surprising that the terms *culture* and *self-culture,* even as they assumed a more distinct shape at mid-century, came loaded down with what we might call heavy ideological burdens. Apart from the more general ethical problem of establishing a secular ideal of *self*-development with a strong "aesthetic" twist, the tradition of *Bildung* in late eighteenth-century Germany had from the beginning implied a rivalry with, even a contempt for, traditional religion. Above all, Goethe's is the haunting shadow-presence, unshakably attached to the word and idea wherever they go.

I offer here a few illustrations of culture and its concurrent embarrassments at midcentury. The free-standing term *culture* pops up here and there in the 1840s, often without ethical entanglements, to meet a new need—for example, in the writings of G. H. Lewes, and, in one memorable place, John Sterling.[10] But it is *self*-culture and *self*-cultivation, in a Goethean context, that generated by far the most interesting responses. Singular in its high intellectual quality and the lonely extremity of its views is Lewes's 1843 essay, which takes up the charge that Goethe was "an *Egoist*" and boldly defends the "dogma of self-culture" in Goethe, a man whose "object in life was . . . to develope his spiritual nature."[11] And *doubts* about Goethe's lifelong devotion to his own "development," which were of course more common, could now be masked in an elaborate pretense of objectivity, as in an 1844 review by Jane Sinnett, one of the most able readers of German literature in the period. She calmly says that Carus, one of Goethe's German apologists, well defends Goethe's "egoism—that complete living for himself which has caused so many expressions of dislike," as well as Goethe's preoccupation with "a career of self-cultivation," indifferent to charges of self-centeredness. And even when she makes a not uncommon contrast between the "two egoists," Rousseau and Goethe—"that between a child crying for the moon, and a Jupiter calmly smiling at the world below him"— the effect of the ostensible praise is certainly chilling and somewhat skeptical.[12] (And if we hear in this a prediction of Matthew Arnold's complex portrait of Goethe, a few years later in "Memorial Verses," calmly and analytically looking down at the maelstrom of modern European history, I do not think we would be wrong.[13])

Less subtle but of even greater importance in the period was the approach of the tart-tongued Herman Merivale, in a widely noticed attack in the *Edinburgh Review* in 1850. "What was left," he asks, "for those who had witnessed the decline of both [Voltaire and Rousseau], except the philosophy which turns from the unsolved enigmas of man's general nature and destinies to the cultivation of the self" and which "teaches men that the real aim of existence in this world is refined enjoyment of it?" There is a cleverly malicious use of paradox in Merivale's concentration on Goethe's "subjecting all irregular impulses to a course of disciplined self-indulgence." Goethe's acclaimed "virtues" take on a sinister tone as Merivale speaks of Goethe's "habits of self-contemplation and self-worship" and his "grand object of harmoniously blending sensual and intellectual delights in the nicest proportions." He concludes: "Genius of the highest order was never employed in developing a system more seductive to human weakness."[14] Heavy-handed as it may seem to us, this review in fact marked an epoch in the lives of some susceptible young readers. G. D. Boyle was a young Oxonian at the time, and almost forty years after the event he remembered J. C. Shairp, who had been at Oxford with Matthew Arnold, exhorting him to read the review. Boyle suggests that Merivale helped dispel the "Goethe worship," as he calls it, that had afflicted so many Oxford men of that generation.[15]

That was in July 1850. Wordsworth had died in April, and *The Prelude* first appeared that summer. Arnold's elegiac poem "Memorial Verses" was written just after the death, and he was not alone in being moved to reassess the significance of the era of Goethe, Byron, and Wordsworth. The liberal clergyman Charles Kingsley, who always "despised and loathed" (to use his own characteristic language) the modern Goethean notion of the "artist,"[16] had written his "Master," the theologian F. D. Maurice, after reading Wordsworth's poem, and Maurice replied:

> I am sure you are right, Wordsworth's Prelude seems to me the dying utterance of the half century we have just passed through, the expression . . . of all that self-building process in which, according to their different schemes and principles, Byron, Goethe, Wordsworth, the Evangelicals (Protestant and Romanist), were all engaged, which their novels, poems, experiences, prayers, were setting forth, in which God, under whatever name, or in whatever aspect He presented Himself to them, was still the agent only in fitting them to be world-wise, men of genius, artists, saints.[17]

As Maurice said later to Kingsley, rather prematurely no doubt, "The age of mere self-culture is over."[18]

The years around 1850 saw a good deal of such intellectual and spiritual resettlement, and decisions were made in the lives of a surprising number of people of two generations. Among those contributing to the clarification of the tangled issues of culture, self-culture, art, and Goethe were two of those "masters of the mind" who were judged by some observers to have unsettled the generation of Matthew Arnold and Arthur Hugh Clough in the 1840s. I am referring to Emerson and Carlyle. In that same busy year, 1850, Emerson—who was widely read and reviewed in England—culminated a long debate among the American Transcendentalists, when, though paying tribute to his realism and unwearied effort, he harshly lashed out against a Goethe "incapable of a self-surrender to the moral sentiment," a man whose devotion was not "to pure truth; but to truth for the sake of culture."[19] Carlyle, meanwhile, had so far moved from his own German "aesthetic" dreams of the 1820s that he had denounced "high art" to Emerson during the latter's visit in 1847: "Yes, [Carlyle insisted] Kunst is a great delusion, and Goethe and Schiller wasted a great deal of time on it."[20] This revulsion against the "Goethean" point of view reached a climax in 1851, in *The Life of John Sterling*, when Carlyle scornfully asserted: "It is expected in this Nineteenth Century that a man of culture should understand and worship Art"—the delusion that had led Sterling astray.[21] (The name of Goethe, however, whom Carlyle regularly protected, is not introduced in this public context regarding issues that were almost universally associated with Goethe in the period.)

I suggest, further, that Matthew Arnold's place in this "1850" situation—whether we consider it the end of the "era of mere self-culture" or the inception of culture's most public and English phase—is much more complex than we have tended to suppose. He himself could use the new term in the modern and neutral sense, though in an amusing context. In March 1853 Arnold was reading the *Memoirs* of the late Margaret Fuller prepared by Emerson and others, and in writing Clough he acknowledged "her exquisite intelligence and fineness of aperçus." But he also deplored the "absence of men of any culture in America," which "must have made her run so wildly, and for many years made her insufferable."[22] (That is also, of course, an implicit indictment of Emerson and his circle.) The "man of culture," it will be recalled, had been Carlyle's rather disgusted usage in 1851. In 1853, the term acquired a new coloration, when in the conclusion to the Preface to his *Poems*, Arnold supports his severe judgment that his is an age wanting in "moral grandeur" and "spiritual health," by appealing to the judgments passed "by the men of strongest head and widest culture whom [the age] has produced; by Goethe and by Niebuhr" (*CPW,* 1:14). It is noteworthy that four years later, in the third edition of the *Poems*, Arnold not uncharacteristically divides his praise more meticulously: now, Goethe is the man "of strongest head," and Niebuhr, the great classical historian, the man "of widest culture" (*CPW,* 1:256). The distinction is, again, prophetic: in the 1860s, although Goethe was acknowledged to be the greatest poet of modern times and the greatest critic of all times, he was never admitted into the circle of the "great men of culture," those more benign Germans such as Herder, Lessing, and Humboldt (*CPW,* 5:113;

3:301). It is as if the very "predominance" in Goethe of "intellectual power" disqualified him as a model for the fullness of Arnold's own gradually emerging "culture"-ideal.[23]

In November 1853, at any rate, Arnold rather gracelessly turned back Clough's praise of "The Scholar-Gipsy," one of Arnold's most "regressive" poems, asking, "What does it *do* for you?" and then citing his own recent lines: "The complaining millions of men / Darken in labour and pain."[24] To put the matter schematically, the unblinkable *facts* of the unsolved nineteenth-century social problem were already forcing Arnold to put aside, however reluctantly, his early dreams of a detached and elevated mode of consciousness and creativity— the Goethean paradigm of the self-culture of the artist, as developed, for example, in the poem "Resignation."

But this drift in Arnold's thought and feeling—in effect a movement away from Goethe—though partially caught and approved by Clough in his review of Arnold's first two volumes,[25] was not evident to most of Arnold's early readers, and the words *culture* and *self-culture* are threaded through the first reviews in an accusatory tone and with a "diminishing" effect. Fittingly, it was Charles Kingsley, again, who established the terms and the disapproving manner with which Arnold's first volumes were received—Charles Kingsley, a fervent disciple of Thomas Arnold. He cries out in 1849, reviewing *The Strayed Reveller:* "To what purpose all the self-culture through which the author must have passed," if, with his "hungry abstractions . . . stolen from the dregs of German philosophy," he offers the public only "dreamy, transcendental excuses for laziness"?[26] Soon thereafter, the satirist W. E. Aytoun, who kept an equally censorious eye on contemporary poetry, expressed his "dissatisfaction at the perversion of a taste which, with so much culture, should have been capable of better things."[27] Arnold's second volume, *Empedocles on Etna* (1852), drew more of the same fire. A young Oxford graduate complained that, though "a man of high culture," of "culture and refinement," Arnold lacked sympathy with the present generation and preached an "indolent, selfish quietism," a "complacent reverie, and refined indolence."[28] The most developed of such reactions was that of Clough, who, after woundingly listing Arnold's virtues—his refined and "highly educated sensibilities,—too delicate, are they, for common service?"—sharply insisted that Arnold's was a philosophy of German "transcendental doubt," an "ascetic and timid self-culture," that embraced "reflectiveness" to the exclusion of "confidence." Clough was suggesting, in effect, that "the dismal cycle of [Arnold's] rehabilitated Hindoo-Greek theosophy" made him the prime English example of "an over-educated weakness of purpose," detectable throughout western Europe, that encouraged "a disposition to press too far the finer and subtler susceptibilities."[29]

Even Arnold's third volume, the *Poems* of 1853, could be similarly pursued—in this case by a "hard" High Church Oxford associate of Arnold's—for presenting "a sceptical train of thought," "clothed with the graces of a refined and scholarlike diction."[30] But perhaps the most interesting use of *culture* is as a form of more subtle disparagement and diminishment. G. H. Lewes writes in this vein of Arnold, as "a scholar, and one of poetical tendencies rather than of poetical genius, a man of culture, reflection, and sensibility" rather than a natural singer; Arnold "naturally looks to Greece for inspiration," and his "fit audience is that of the cultured few."[31] And yet another of Arnold's fellow Oxonians presents him as "a man of undeniable culture," with a mind "of the cultivated and artistic order," who aspires to "a place among the learned and artistic poets," instead of the natural or unlearned race of poets. He disapproves of Arnold's philosophy of "blank dejection and fatalistic apathy" and advises him "to forget all his poetic theories, ay, and Homer and Sophocles, Milton and Goethe, too," and to speak directly from his experience.[32]

This derogatory view of the poetry of "culture" (not wholly unlike the modern disparagement of "academic poetry") goes back at least to John Stuart Mill's discussion of "the two kinds of poetry" in 1833: he had contrasted the "poet by nature," the creature of "intense sensibility," represented by Shelley, with the poet of "mere culture," who had "a cultivated but not naturally poetic mind," represented by Wordsworth.[33] And so Matthew Arnold is, in effect, the second "poet of culture": but in the intervening two decades the newly emergent term, as we have seen, had quickly acquired troublesome overtones. Arnold was the poet of culture, not merely because he was classical and scholarly and (as we might say) elitist, but because he had almost single-handedly created in mid-Victorian England a new and challenging view of life—*his* culture and *his* self-culture were too Greek, too "pagan," too German and Goethean, too quietistic, to be endorsed readily in an England absorbed by prosperity, activism, and the splendors of the Crystal Palace. In fact, perhaps the most adequate and serious response to Arnold's early Hellenism, paganism, and culture is that embodied in Robert Browning's "Cleon." We now know that the Brownings were reading Arnold and Clough from the very first; and it is evident that Robert Browning at once singled out Arnold as a new and serious challenge to his own most deeply held views of life. More specifically, "Empedocles on Etna" solidified Browning's suspicions and provided a constantly revisited basis for the lifelong ironies he directed against the modern culture ideal.[34]

A further sure sign of the complexity and challenge of the term *culture* is the quick rise of its comic or ironic possibilities. Clough, for example, in *Amours de Voyage* (begun in 1849), uses the term in a deliberately weary and knowing way; the antihero Claude speaks about the social pretensions of the hapless middle-class Trevellyns: "Is it not fitting that wealth should tender this homage to culture?"[35] And David Masson, later to be famous as a Milton scholar, in an elaborate contrast of Goethe with Shakespeare in 1852, speaks in deadpan fashion of Goethe as an Apollo, "a Jupiter, composed, stately, serene," "daily doing something for his own culture and for that of the world," and suddenly he suggests that of Shakespeare's daily thoughts a much smaller space was occupied by "literature and culture and all that."[36] This, at the very beginning of the era of "Arnoldian" culture, is a "modern," nervous usage of the sort we might employ ourselves.

Perhaps not surprisingly, *culture* and *self-culture*, in a derogatory sense and in a Goethean context, were to plague estimates of Arnold's poetry to the very end of his life. Part of this "comedy" of culture became evident much later, in Arnold's discomfort over Swinburne's extravagant praise of his *New Poems* of 1867. What the midcentury critics had so deplored in

Arnold, Swinburne now converted into virtues, making Arnold's early "poetry of the intellect" a sort of sublime "Greek" paganism, preaching "the creed of self-sufficience" and the duty of "intellectual self-reliance" and "self-dependence." Arnold, then in the act of planning the defense of his now much more benign culture ideal as presented in "Sweetness and Light," bemoaned that Swinburne's inconvenient praise had inclined the religious journals to see in his writings "a crusade against religion."[37]

It seems not to have been noticed that throughout the 1850s, as John Stuart Mill developed his defense of the greatest variety of human development through the "culture" and the "cultivation" of the human faculties (with a nod to the Germans, especially Humboldt), culminating in *On Liberty* (1859), he was continually aware of Goethe as an attractive threat to his social and morally "militant" version of culture. This is the Goethe who, as Mill said, tried to defend his indefensible "views of morals and of conduct in life" by incessantly invoking "the theory of the right and duty of self-development."[38] In 1838, Mill had rejected the Carlylean reading of Goethe's career: "that a thoroughly earnest mind may struggle upwards through the region of clouds and storms to an untroubled summit, where all other good sympathies and aspirations confound themselves in a serene love and culture of the calmly beautiful—looking down upon the woes and struggles of perplexed humanity with as calm a gaze (though with a more helping arm), as that of him who is most placidly indifferent to human weal."[39] In February 1854, the year Mill wrote the first version of *On Liberty* as a short essay, he elaborated further on his disapproval of Goethe's preoccupation with "the Beautiful" and his own "mental tranquillity and health."[40] In his diary Mill firmly rejected Carlyle's holding up of "Goethe's ideal of life" as the model for modern life and the modern mind: "He [Goethe] wished life itself, and the nature of every cultivated individual in it, to be rounded off and made symmetrical like a Greek temple or a Greek drama," whereas modern life demands, not "symmetry, but bold free expansion in all directions," strong and varied faculties, not the "well-proportioned" faculties of an Apollo.[41] There was no greater threat to the stilted moral posture of Mill and his fellow English freethinkers than the possibility that the ideal of development "on all sides" might well lead not only to the flagrant service of the French goddess Lubricity but also to the more subtle allure of a Goethean "aesthetic" moral indifference.[42]

As is evident, I see the powerful and paradoxical figure of Goethe—the "glorious devil" of Tennyson's "The Palace of Art"—haunting these extraordinarily tangled issues of culture and self-development and forcing critic after critic to adopt special and sometimes uncomfortable strategies. I end with three citations that convey some of the hard-to-describe aftertaste of the "Goethean" element in nineteenth-century English intellectual life. F. D. Maurice, who agreed with Kingsley that the era of self-culture was at an end, declined to join Kingsley in wishing that Goethe had never existed: "He seems to me the most perfect specimen of a genius of which I do not desire the multiplication, but which in itself is very valuable"[43]—a generous concession, coming as it does from an essentially cautious clergyman.

And there is John Morley, one of the "hard" freethinkers of the period and a disciple of John Stuart Mill, who had several years before, in a notorious outburst, excoriated the lasciviousness and immorality of Swinburne's poetry. But he seemed unaffected by his master's misgivings about Goethe: in 1870, speaking in the solemn tones he was capable of, he says that Goethe is the poet of "that new faith which is as yet without any universally recognized label, but whose heaven is an ever-closer harmony between the consciousness of man and all the natural forces of the universe; whose liturgy is culture, and whose deity is a certain high composure of the human heart"—precisely that pseudo-Greek and Goethean ideal of serenity and elevation already severely challenged by Mill, even if mostly in private.[44] And finally, the great Liberal statesman and troubled defender of traditional Christianity, William E. Gladstone, may have been speaking for many when he said, as late as 1880 and in a puzzled tone of voice, "I am unable to answer the question whether he has or has not been an evil genius of humanity."[45]

These are some of the episodes in a comedy, a high and

serious intellectual comedy, and one of the most significant of the nineteenth century. An unchallengeable shibboleth of our time is that of the paradoxical *duty* of "self-development" and "self-realization," ranging from the jargon of child psychology to California psychobabble. The Victorian debate over the issues, though certainly diffuse, helps us grasp the more underlying cultural issues and fills in the backdrop of our own unexamined certainties—including that even larger and related idea of "progress." We may wonder whether, in our more detached and academic way, we are not confused about these issues still though less aware of their ethical, social, and philosophical dimensions, as well as their genesis.

NOTES

1. I have treated the earlier history of the term in English, starting in the 1820s, in "Heroic Egotism: Goethe and the Fortunes of *Bildung* in Victorian England," in *Johann Wolfgang von Goethe: One Hundred Fifty Years of Continuing Vitality,* ed. Ulrich Goebel and Wolodymyr T. Zyla (Lubbock: Texas Tech University Press, 1984), pp. 41–60.

2. In *The Reception of Classical German Literature, 1760–1860,* ed. John Boening, 10 vols. (New York: Garland, 1977). Because Boening's format makes it difficult to determine page numbers in the original, I hereafter give the source first, with full pagination, followed by the exact reference in Boening.

3. *Spectator* 28 (1835):1138–40; Boening 7:400.

4. Quoted from G. H. Lewes, *The Life of Goethe,* 2d ed. (London: Smith Elder, 1864), p. 260.

5. Quoted from Sarah Austin, *Characteristics of Goethe, from the German of Falk, von Müller &c.,* 3 vols. (London: Effingham Wilson, 1833), 2:121.

6. *The Works of Thomas Carlyle,* ed. H. D. Traill, Centenary Edition, 30 vols. (London: Chapman & Hall, 1896–99), 23:22.

7. Ibid., 26:20, 19.

8. John Colmer, ed., *On the Constitution of the Church and State, The Collected Works of Samuel Taylor Coleridge* (Princeton: Princeton University Press, 1976–), 10:42–43.

9. Williams discusses the passage in Pt. I, chap. 3, of *Culture and Society, 1780–1950* (New York: Columbia University Press, 1958).

10. "Characteristics of German Genius" (1842), *Essays and Tales by John Sterling*, with a Memoir of His Life by Julius Charles Hare, 2 vols. (London: Parker, 1848), 1:409. *"Earnestness of heart"* is the source from which flows "culture, knowledge, and reflection, the seriousness that will to careless eyes appear mysticism, the affectionateness that fills a a life and book with warmth." Culture here fits at the extreme "knowledge" end of a spectrum of approved human qualities. And see Morris Greenhut, "George Henry Lewes and the Classical Tradition in English Criticism," *Review of English Studies* 4 (1948):126–37, esp. 127: "In his conception of culture and the function of criticism [Lewes] anticipates many of the fundamental ideas of Matthew Arnold." But the uses he cites are, in my judgment, almost casual and lacking in "weight." A benign usage in a directly educational context occurs in the Prologue (written in 1842) of Tennyson's *The Princess* (1847): the maiden Aunt "preached / An universal culture for the crowd, / And all things great" (*The Poems of Tennyson*, ed. Christopher Ricks [London: Longmans, Green, 1969], p. 746). A very early and prophetic but equally unproblematic usage became available in 1850, in Wordsworth's *The Prelude* 13:197–98: "where grace / Of culture hath been utterly unknown"—about human development in its relation to "courteous usages refined by art" (William Wordsworth, *The Prelude, 1799, 1805, 1850*, ed. Jonathan Wordsworth, M. H. Abrams, and Stephen Gill [New York: Norton, 1979], p. 447).

11. *British and Foreign Review* 14 (1843):78–135; Boening 7:304, 311, 315.

12. *Foreign Quarterly Review* 32 (1843):99–103; Boening 7:330, 331.

13. On Arnold's relations with Goethe, see David J. DeLaura, "Arnold and Goethe: The One on the Intellectual Throne," in *Victorian Literature and Society: Essays Presented to Richard D. Altick*, ed. James R. Kincaid and Albert J. Kuhn (Columbus: Ohio State University Press, 1984), pp. 197–224.

14. *Edinburgh Review* 92 (1850):188–220; Boening 7:351, 352, 355, 360.

15. G. D. Boyle, in William Knight, *Principal Shairp and His Friends* (London: John Murray, 1888), p. 152.

16. See, e.g., "The Poetry of Sacred and Legendary Art," *Fraser's Magazine*, Mar. 1848, cited here from his *Literary and General Lectures and Essays* (London: Macmillan, 1880), p. 199: he praises Anna Jameson for not viewing pious legends "with the cold unbelieving eye of a Goethe, merely as studies of 'artistic effect.'"

17. Letter to Charles Kingsley, Feb. 25, 1851, in *The Life of Frederick Denison Maurice*, ed. Frederick Maurice, 2 vols. (London: Macmillan, 1884), 1:63. We lack Kingsley's prior letter to Maurice.

18. Letter to Kingsley, Aug. 29, 1855, in ibid., 2:266. Kingsley in his letter of August 6 (in Margaret Farrand Thorp, *Charles Kingsley, 1819–1875* [Princeton: Princeton University Press, 1937], p. 124), had said: "I despise and loathe the notion [of being "an artist"] from the bottom of my heart. I have felt its temptation: but I *will* by God's help, fight against that." He announces his intention of including in his next novel "a man who wants to be an 'artist' like old Goethe, (of whom I think less, if not worse, the longer I live) and finds that he becomes, artist or none, a very confused fellow rapidly going to hell." The reference is to Elslie Vavasour (alias John Briggs) in *Two Years Ago* (1857). Early in chapter 9, Marie, a viscountess, speaks scornfully of expenditure on "self-education, and the patronage of art, and the theatre": "Christ was of old the model, and Sir Galahad was the hero. Now the one is exchanged for Göthe, and the other for Wilhelm Meister" (*Two Years Ago* [New York: Publishers Plate Renting Co., n.d.], p. 152).

19. *Representative Men* (1850), in *The Complete Works of Ralph Waldo Emerson*, ed. Edward Waldo Emerson, 12 vols. (Boston: Houghton Mifflin, 1903), 4:284.

20. *English Traits* (1856), in ibid., 5:274.

21. *Life of John Sterling* (1851), in Carlyle, *Works* 11:174.

22. Letter of Mar. 21, 1853, in *Letters of Matthew Arnold to Arthur Hugh Clough*, ed. Howard Foster Lowry (London: Oxford University Press, 1932), p. 132 (hereafter cited as *LC*).

23. Letter of Dec. 17, 1860, in *Letters of Matthew Arnold, 1848–1888*, ed. George W. E. Russell, 2 vols. in 1 (New York: Macmillan, 1900), 1:147 (hereafter cited as Arnold, *Letters*).

24. Letter of Nov. 30, 1853, citing "The Youth of Nature," ll. 51–52; *LC*, p. 146.

25. "Recent English Poetry," *North American Review*, July 1853, cited here from *Selected Prose Works of Arthur Hugh Clough*, ed. Buckner B. Trawick (University, Ala.: University of Alabama Press, 1964), pp. 142–71, esp. 159.

26. Charles Kingsley, *Fraser's Magazine* 29 (1849):575–80, quoted here from *Matthew Arnold: The Poetry: The Critical Heritage*, ed. Carl Dawson (London: Routledge, 1973), pp. 42, 44, 45 (hereafter cited as *ACH*).

27. W. E. Aytoun, *Blackwood's Magazine* 66 (1849):340–46; *ACH*, p. 52.

28. Apparently G. D. Boyle, *North British Review* 9 (1853):209–14; *ACH*, pp. 68–70.

29. *Selected Prose Works of Clough*, pp. 153, 163, 164.

30. J. D. Coleridge, *Christian Remembrancer* 27 (1854):310–33; *ACH*, pp. 110–11.

31. G. H. Lewes, *Leader*, Nov. 26 and Dec. 3, 1853, pp. 1146–47, 1169–71; *ACH*, p. 83.

32. Probably J. C. Shairp, *North British Review* 21 (1854):493–504; *ACH*, pp. 122, 119.

33. "The Two Kinds of Poetry," *Monthly Repository* n.s., 7 (Oct. 1833):714–24, quoted here from *Autobiography and Literary Essays*, ed. John M. Robson and Jack Stillinger, *Collected Works of John Stuart Mill* (Toronto: University of Toronto Press, 1981–), 1:354–65 (hereafter cited as Mill, *Works*).

34. For the Brownings reading Arnold and Clough in December 1849, see *The Letters of Elizabeth Barrett Browning to Mary Russell Mitford, 1836–1859*, ed. Meredith B. Raymond and Mary R. Sullivan, 3 vols (Winfield, Kan.: Armstrong Browning Library, Browning Institute, Wedgestone Press, and Wellesley College, 1983), 3:286. The relationship between the two poems was first pursued by A. W. Crawford, "Browning's 'Cleon,'" *Journal of English and Germanic Philology* 20 (1927):485–90. A perceptive recent treatment is that by John Coates, "Two Versions of the Modern Intellectual: 'Empedocles on Etna' and 'Cleon,'" *Modern Language Review* 79 (1984):769–84.

35. *The Poems of Arthur Hugh Clough*, 2d ed., ed. F. L. Mulhauser (Oxford: Clarendon Press, 1974), p. 98.

36. *British Quarterly Review* 16 (1852):512–43; Boening 7:375.

37. Letter to his mother, Nov. 16, 1867, Arnold, *Letters*, 1:436.

38. Mill, *Works*, 1:260.

39. Ibid., pp. 477–78.

40. Ibid., p. 249.

41. Mill's diary, Feb. 6, 1854, in *The Letters of John Stuart Mill*, ed. Hugh S. R. Elliot, 2 vols. (London: Longmans, Green, 1910), 2:368.

42. "on all sides": *On Liberty*, in Mill, *Works* 18:263.

43. Letter of Aug. 29, 1855, in *Life of Maurice* 2:266.

44. John Morley, *Fortnightly Review*, Dec. 1870, quoted from *Byron: The Critical Heritage*, ed. Andrew Rutherford (New York: Barnes

and Noble, 1970), p. 388. Morley's excoriation of *Poems and Ballads,* in *Saturday Review,* Aug. 4, 1866, pp. 145–47, is most readily available in *Swinburne: The Critical Heritage,* ed. Clyde C. Hyder (New York: Barnes and Noble, 1970), pp. 22–29.

45. Letter of Oct. 9, 1880, quoted in John Morley, *The Life of William Ewart Gladstone,* 3 vols. (London: Macmillan, 1903), 2:534.

RUTH apROBERTS

TWO

Arnold and Natural Supernaturalism

In 1956 Kathleen Tillotson said that it might "seem surprising" to link the names of Carlyle and Arnold. She did her work so well that now no Arnoldian can ignore Carlyle, and Carlylean lineaments appear everywhere below the surface of Arnold's writings. She amassed an impressive set of echoes in the poetry: the *languid doubt,* the *spark from heaven,* the *ignorant armies clash by night*—all are echoes in Arnold's poetry of Carlyle's poetic prose. There seems no end to these; I have especially noted the original of the Scholar Gipsy's listening "with enchanted ears, / From the dark dingles, to the nightingales!" (ll. 219–20) in Carlyle's translation of *Wilhelm Meister.*[1] Kathleen Tillotson also indicates some of the vital intellectual connections—and the persistent ambiguity of Arnold's attitude to Carlyle—and observes how Arnold repeatedly praises Carlyle only to explain how wrong he is. The rhetorical device, she says, "might be called presenting a bunch of snakes tied up with flowers."[2] David DeLaura enlarged the investigation with his classic *PMLA* essay of 1964, "Arnold and Carlyle," which focuses mainly on the Carlylean elements in the prose of the 1860s, showing how Arnold "suppresses consciously or otherwise, the degree of his substantive agreement with Carlyle's views on the nature of the social and moral crisis of the nineteenth century, as well as some of its solutions."[3] This peculiarly suppressed debt becomes more apparent the more familiar one is with Arnold. One becomes more and more aware of a sort of ground-base of Carlylean thought, not to mention the melodic verbal echoes. And it seems to me in the area of religion, the connection is more radical, more basic, than in the social and moral lines.

I propose to take up just one Carlylean text, the first lecture in *Heroes and Hero-Worship*, "Odin, the Hero as Divinity," and trace some of its effects in Arnold's writings.

The Odin lecture is among other things a fine *teaching* piece, on the then little-known Norse mythology. Carlyle used Paul Henri Mallet's *Northern Antiquities* (1770) in Bishop Percy's translation from the French, and Mallet used Saemund's Elder or Poetic Edda, Snorri Sturluson's Younger or Prose Edda, and Saxo Grammaticus's *Gesta Danorum;* Carlyle also used the more recent Jakob Grimm's *Deutsche Mythologie* and Ludwig Uhland's *Der Mythus von Thor.* It seems to me somewhat more than probable that Arnold's interest was piqued when Carlyle described Balder: "the White God, the beautiful, the just and benignant (whom the early Christian Missionaries found to resemble Christ)."[4] There is little question that the Odin lecture was the inspiration for Arnold's poem "Balder Dead." Arnold did go back to Carlyle's main source, Mallet, but there are certain marks of Carlyle's own lecture on Arnold's poem. In the course of the lecture, Carlyle summarizes the Balder story from the death of Balder to the end of Hermoder's visit to him in Hela. Arnold develops from his source in Mallet Balder's vision of the future and prediction of his return— which Carlyle does not mention—but otherwise Arnold uses just the narrative section of the Balder material that Carlyle had summarized.[5] When the poem was published, with Arnold's other exercise in the epic vein, "Sohrab and Rustum," A. P. Stanley urged Arnold to write "a first book with an account of the circumstances of the death of Balder himself"[6] Arnold did not, but he put these "circumstances" into a prefatory note to the 1869 edition: how Frigga extracts an oath from all things to do no harm to Balder—all things except the feeble mistletoe; but the evil Loki persuades blind Hoder to throw the mistletoe at Balder, and it pierces and kills him. And Arnold stuck to his epic opening *in medias res:* "So on the floor lay Balder dead" (i, l. 1).

The poem itself, never liked by the critics as much as by

Arnold himself, is troubled, I think, by the logic of its cosmology. There is an anomaly in Asgard being the home of the gods and also of dead heroes: a hero dies and goes to Asgard, a god dies and goes to Hela. But unquestionably "Balder Dead" has its moments and achieves at times something of the true Virgilian pathos. What, though, is there of Carlyle in it? The emphasis on a place for the apotheosis of *Heroes* might be thought a nod in Carlyle's direction, but that is speculative. Besides using Carlyle's exact segment of the Balder material, Arnold echoes the special epithet that Carlyle twice applies to Balder: *benignant* (*H,* 18, 34).[7] He develops from Carlyle's cue the vision of Balder as Christ-figure: Balder in the myth, being a sun-god, has rays of light round about him; Arnold seems to convert these into a Christian halo (i, l. 284). He gives him Christlike qualities: meekness, nonviolence; he is the mild, the lowly of heart, the compassionate, the much *loved,* and he has the secret of recalling the dead to life (i, l. 209). And Balder is described with biblical echoes: "Unhappy! but that art he did not know / To keep his own life safe" (i, ll. 212–13) evokes the gospels' "He saved others; himself he could not save." Balder's words,

> Mourn not for me! Mourn, Hermod, for the Gods;
> Mourn for the men on earth, the Gods in Heaven,
> Who live, and with their eyes shall see that day!"
>
> (iii, ll. 484–86)

echo Jesus' words in Luke, "Daughters of Jerusalem, weep not for me, but weep for yourselves, and for your children." Arnold, as Carlyle before him, inclines to see the Christian myth *comparatively.*

One of the greatest appeals of Norse myth for Carlyle was its ideology. He loved the energy and humor and pathos of these northerners with whom he felt a strong kinship, but certain metaphorical concepts he loved even more, such as the tree Igdrasil, with its

> roots deep-down in the kingdoms of Hela or Death; its trunk
> ... heaven-high ... at the foot of it ... sit Three *Nornas,*
> Fates,—the Past, Present, Future. .... Its "boughs," with their

buddings and disleafings,—events, things suffered, things done, catastrophes,—stretch through all lands and times. Is not every leaf of it a biography, every fibre there an act or word? Its boughs are Histories of Nations. The rustle of it is the noise of Human Existence, onwards from old. . . .—I find no similitude so true as this of a Tree.   (*H*, 20–21)

Carlyle knows the surpassing shaping power of our radical metaphors. But further, when we know how the vital principle of his German learning is Herderian historicism, the concept of differing civilizations with their differing religious and autonomous developments, each flourishing in varying degrees and giving way at last to another, we can understand how struck he was to find in Norse myth itself this very idea of organic cyclicism, in the Igdrasil image, and even more in the "old prophetic idea of the *Ragnarök,* consummation, or Twilight of the Gods."

The old Universe with its Gods is sunk; but it is not final death: there is to be a new Heaven and a new Earth; a higher supreme God, and Justice to reign among men. Curious: this law of mutation, which also is a law written in man's inmost thought, had been deciphered by these old earnest Thinkers in their rude style; and how, though all dies, and even gods die, yet all death is but a phoenix fire-death, and new-birth into the Greater and the Better! It is a fundamental law of Being for a creature made of Time, living in this Place of Hope.   (*H*, 39)

Curious, he is saying, that these old earnest thinkers intimate the idea of cyclic historicism. The myth itself affords its own self-cancellation, what he himself had described in *Sartor* with his figure of the Phoenix death and rebirth.

The tree Igdrasil is also lovingly noted by Arnold, and

> his fount
> of wisdom, which beneath the ashtree springs;
> And . . . the Nornies watering the roots
> Of that world-shadowing tree.   (iii, ll. 217–22)

But above all it is the Twilight of the Gods that is important in his poem and gives it the distinctive millennial vision, in the concluding prophecy of Balder:

> The day will come, when fall shall Asgard's towers,
> And Odin, and his sons, the seed of Heaven;
> ....
>   I attend the course
> Of ages, and my late return to light,
> In times less alien to a spirit mild,
> In new-recovered seats, the happier day.
> ....
> Far to the south, beyond the blue, there spreads
> Another Heaven, the boundless—no one yet
> Hath reached it; there hereafter shall arise
> The second Asgard, with another name.
> Thither, when o'er this present earth and Heavens
> The tempest of the latter days hath swept,
> And they from sight have disappeared, and sunk,
> Shall a small remnant[7] of the Gods repair;
> Hoder and I shall join them from the grave.
> There re-assembling we shall see emerge
> From the bright Ocean at our feet an earth
> More fresh, more verdant than the last, with fruits
> Self-springing, and a seed of man preserved,
> Who then shall live in peace, as now in war.
>   (iii, ll. 487–531)

Here the Christ figure eschews the exclusively Christian miraculous resurrection, as Arnold is to do in *God and the Bible*, but underwrites the Herderian-Carlylean historicist vision of succeeding cultures in slow spirals evolving into a better, more human and humane civilization. The death of Balder is a portent of the fall of the old and the ultimate evolution of the new and better. This is the vision of *Sartor*, and the culture that is outworn, while the world awaits a new gospel yet to take form. It is also the vision of the poet

> Wandering between two worlds, one dead,
> The other powerless to be born.   (ll. 85–86)

Furthermore, Arnold's "Grande Chartreuse" stanzas are slightly reminiscent of the Norse myth of "Balder Dead" on the same theme: the poet sees himself

> as, on some far northern strand,
> Thinking of his own Gods, a Greek
> In pity and mournful awe might stand
> Before some fallen Runic stone—
> For both were faiths, and both are gone.   (ll. 80–84)

Carlyle's Odin and *Sartor* are clearly visible behind these most doctrinal of Arnold's poems.

There is another vital connection between the Odin lecture and Arnold's thought. With Carlyle, *Sartor* is of course the best and most complete unfolding of the doctrine of "Natural Supernaturalism," but the Odin lecture restates it in a daring and original way, which I believe Arnold took deep cognizance of. Here I must explain how I read the Odin lecture. Unquestionably, it is a fine amalgam of Norse lore but it is, I believe, much more than that. A second pattern of significance is discernible under the Norse material. As we imagine the occasion of the lecture in the spring of 1840, the choice of Odin appears both a stunning *coup-de-theâtre* and a well-considered strategy. One imagines the run-of-the-mill lecturegoer's first reaction to "The Hero as Divinity"—"Divinity"? with a little *frisson* of shock. But Jesus Christ is *the* example of divinity: how unorthodox to treat him as a *hero*—Ah, I see it is *Odin* as divinity—we will hear something new, of the Germans' mythology. But in fact that original little shock was the significant reaction. For the whole lecture on Odin can be seen as a disguised account of the nature of Christ and the early development of Christianity, in terms essentially as rationalistic and nonsupernaturalist as those of D. F. Strauss's *Leben Jesu* (1835–36). Strauss, as is well known, applies the myth theory to the life of Jesus, denies the historical basis of supernatural elements in the Gospels, and assigns them to an unintentionally creative legend (the "myth"), developed between the death of Jesus and the writing of the Gospels. So the Odin lecture is a declaration that Christianity does not depend on supernatural manifestations and has a great worth in it that withstands and survives Enlightenment reductionism.

"The Hero as Divinity—Odin," concerns the "oldest primary form of Heroism," and it can be read to refer, all the way through, to Jesus. He that hath ears to hear, let him hear. This paganism—that is, supernaturalism—is a strange-looking thing these days, Carlyle says, "almost inconceivable to us. . . . A bewildering, inextricable jungle of delusions, confusions, falsehoods and absurdities covering the whole field of life." We are filled with astonishment, "Almost, if it were possible, with incredulity. . . . That men should have worshipped their poor fellow-man as a God . . . and fashioned for themselves such a distracted chaos of hallucinations by way of Theory of the Universe: all this looks like an incredible fable. . . . Nevertheless it is a clear fact that they did it. . . . This is strange." Yet "Such things were and are in man; in all men; in us too" (H, 4). You see here the experiential approach, like that of William James. Religious experiences are our facts, as Arnold also was to insist. And so pagan religion (let us continue to read *Christianity*) is not "mere quackery, priestcraft, and dupery." Paganism and all other *isms* "have all had a truth in them, or men would not have taken them up." Carlyle here calls Christianity *Christianism* to enforce the parallel with pagan*ism*. In the comparative way he cites also the "Lamaism" of Tibet as another form of that need for a "greatest" man to look up to (H, 4).

There was a firm belief, he says, in the "miracle" of nature and the universe, "beautiful, awful, unspeakable": "Hardened round us, encasing wholly every notion we form, is a wrappage of traditions, hearsays, mere words. We call that fire of the black thunder-cloud 'electricity' and lecture learnedly about it—" (H, 8) and forget the marvel and unknown of it. In Odin's time there were no "hearsays" to chain up experience, and so men were open to the worship of the transcendent unknown.

> Science has done much for us; but it is but a poor science that would hide from us the great deep sacred infinitude of Nescience. . . . That great mystery of *Time*, were there no other . . . on which we and all the Universe swim like exhalations. . . .

> This Universe . . . a Force . . . a Force which is not *we*. . . . In
> such a time as ours it requires a Prophet or Poet to teach us,
> namely, the stripping-off of those poor undevout wrappages,
> nomenclatures and scientific hearsays,—this, the ancient ear-
> nest soul, as yet unencumbered with these things, did for itself.
> All was Godlike or God. . . . But now if all things whatsoever
> that we look upon are emblems to us of the Highest God, I add
> that more so than any of them is man such an emblem. You
> have heard of St. Chrysostom's celebrated saying in reference to
> the Shekinah, or Ark of the Testimony, visible Revelation of
> God, among the Hebrews: "The true Shekinah is Man!" . . . we
> are the miracle of miracles,—the great inscrutable mystery
> of God.   (*H,* 19)

Spinoza too said something like this. But Carlyle finds it pru-
dent to cite the saint, not Spinoza, teacher of the Germans,
whose name still carried an aura of fearful heterodoxy. It was
Arnold who would give Spinoza the credit. Carlyle continues
in a Herderian historicist vein: "The young generations of the
world, who had in them the freshness of young children, and
yet the depth of earnest men, who did not think they had fin-
ished-off all things in Heaven and Earth by merely giving them
scientific names. . . . They felt better what of divinity there is in
man and Nature" (*H,* 11). If there was meaning even in the
worship of a star, how much more in the case of a man: "Hero-
worship, heartfelt prostrate admiration, submission, burning,
boundless, for a noblest godlike Form of Man,—is not that the
germ of Christianity itself? The greatest of all Heroes is One—
whom we do not name here! Let sacred silence meditate that
sacred matter; you will find it the ultimate perfection of a
principle extant throughout man's whole history on earth."
(*H,* 11).

By his "sacred silence" Carlyle can avoid committing himself on the divinity of Christ and at the same time invites med-
itation—he that hath ears to hear, let him hear—and invites
some to recognize that Christ is the subject of this lecture. The
bold scheme of *Heroes* is essentially that the sacred and secular
are one—our reverence for Dante, Shakespeare, Johnson, Luther, Calvin, Napoleon, Cromwell, is one with our reverence

for Mahomet the prophet and for Odin/Christ—"from Norse
Odin to English Samuel Johnson, from the divine Founder of
Christianity to their withered Pontiff of Encyclopedism [Vol-
taire], in all times and places" (*H*, 15). In fact, Carlyle's taking
a "god" as hero is in itself the bold step and a clear declaration
against supernaturalism.

In old paganism, then, Carlyle finds "truth, only under an
ancient obsolete vesture, but the spirit of it is still true"; "vesture" recalls *Sartor*, and the principle applies equally to Christianity. These Norse poems "have a *truth* in them, an inward
perennial truth and greatness,—as, indeed, all must have that
can very long preserve itself by tradition alone [read Christian-
ity] (*H*, 36). The Norse mythology is marked, he says, by "Im-
personation of the visible workings of Nature" (figures,
metaphors, characteristic of Scriptures as the German critics
were declaring), which are "simple recognition of . . . Nature
as a thing wholly miraculous, stupendous and divine" (*H*, 17).

"How the man Odin came to be considered a *god*, the chief
god," that is the question. Part of the Odin lore that might have
been known to Carlyle is the account in one of the verse Eddas
of how Odin was hanged on the Ash Tree, wounded, in order
to learn the great secret of the runes of wisdom. Some mythog-
raphers consider the development of this aspect of the Odin
material to be an effect of the influence of Christianity. But for
Carlyle, all we need note is the parallel, which might have been
what gave him the idea for the lecture. But the point about the
account of Odin's apotheosis from man to God is that it is written with great passion, precisely because it is written about
Jesus.

> People knew no limits to their admiration. . . . Fancy your own
> generous heart's-love of some greatest man expanding till it
> *transcended* all bounds, till it filled and overflowed the whole
> field of your thought! Or what if this man Odin,—since a great
> deep soul, with the afflatus and mysterious tide of vision and
> impulse rushing on him he knows not whence, is ever an
> enigma, a kind of terror and wonder to himself,—should have
> felt that perhaps *he* was divine. . . . He was not necessarily false;
> he was but mistaken, speaking the truest he knew [this state of

mind had been ascribed by rationalists to Jesus]. . . . And then consider what mere Time will do in such cases; how if a man was great while living, he becomes tenfold greater when dead. . . . Why, in thirty or forty years [the period between the Crucifixion and the Gospels], were there no books, any great man would grow *mythic*, the contemporaries who had seen him, being once all dead. And in three-hundred years, and in three-thousand years!—   (*H*, 25)

Well, he means eighteen hundred years. Our needs and wishes shape our perceptions: "Curious to think how, for every man, any the truest fact is modelled by the nature of man!" Even number—here is Carlyle the mathematician: "The number *Twelve*, divisiblest of all, which could be halved, quartered, parted into three, into six, the most remarkable number,—this was enough to determine the *Signs of the Zodiac*, the number of Odin's *Sons*, and innumerable other Twelves" (*H*, 12). It would be a slow mind that would not leap to think of *twelve* tribes of Israel and *twelve* apostles and recognize the mythic elements there.

In conclusion he tells the touching story that belongs to what the folklorists call the Heavenly-Visitor category. King Olaf has been zealous in promulgating Christianity. As he is sailing along the shore of Norway, at a certain haven there steps into his ship

> a stranger, of grave eyes and aspect, red beard of stately robust figure. . . . The courtiers address him; his answers surprise by their pertinency and depth: at length he is brought to the King. . . . As they sail along the beautiful shore . . . he addresses King Olaf thus: "Yes . . . it is all beautiful, with the sun shining on it there; green, fruitful, a right fair home for you; and many a sore day had Thor, many a wild fight with the rock Jötuns, before he could make it so. And now you seem minded to put away Thor. King Olaf, have a care!" said the stranger, drawing-down his brows;—and when they looked again, he was no-where to be found.—This is the last appearance of Thor on the stage of this world!   (*H*, 40)

This is as though to say: Have a care, you Saint-Simonians, Comptists, Benthamites, Utilitarians, Atheists, Scientists, lest you put away Christianity! It is all beautiful, this great European cultural shore, and many a sore day had Christianity to make this tradition we live in and profit by. On Thor's apparition, Carlyle continues, "Do we not see well enough how the Fable might arise, without unveracity on the part of any one? It is the way most gods have come to appear among men: thus, if in Pindar's time, 'Neptune was seen once at the Nemean Games,' what was this Neptune too but a 'stranger of noble grave aspect'" (*H*, 40). And *we* call to mind some other Visitors, the three mysterious "men" who appeared to Abraham in the plains of Mamre, as he sat in the tent door in the heat of the day; or the Stranger who appeared to the disciples on the road to Emmaus. These appearances were recorded "without unveracity" and are full of significance, just as this little story of Thor and King Olaf is full of significance. It is a beautiful metaphor for Carlyle's sense of the cyclical in history and for the invaluable humanity that exists in each religion, in each culture, each a unique and invaluable *Vorstellungsart* of man's spirituality.

The gist of this reading of the Odin lecture is finally to enhance its discretion and its artistry. The strategy of the bilevel meanings seems to have been widely successful. Carlyle's own pious mother, whose searching, interrogative gaze one must imagine as dominant in Carlyle's consciousness, she and other pious or naive souls could have read the Odin lecture without a tremor. But anyone conscious of German biblical scholarship—anyone aware of the new (1836) *Leben Jesu* by Strauss—would be liable to catch the clues and recognize that Carlyle, for all his sounding so religious, was in fact exploding the supernaturalist Christian myth.

Matthew Arnold, I believe, understood perfectly. He holds that a nonsupernaturalist religion such as Carlyle's is legitimate. For him, this nonsupernaturalist religion is compatible with Anglicanism (for Carlyle of course it was *not*). He acquired the Carlylean technique of demythologizing: What is "God"? That man has such a word, such a concept, is man's recognition of, in Carlyle's words, "a force, and thousandfold Complexity of Forces; a Force which is *not we*. That is all; it is not we, it is altogether different from *us*" (*H*, 8). Carlyle demythologizes the Odin material as Arnold is to do with the Jesus material in *God and the Bible.* Even Arnold's anathema to dogma has its clue in *Heroes:* "How the man Odin came to be considered a *god,* the chief god?—that surely is a question which nobody would wish to dogmatise upon" (*H,* 24). Nor can anybody legitimately dogmatize on the "truths" of any religion. Dogma is irrelevant to the humane values of our great myths. Dogma is the mistreatment of Scripture or poetry, taking it as science, with literalist readings. Religion is to be found rather in the metaphors of the great myths.

Carlyle's Thor in his last appearance on earth had a warning for King Olaf: "Have a care"—lest you put away the old religion, that inestimable treasure of culture. Arnold devoted his career to that care, lest the contemporary Victorian society put away Christianity, the treasure of eighteen hundred years of culture. Hence his great effort in *Literature and Dogma* and *God and the Bible* to save Christianity from the literalists on one hand and from the scientific reductionists on the other. If Christianity is made to depend on literalist interpretation of the metaphors of miracle and resurrection, it is doomed. Man's increasing rationalism makes miracles absurd. And scientific reductionists dismiss the need for stories, for metaphors, for myth that the Christian tradition so richly supplies. We can no more afford to let Christianity go than we can let Sophocles, Homer, Dante, or Shakespeare go. They and Christianity have made our beautiful, green, and fruitful cultural shore.

NOTES

1. *Wilhelm Meister, Works,* 23:113 (Bk. 2, chap. 2).

2. Kathleen Tillotson, "Matthew Arnold and Carlyle," *Proceedings of the British Academy* 42 (1956):146.

3. David DeLaura, "Arnold and Carlyle," *PMLA* 79 (Mar. 1964):128.

4. Thomas Carlyle, *Heroes and Hero-Worship,* in *Works,* Centenary Edition, 30 vols. (New York: Charles Scribner's Sons, 1896–1901), 5:18 (hereafter cited in the text as *H* with page numbers).

5. Kathleen Tillotson notes that Carlyle again recounts the story

of Balder's death and Hermod's journey in chapter 1 of *Oliver Cromwell's Letters and Speeches* ("Matthew Arnold and Carlyle," p. 149n.).

6. See *The Poems of Matthew Arnold,* ed. Kenneth Allott, 2d ed., ed. Miriam Allott (London: Longman, 1979), p. 376.

7. *Remnant:* the biblical term so much to be used in *Literature and Dogma.*

James C. Livingston

THREE

Matthew Arnold's Place in the Religious Thought of the Past Century

In his excellent biography of Arnold, Park Honan remarks that "no other aspect of Arnold studies late in the twentieth century was more in motion" than that of Arnold and religion. The great interest in this side of Arnold, at first perhaps surprising, may well be because many of us in the humanities still feel the pathos of "standing between two worlds." Whether or not we wish to or can follow him, we are attracted to Arnold's effort in religious criticism to carry out what Paul Ricoeur calls "a hermeneutics of retrieval" or "restoration of meaning."[1]

My own work on Arnold has focused on the years following the 1860s, the period of his prose writings on religion. My work itself represents something of "a hermeneutics of retrieval" in that it is an attempt to retrieve Arnold's religious criticism from the suspicions that commenced with the influential tradition of interpretation associated with T. S. Eliot, I. A. Richards, and Lionel Trilling. It is a current of interpretation whose confluence, for a time, became something of a tideway. This tradition charged Arnold with religious aestheticism and emotivism, with having reduced religion to poetry, to a moral subjectivism. Religion is charming, religion is lovely, religion is natural, but it is not true. This position is condensed in Eliot's charge that "the total effect of Arnold's philosophy is to set up culture in the place of religion," with the result that religion is left "to be laid waste by the anarchy of feeling." It is present in Trilling's charge of religious dilettantism, that Arnold is but "a connoisseur of Christianity."[2]

I am told by some Arnold scholars that this tradition of interpretation is passé, and yet I encounter excellent studies of Arnold that appear to continue under its spell. It is a critically important issue because it has to do with such fundamental matters as our understanding of Arnold's view of the relationship between religion and culture, his conception of the nature and status of poetic-religious language, the claims of religious experience, and his own substantive reconception of Christianity.

I want to propose here that Arnold's mature religious position must not be viewed simply as that of a maverick or a dilettante but rather that it must be seen as standing squarely in a tradition of liberal-modernist theology, which in the last century has established itself in the mainstream of Christian thought. We may not approve of this theological tradition; we may find it personally unsatisfactory; but, historically speaking, we no longer can claim that it is a minor sectarian aberration. Arnold was, in Mrs. Humphry Ward's words, "A Modernist before the time."[3]

Arnold's religious writings, we know, did speak to large numbers of the educated class, including many eminent theologians and ecclesiastics in Britain and America, for two generations after 1870. This wide audience is well documented by a review of the best liberal religious literature to about 1920. References to his religious essays and discussions of his striking ideas are scattered throughout the theological literature of this period—with a mixture of censure and praise. Scores of influential liberal clergymen concurred with Llewelyn Davies's judgment "that there are characteristics of Mr. Arnold's creed which are likely to make it, to a large section of Englishmen, more attractive than any rival."[4] An analysis of these "characteristics" gives us a clue to how we should locate Arnold in relation to the movements of religious thought of the past century. The answer is, paradoxically, both simple and complex.

Unmistakably, Arnold stands in the tradition of nineteenth-century Protestant liberal theology with its roots in a

Kantian skepticism regarding metaphysics and the founding of a rational religious faith on moral experience, as well as in Friedrich Schleiermacher's experiential grounding of theology in the religious affections. The key to this liberal tradition is the experiential and the moral foundations of religious belief—ideas very much in the air in the mid- and late nineteenth century.

In his (at the time) influential *Rise of Modern Religious Ideas* (1915), Arthur C. McGiffert summarized the modern Protestant liberal position simply yet authoritatively, placing Arnold centrally within it. The position, he wrote,

> interprets the larger whole in terms of moral purpose, and makes religion consist in the recognition of this divine purpose and virtue life in sympathy with and devotion to it. Matthew Arnold's description of God as "the power not ourselves that makes for righteousness" illustrates this position, and, in the teaching of the German [Kantian] theologian Ritschl, it finds its completest and most consistent theological formulation. We are religious when we rise above our separate or single selves into the consciousness of a divine purpose, and, when we devote ourselves to its accomplishment we put religion into practice and are righteous in the highest sense. The influence of this conception upon the religious thought and life of the present day it would be hard to exaggerate.[5]

What is critical to this theological position is the belief that God must be envisioned as the ground of moral values and, therefore, conceived essentially as a moral influence, rather than in abstract or metaphysical categories. God is known neither by intellectual demonstration nor by mystical vision but rather by the exercise of conscience and the moral will. This approach to theology informed the writings of John Baillie, who, with William Temple, is considered foremost among British theologians of the first half of the twentieth century. Baillie specifically commended Arnold for his insistence on grounding religion in moral experience and his refusal to consider any antithesis between the two. Baillie suggests, with particular reference to Arnold, that he should himself "be inclined to say that this tendency to look upon religion as being essentially and in the first place a practical thing is the most characteristic contribution which the last two or three generations have made to religious thought."[6]

The dominant movement of liberal Protestant thought between 1870 and World War I was the Ritschlian school, named for Albrecht Ritschl (1822–89), the foremost Protestant theologian between Schleiermacher and Karl Barth. Ritschl's writings had a leading influence for half a century. As we know, Arnold was not familiar with Ritschl's important works of the 1870s; nevertheless, Arnold does reflect the philosophical soundings of his day, which have much in common with the Ritschlian program. The parallels are striking. For example, Arnold shares with the Ritschlians an abhorrence of metaphysics and speculative theology; the rejection of ecclesiastical dogma as normative for religious faith; a practical, moral conception of religion and thus a sharp contrast between religious and scientific knowledge; the restriction of theological knowledge to the contents or effects of divine action on the moral consciousness and the affections; the perception of Jesus' life and message as the normative revelation of the Christian "idea" or gospel; an adoptionist Christology; and the use of the Kingdom of God as the regulative principle of the Christian community and its moral activity. In all of these respects Arnold's religious thought is representative of classic nineteenth-century Protestant liberalism.

Arnold was not, however, simply a liberal Protestant. He was an Anglican deeply attracted to aspects of Catholic spirituality and tradition, religious tendencies which Protestant liberalism neither found congenial nor could nurture. Arnold's religious position is, therefore, more complex. It has a kinship as well with the Anglican and Catholic modernism that briefly flourished between 1890 and 1910 and with certain aspects of Anglican "Empirical Catholicism" of the 1920s and 1930s. Arnold often opposed the more extreme forms of liberal Protestant rationalism and as early as 1863 had denounced such theological liberalism: "[Christianity] will even survive the handling of 'liberals of every shade of opinion.' But it will not do this by losing its essence, by becoming such a Christianity as those liberals imagine . . . a Christianity consisting of half-a-dozen moral rules deduced from them. It will do it by retaining the religious life in all its depth and fullness in connexion with new intellectual ideas" (*CPW,* 3:78).

Arnold shared with the turn-of-the-century Catholic and Anglican modernism an antipathy to metaphysics and scholastic theology; the belief that religion has essentially to do with living experience and that doctrines containing spiritual truth derived from such vital experience can never be wrong, no matter what science or history may say about the nature and claims of the original sources of revelation; the recognition that religious language is essentially symbolic and analogical, not literal and scientific; the rejection of any sharp antithesis between natural and revealed religion; the recognition of the critical need to adapt Christianity to the intellectual needs of the time and the radical implications of this fact for the development of religious doctrine; and, most significantly, the importance of the corporate life and worship of the church, what the Catholic modernist George Tyrrell called the collective subconscious of the "Populus Dei," people of God.

Modernists such as Tyrrell, Percy Gardner, and F. C. Burkitt found in Arnold a spiritual confrère, the balance of openness to criticism and devotion to Catholic spirituality which they found lacking in Protestantism. "My ideal would be," Arnold wrote to the French Protestant pastor Ernest Fontanès, "for Catholic countries, the development of something like old Catholicism, retaining as much as possible of old religious services and usages, but becoming more and more liberal in spirit."[7] It was also his hope for the future of the Church of England.

At bottom and in many essentials, Arnold found the religious life of Catholics and Protestants to be much alike. In the "accessories," however, in the outward form and setting, there is, Arnold knew, a very great difference, and in these "externals" he placed immense significance:

> Catholicism has these so different from Protestantism! and in Catholicism these accessories have, it cannot be denied, a nobleness and amplitude which in Protestantism is often wanting to them. In Catholicism they have, from the antiquity of this

form of religion, from its pretensions to universality, from its really widespread prevalence, from its sensuousness, something European, august, and imaginative: in Protestantism they often have from its inferiority in these respects, something provincial, mean, and prosaic. . . . The signal want of grace and charm in English Protestantism's setting of its religious life *is not an indifferent matter; it is a real weakness.*

(*CPW,* 3:96–98; emphasis added.)

Arnold's strong attraction to worship with what he saw as Catholicism's "consecration of common consent, antiquity, public establishment, and long-used rites" (*CPW,* 5:197) set him apart from Protestantism. He felt deeply that "unity and continuity in public worship are a need for the human race, an eternal aspiration of Christendom" (*CPW,* 8:110), which could not be nurtured by "the Protestantism of the Protestant religion." Arnold predicted that Catholic worship would prevail long after what he regarded as the intellectual liabilities of Catholic dogma "tired out men's patience" (*CPW,* 8:333).

Arnold was in many respects the precursor of the Anglican modernism of the next two generations and beyond. The recent authoritative history of English modernism summarizes the principal modernist tenets. They can, with hardly any exceptions, be taken as Arnold's credo: "The English Modernist believes," writes Alan Stephenson,

in a God who was in everything and that everything was in God, but a God who worked only through the evolutionary process. . . . He had no doubt about the existence of Jesus Christ, though he was prepared to admit that if it were proved that Jesus had never existed, that would not mean the end of his religious faith. His Christology was a degree Christology and adoptionist. His Jesus was not an eschatological figure but rather "The Lord of Thought" who proclaimed the Fatherhood of God and the Brotherhood of Man. His doctrine of the atonement was Abelardian or exemplarist. He had no hesitation in accepting all that biblical criticism had to say. . . . He maintained that he believed in the supernatural, but not in the miraculous. His Jesus, therefore, did not perform miracles. He was not born of a Virgin and his resurrection was a spiritual one.

The tomb was not empty. He had a strong belief in the life after death and was a universalist. He was not so naive as to think one could exist without dogma, but he wished dogmatic definition to be kept to a minimum. He thought there was such a thing as essential Christianity. For the English Modernist ethics were more important than doctrine. Life was more important than belief. He did not relish ecclesiasticism or see a great divide between the secular and the sacred.[8]

Arnold would have been disturbed by a skepticism regarding the historical Jesus, which little concerned some English idealists in the modernist camp. And depending on how it were to be interpreted, Arnold might express a reservation about "a strong belief in life after death"; he spoke, rather, of eternal life as a present reality.

Augustin Renaudel has remarked that the religious *modernisme* of Erasmus was neither wholly Protestant nor Catholic. What Erasmus wanted was a "troisième Eglise," a third church, which would be spiritual Catholicism profoundly reformed by the principle of critical light and prophetic protest. This, too, was Arnold's vision and hope. Like Erasmus, Arnold saw the need for a third way that would join the two in an unerring balance. We will fail, then, to plumb the true depths of Arnold's spiritual life and ideal if we focus too exclusively on the moral and critical sides of his religious reconstruction. Arnold was a religious liberal but a liberal with a difference. Compared to W. K. Clifford, the Victorian rationalist, Arnold considered the evangelists Dwight L. Moody and Ira Sankey "masters of the philosophy of history" (*CPW,* 7:38).

If we extend our placing of Arnold backward as well as forward, he can perhaps best be understood as standing in the modern tradition of Christian humanism, in which Christianity is first and foremost "a temper, a behavior." The characteristics we often associate with Christian humanism and with Arnold, but which often have displeased the critics of both, are well described by a modern cultural historian: "We are troubled," he writes,

> by the frivolous lightness of his humanistic style when he writes about things sacred. . . . It is hard for us to accept piety with

such a strong aesthetic tinge as serious. . . . [His] religious sentiments, it seems to us, more often moved in a middling sphere of poetic learning than cry toward heaven out of the deep. . . . His theology seems too vacillating and too vague. . . . He placed little value on definitions. As a consequence he had no desire to advance toward a profound and clearly defined philosophical foundation of his beliefs, and the direct, mystical basis of his theological thinking was also weak. He was just as little a rationalist. His beliefs were rooted in deep ethical needs. . . . Sacred truth cannot bear subtle definition. . . . It was but little service to piety for one to attempt to penetrate further than was seemly, into the cave of the unfathomable mystery.[9]

The person Johan Huizinga is here describing is not Matthew Arnold but the Christian humanist Desiderius Erasmus. One could expatiate at length on the extraordinary filiation between the humanistic and spiritual principles and ideals of the two men. A brief enumeration of some of them will suggest, I believe, the extent of their religious kinship. Both men viewed Christianity in essentially moral terms and were suspicious of rationalism and mysticism; they disliked scholastic metaphysics; they recognized the profound spiritual importance of tradition, comprehensiveness, and Christian unity; they were engaged and yet detached observers of their age; they shared a passion for the disinterested truth of scholarship and knowledge and yet each found himself deeply involved in a mission to edify and to put something in the place of reductive criticism; in this mission to edify they used humor, scorn, and irony, but they also shared a faith in the morally directing and energizing power of key precepts or maxims which they collected and used; as humanists they were alike in their devotion to the classics and were drawn especially to the spiritual resources of the Stoic philosophers, but it was a Stoicism touched and transformed by Christian sentiment; they shared a love of simplicity and a dislike of a materialistic and commercial spirit, of narrowness and "the one thing needful"; both men were noted for their defense of religious toleration. Arnold was one with Erasmus in affirming "the old and true Socratic thesis of the interdependence of virtue and knowledge (*CPW,* 8:162) and the harmonious expansion of all human powers. Both men worked to achieve this balance and the breadth that culture alone could give to religion, but they also sought to reconcile autonomous classical culture with the moral and spiritual temper of Christianity.

Aby Warburg suggests that the central intellectual problem of the Renaissance was to find a compromise formula, "an *Ausgleichsformel*," that would enable men to live comfortably with classical forms and Christian convictions, with trust in man and trust in God, with vigorous secular energies and a tenacious ascetic ideal.[10] Erasmus epitomized this quest, but it was also a burning problem in the high Victorian age, perhaps best seen in the dialectical tension of Arnold's essays on religion and culture, and certainly in his own life. This quest for the interdependence and balance of these competing values and forces has led students of Erasmus to observe and comment on the unique juxtaposition of strong traditional and yet intensely reformist predispositions in his life and work. It is a telling mark of the Christian humanist—and of Matthew Arnold, the Anglican modernist.

NOTES

Portions of this essay are reprinted with permission of the publisher from my book *Matthew Arnold and Christianity: His Religious Prose Writings* (Columbia: University of South Carolina Press, 1986).

1. Park Honan, *Matthew Arnold: A Life* (New York: McGraw-Hill, 1981), p. 476; Paul Ricoeur, *Freud and Philosophy* (New Haven: Yale University Press, 1970), p. 28.

2. T. S. Eliot, *Selected Essays, 1917–1932* (London: Faber and Faber, 1932), p. 382; Lionel Trilling, *Matthew Arnold* (New York: Harcourt Brace Jovanovich, 1977), p. 363.

3. Mrs. Humphry Ward, *A Writer's Recollections* (London: W. Collins Sons, 1918), p. 235.

4. J. Llewelyn Davies, "Mr. Matthew Arnold's New Religion of the Bible," *Contemporary Review* 21 (1872–73):842.

5. Arthur C. McGiffert, *The Rise of Modern Religious Ideas* (New York: Macmillan, 1915), pp. 74–75.

6. John Baillie, *The Roots of Religion in the Human Soul* (London: Hodder and Stoughton, 1926), p. 51.

7. *Letters of Matthew Arnold, 1848–1888,* ed. George W. E. Russell, 2 vols. (New York: Macmillan, 1895), p. 114.

8. Alan M. G. Stephenson, *The Rise and Decline of English Modernism* (London: S.P.C.K., 1984), pp. 7–8.

9. Johan Huizinga, *Men and Ideas* (New York: Meridian Books, 1959), p. 314.

10. Peter Gay, *The Enlightenment: An Interpretation I* (London, 1973), p. 270.

SIDNEY COULLING

FOUR

Matthew Arnold and the American South

In the concluding part of *A French Eton,* written as the American Civil War neared the end of its terrible third year, Matthew Arnold declared that "lovers of perfection in America" should rejoice that the nation had been compelled, "even at any cost of suffering," to transform itself "in the furnace of civil war" and "become something higher, ampler, more gracious" (*CPW,* 2:319).[1] In the same year (1864), writing from beleaguered Richmond, Virginia, to a friend in another city, Mrs. Robert E. Lee employed precisely the same image to express a similar hope: "We must pray for the good time when we shall all meet again in peace & comfort a better people purified in the furnace of affliction."[2] I have juxtaposed these two passages—neither, of course, known to the author of the other—as a way of suggesting the thesis of this essay: namely, that there was a fundamental bond of sympathy between Arnold and the South that helps to account for his idealizing, not to say romanticizing, the Civil War and especially the Confederate cause,[3] and to explain why, although his single visit to the South in 1883 failed to advance the transformation of which he had spoken, it was nevertheless one of his most successful appearances in America and established a warm relationship that has continued to the present day.

Arnold's sympathy with the South had been apparent even before the outbreak of hostilities. As early as January 1861 he wrote to his sister Jane, Mrs. Forster, whose husband was a vigorous and outspoken advocate of the North, that he had little faith "in the nobility . . . of the Northern Americans" and that secession by the South would contribute to developing a nation of "grandeur and richness."[4] After the *Trent* affair, which he viewed as the insolent expression of an upstart country, Arnold thought it "indispensable to give the Americans [i.e., the North] a *moral lesson*" and "fervently" hoped it would be given (*L*, 1:182). Later his sympathy seems to have shifted somewhat toward the North, as was pointed out long ago by Hugh Kingsmill,[5] and the final events of the war elicited the comment that they "had raised America in one's estimation," even the assassination of Lincoln having brought into its "history something of that dash of the tragic, romantic, and imaginative, which it has had so little of" (*L*, 1:300). But that these were ultimately for Arnold characteristics of the South rather than of the North is made clear in the essay on Ulysses S. Grant, in which Arnold defends English partiality for the Confederates as favoring "the weaker side which was making a gallant fight" and asserts that the real hero of the conflict was not Grant but Lee, who had "pathos," "dignity," and the "power of captivating the admiring interest, almost the admiring affection . . . of the world" (*CPW,* 11:144, 154, 157).

It thus seems appropriate that *Essays in Criticism*, the preface to which concludes with the famous apostrophe to Oxford as the "home of lost causes . . . and impossible loyalties" (*CPW,* 3:290), apparently was the first of Arnold's works to reach a southern audience.[6] Nearly twenty years after its publication he was told in Richmond that "an aide de camp of Gen. Lee had smuggled over" a copy of the volume "at the height of the blockade,"[7] a story which, if true, would indicate the English rather than the American edition (see *CPW,* 3:400–401). It was certainly the latter that was read by another southerner, Alexander H. Stephens, former vice-president of the Confederacy, who was sent a copy by a Boston woman during his imprisonment.[8] A writer of greater literary distinction than Stephens, William Gilmore Simms, read the book under less trying circumstances and described it, in the earliest (as well as the vaguest) critical comment by a southerner on Arnold's work that I can find, as "charming . . . graceful, scholarly, interesting."[9]

Arnold's subsequent volumes attracted the occasional notice of southern periodicals, often as severe in their criticism as some of their counterparts across the Atlantic, but they also won devoted readers and sometimes the qualified respect of even hostile critics. A persistent antagonist was the *Southern Review*, which in the 1870s, to the dismay of William Hand Browne, became the organ of the Southern Methodists.[10] In the course of a review of translations of the *Iliad* by the Earl of Derby and William Cullen Bryant it gratuitously rebuked Arnold for his "dogmatism" (an old complaint) and his "presumptuous pedantry" (a new and curious one);[11] and in a long, sarcastic, emotionally charged review four years later it characterized *Literature and Dogma* as "one of the most conceited and shallow atheistical performances which this or any other age has produced." The hyperbole seems intended to counteract the effect the book was apparently having, as in the case (cited by the incredulous reviewer) of "a learned doctor of divinity in the Methodist Episcopal Church, South," who "had read the book through 'three times,' . . . every time with increasing admiration and delight," and had "pronounced it 'one of the very greatest works of the age.'"[12] In essence this was the response of the religiously troubled Walter Hines Page, whose closest friend at Randolph-Macon College presented him as his last gift—"a gift from his deathbed"—his copy of *Literature and Dogma;* and later, at Johns Hopkins, according to Page's biographer, the works of Arnold were among his "ever-present companions."[13]

Some sense of Arnold's impact on the South during the two decades between the Civil War and his American visit may be gleaned from the ambivalent attitude toward him expressed by the *Southern Presbyterian Review* (published in Columbia, South Carolina), a conservative journal, as its title indicates, but also a literate one, in keeping with the emphasis of its denomination on an educated clergy. Not surprisingly it gave *God and the Bible* an adverse (though intelligent and fair-minded) review, the tone of which is suggested by an exclamation of sadness in a comment the following year on A. P. Stanley's *Life of Dr. Arnold:* "How the vagaries of his son Matthew would have shocked the master of Rugby!" But two years later, in a notice of Arnold's edition of Johnson that led the writer into a comparison of Arnold with Sainte-Beuve, the paper maintained that Arnold was "as fine and discerning in his appreciation" as the French critic, declared that the "literary instinct of the two men (where unbiassed) [was] seldom at fault," and concluded that although both "may be set down as delicately tutored pagans," Arnold was the superior because he possessed "the synthetic as well as the analytic faculty; he is poet no less than critic and scholar." And after Arnold's return to England, in a notice of the seven-volume edition of his works published in America to coincide with his visit, it found itself torn between the irresistible attraction of Arnold's style and the ineradicable conviction that his ideas were unacceptable:

> [Mr. Arnold's] literary merits are indeed of a high order. His poems are full of masculine strength and beauty, though also of a sort of pessimistic scepticism, and his prose style is really almost unequalled for its exquisite clarity and precision, and for a certain nameless satisfying charm. His opinions are of varied quality. . . . His vaunted theology of culture is nothing but the extremest form of sublimated rationalism strongly tinged with the conservative glow of a warm attachment to the institutions and monuments, including the Prelatic Church, of England. We regard Mr. Arnold as on the whole one of the most fascinating, and at the same time (on important subjects) one of the most dangerous and pernicious thinkers and writers of our time.[14]

The ambivalence of this review reflects the paradoxical state of the South at the time of Arnold's visit. On one hand, there was the poverty of a war-ravaged land, later epitomized by Ellen Glasgow (a ten-year-old girl in Richmond when Arnold came to the city) in her account of having asked for a doll and being told that she could not have it because "we had 'lost everything in the war'": deprivation, either real or self-imposed, was the price of defeat.[15] But at the same time there was a burgeoning industrialism—in tobacco, textiles, and iron—from which emerged an affluent middle class that had been heralded in the 1870s by the *Richmond Whig and Advertiser*: "We find a new race of rich people have been gradually springing up among us. . . . [They] are taking the leading place not only in our political and financial affairs, but are pressing to the front for social recognition. . . . They may be parvenuish, and want something of the polish which is the heritage of birth or only acquired by many generations of refining influences; but these are trifling matters. . . . Our provincial characteristics are fast disappearing, and we . . . are losing our petty, narrow prejudices."[16] Here in Richmond, then, were the same decline in the prestige and power of a landed aristocracy, replaced by captains of industry, that Carlyle had depicted earlier in England and the corresponding increase in influence of a middle class that in Arnold's view would determine the future.

But at roughly the same time—the 1880s—the South also began a retreat into the past that gave birth to the cult of the Old South and the myth of the Lost Cause. "All Confederate leaders became stainless and true," Louis Rubin has written, and soldiers who "had battled profanely and unwashed in the hot, savage summer campaigns became now . . . heroic, dauntless knights." The phenomenon puzzled the young James Branch Cabell (four years old when Arnold visited Virginia), who thought "Richmond was not at all like Camelot," and led another Richmond novelist, Ellen Glasgow, to show in *The Deliverance,* her novel about Reconstruction, how "the entire South, unaware of the changes about [it, clung], with passionate fidelity, to the ceremonial forms of tradition."[17]

It was a tradition, however, without a strong literary component. "A little literature goes a long way in Richmond," the caustic Mary Chesnut had observed during the war, a comment echoed in peacetime in Ellen Glasgow's remark that "books have always been regarded by Southerners as the last of the luxuries."[18] In his correspondence with John G. James (later president of Texas A&M College) Walter Hines Page repeatedly complained of southern indifference to literature. The more outspoken Joel Chandler Harris publicly stated, "The truth might as well be told: we have no Southern literature worthy of the name."[19]

This was an unpromising setting, consequently, in which to speak on literature and science, which Arnold had thought a "stupid" lecture topic for Washington (*L,* 2:281), and to proclaim the preeminent importance of letters. He would have done well, one is tempted to say, to choose "Numbers," a lecture clearly appealing to those members of his audience who continued to think of the South as the saving remnant by which the entire nation might eventually be redeemed.[20] Still, in retrospect his appearance in Richmond must have seemed to him a welcome interlude between lectures in two other cities, in one of which he was outrageously treated and, in the other, he was tactlessly made to appear the prelude to more important matters.

In Washington, where he spoke on December 17, William E. Chandler, secretary of the navy and a hardened polemicist, attempted to use the lecture for attacking John G. Carlisle, who had just been elected Speaker of the House (it has been said that he became one of the few great Speakers[21]) and who was to have introduced Arnold. But that was only the beginning, and the next day, as he was leaving for Richmond, Arnold read in the *Washington Post* an account of the previous evening that was so "characteristic" and "common" in America, he told his younger daughter, that "one does not think of cutting it out and sending it" (*L*, 2:283):

> Mr. Matthew Arnold appeared somewhat surprised, agreeably astonished, at the character of the audience which greeted him at the Congregational church last night. He made an apology for his theme, saying that he spoke by request, as he understood it, upon what the staple of modern education ought to be, a theme more suited for an academic audience than one gathered from a great political center. But a glance at the auditors appeared to satisfy him that all he should say would be appreciated and understood.
>
> Secretary Chandler introduced Mr. Arnold, reading a letter of apology from Speaker Carlisle, whose official duties precluded his presence. Mr. Chandler thought it becoming to express his sincere regrets that Mr. Carlisle had been elected Speaker.

Arnold spoke for some two hours, and after the applause that followed his "eloquent peroration had subsided," Chandler rose to make the extraordinary request that some one of the scientists present should controvert the views "so eloquently expressed" by Mr. Arnold. No response being forthcoming, he called upon the gentlemen occupying the platform . . . for remarks.

Rev. Edward Everett Hale said that so much had been said, and so well, that he had nothing more to add.

Commissioner Loring expressed his opinion by asking the privilege of publicly taking the lecturer's hand in his, which he did amidst applause.

Congressman W. W. Phelps, introduced as a reformed politician, in a few well chosen phrases voiced the feeling of gratification, which all must feel at the rich treat they had enjoyed.

Frederick Douglass moved that a tremendous vote of thanks be tendered the speaker by a rising vote. This was done most promptly to the astonishment of Mr. Arnold.[22]

There were no elements of farce three nights later, when Arnold lectured on "Numbers" in Baltimore, but he could scarcely have found the evening more gratifying. His audience was unusually small—"a mere remnant," said a reporter—and many of those present had come only because of the large reception that followed honoring J. J. Sylvester, a professor of mathematics who was leaving Johns Hopkins for Oxford.[23] Later in the week, when Arnold delivered a second lecture in the city, he asked the indulgence of his audience because of the severe cold he had contracted during his earlier appearance, "the hall having been very chilly, and the audience not sufficiently large to warm it." Those who had come seem to have been further chilled by the lecturer himself. Arnold's "manner of speaking was mechanical and rather awkward," the writer for the *Baltimore Sun* reported. "He would turn his head as though it were on a pivot, glance hurriedly at his manuscript, and then face the audience again and deliver a fresh sentence." But even a theatrical performance could not have saved Arnold, who was giving a lecture that the *Sun* had already published, after its delivery in New York.[24]

Compared to such debacles as these, the appearance in Richmond on December 18 was a stunning success. Arnold's agents had opposed his going there, but the lecture, despite being given "in a tumble-down old hall," went "very well, as [Arnold] was sure it would." He "had all the 'old families,' who in general do not go to lectures," he told his younger daughter (*L*, 2:285), and if the audience hardly rivaled the crowds attracted by Lily Langtry, whose American tour crisscrossed Arnold's and who the following week was to begin a three-nights engagement in the city,[25] it nonetheless numbered a respectable "three hundred and included many of Richmond's most cultured people."[26] Before such an audience of "old families"—which, in Ellen Glasgow's words, had preserved "custom, history, tradition, romantic fiction, and the Episcopal Church"[27]—Arnold was at his best. He was no orator, the *Daily Dispatch* reported in a front-page story, but he "delivered his lecture . . . with only occasional reference to the printed page which he had before him," "his pronunciation was rather musical," and "he appeared every inch the great thinker the world concedes him to be."[28]

But of greater importance to Arnold than his lecture was the opportunity afforded by Richmond—as far south as he was to travel—to observe firsthand a part of America that had suffered "in the furnace of civil war." His host was General Joseph R. Anderson, a West Point graduate who more than forty years earlier had undertaken direction of the nearly bankrupt Tredegar Iron Works in Richmond and before the outbreak of war had turned it into the largest foundry in the South, in the process becoming one of the richest and most influential men in the city. After brief service as a Confederate officer he resigned to resume direction of the company, which was essential to the South in supplying its forces with the matériel of war.[29]

Following the death of his first wife Anderson married Mary Pegram, a pretty, accomplished member of a distinguished family who had once conducted a fashionable school for young women and was regarded in Richmond as "the most noted conversationalist of her day."[30] Her brother John had been a classmate and intimate friend of Lee's eldest son, Custis, at West Point and during the war rose to the rank of general. Early in 1865, in the social event of the Confederate capital, he was married at Saint Paul's Church to Hetty Cary of Baltimore, the most famous belle of the time, and exactly three weeks later, after being killed in action, was buried from the same church. His younger brother, known as "Willie," had been a shy, retiring student at the University of Virginia when war broke out and awakened in him a thirst for battle. Rapidly promoted, he had become a colonel of artillery by the time he was twenty-three, when he was fatally wounded less than a week before Appomattox.[31]

Reminders of the war such as these appeared everywhere Arnold went. On the train from Washington to Richmond he passed through the densely wooded area of northern Virginia known as the Wilderness, where some of the most savage fighting had taken place and where Stonewall Jackson had been mortally wounded by one of his own men. In Richmond he observed sections of the city still impoverished by the war and toward dusk was driven with Mrs. Anderson through the serenely beautiful Hollywood Cemetery, where hundreds of Confederate dead—including her two brothers—lay buried. At dinner he met William Gordon McCabe,[32] who had fought throughout the war with "Willie" Pegram (of whom, he said, he could never think without recalling Clarendon's eulogy of Falkland) and had been with him at the time of his death.[33] In Mozart Hall, where he lectured, Arnold was introduced by Colonel Archer Anderson, General Anderson's son and a former chief of staff in the Confederate armies. Afterward, at a charity ball, he met the widow of Jackson (whose first wife was the sister of Margaret Junkin Preston, known as "the poetess of the Confederacy") and Jackson's daughter Julia, who the preceding spring had unveiled the recumbent statue of Lee by the Richmond sculptor Edward Virginius Valentine, whose studio Arnold visited the following day.[34] And as if all this were not enough, on his return to the Andersons' at the end of a long day Arnold "heard much about the war" before at last being allowed to go to bed (*L,* 2:285).[35]

Yet there is no evidence that he felt surfeited. On the contrary, he wished for more. "If I ever come back to America," he wrote from Washington to Mrs. Forster, "it will be to see more of the South" (*L,* 2:288). To Charles Eliot Norton he wrote from New York, "I was extremely interested with Virginia, and begin to think of really coming back once more before I die, in order to see the South and California." And two years later, just before his second trip to America, he wrote to Gordon McCabe, "It will go hard with me if I do not manage to see you in Virginia somewhere—the most attractive of all the States."[36]

The attraction that Virginia and the South held for Arnold is not easy to account for, though clearly it involved more than his pleasure in leaving the snow of the North for the comparative warmth of a region that had been "colonised not by the Puritans, but by English gentry" (*L*, 2:284); more than his enjoyment of amenities like excellent Madeira and the observance of such old English customs as the drawing of the cloth after dinner; more even than his relief in escaping from the wrath of Emerson's admirers and the impertinence of newspaper reporters.

A major reason the visit to Richmond engaged his interest, I suggest, is that it touched the deep vein of melancholy that was part of Arnold's temperament. "I have a great *penchant* for the Celtic races," he had confessed to Lady de Rothschild almost twenty years earlier, "with their melancholy and unprogressiveness (*L*, 1:279). He identified the "sweetest note" of the stricken Heine as his "plaintive note, his note of melancholy" and traced the source of the melancholy of the Celts to their "adverse destiny" and "immense calamities" (*CPW*, 3:131, 370). And in language closely akin to that in which he later spoke of Lee, he found in Lord Falkland's courage and melancholy the qualities of "a hero to the imagination of mankind in general" and in the inescapable fate he suffered the crown of his "indefinable" and "irresistible charm" (*CPW*, 8:196, 198).[37]

This side of Arnold appears to have become pronounced during the period of his American tour. In the spring of 1883 he described himself as having grown "very grave and solemn" (*CPW*, 10:493). Andrew Carnegie, who greeted him in New York, later remarked on his "grave silences,"[38] and in the opening paragraphs of his essay on Emerson, composed after his arrival in America, Arnold recalled the "mournful" voice of Newman and the "pathetic eloquence" of Carlyle (*CPW*, 10:165–66). The writer for the *Daily Dispatch* (Richmond) reported that his lecture contained "but a few sparkles of humor" and that he "spoke like a man in earnest," and less than three weeks later Henry Adams, who had canceled another engagement so he could have dinner with Arnold in Washington, called him "a melancholy specimen of what England produces at her best."[39] Although their appeal derived largely from their natural beauty, the only places in Virginia to win Arnold's unqualified praise were cemeteries associated with the Civil War—Hollywood in Richmond and (on his second visit to America) Arlington National Cemetery, where both Union and Confederate dead lay buried below the stately house in which the Lee family had lived before the war (*L*, 2:285, 389).

Yet however we account for Arnold's interest in the South, his visit to Richmond must be seen as a disappointment to "lovers of perfection in America." He came at a time when, as a recent historian of the city has written, "Richmond was becoming more like a city of the Old South than of the New," when racism and conservatism were growing increasingly "embedded in its society," and when "much of the antebellum graciousness, noblesse oblige, and disdain for money was gone, replaced by a materialism and a superficiality vividly perceived by Ellen Glasgow."[40] Arnold, to be sure, did not approve of all he saw. He remarked on "the dirt, untidiness, and spitting" that reminded him of reports by Trollope and Dickens, and he expressed astonishment at the segregation of the races. But he was pleased to avoid one of Richmond's bad hotels by accepting the hospitality of General Anderson, who seems not to have been badly burned "in the furnace of civil war" but rather to have emerged from it richer than before, living in "a capital house standing alone," with a garden behind extending almost a full city block,[41] and attended by unnumbered black servants; and Arnold was touched by "the interest of people in seeing [him] and in speaking of England, 'the mother country,' as they still call it" (*L*, 2:288). Writing uninhibitedly to members of his family, in letters later published with relatively few deletions, Arnold opened himself to charges like Howard Mumford Jones's that the culture of which he spoke always seemed the "possession of the saving remnant, *i.e.*, the richer Anglo-Saxons."[42]

If this is true, then there was a hollowness in Arnold's Richmond visit that found symbolic expression in the anecdote that concludes the story of his trip to the South. Nearly three years later, toward the end of his second visit to America, he was invited to Bar Harbor by Mrs. Burton Harrison, a minor novelist of the period, whose apparent purpose in life was to demonstrate the truth that in Virginia everyone is related to everyone else. She was a member of the family of Viscount Falkland; a great-great niece of Thomas Jefferson; a cousin of John Pegram's widow; the wife of the private secretary to Jefferson Davis during the war; and a sister of the Jennie Cary who had set James Ryder Randall's "Maryland, My Maryland" to an old German air to create the most famous of Confederate war songs. Because of chest pains Arnold declined her invitation to an entertainment she had planned for him—"a water pageant of Indian birch-bark canoes"—but later, during the entertainment, there was confusion when it was announced that the guest of honor was unable to be present, and "most canoeists went home firmly believing that they had been seen and admired by the famous apostle of sweetness and light."[43]

But to pursue this line of argument—to suggest that both the apostle and the doctrine of culture were shams—is patently unfair. It is as absurd to believe that Arnold could have done anything to arrest a retreat into the past that continued in Richmond for decades as it is unreasonable to imply that he should have declined to enjoy pleasures that might lighten an arduous tour. To be sure, one might wish that at some point he had proclaimed the truth uttered by Henry James after his visit to Richmond twenty years later—that the city had "worshipped false gods."[44] But that is not to say that Arnold failed to perceive this truth or that it was the only truth to be discovered in Richmond. Far more than James, whose lugubrious account of his visit is written in the manner in which Oscar Wilde thought his fiction was written (as if it were a painful duty), Arnold expressed the broad sympathies of a poet and humanist who could admire the flora of Hollywood Cemetery and the pretty young women of Richmond as well as appreciate the memories of a conflict that bore the classic attributes of tragedy, forcing men like Lee to choose between antithetical loyalties and dooming others like the Pegrams to die in a hopeless cause.

Arnold never returned to the South, but his reception in Richmond and his response to it marked the beginning of a friendship that has grown steadily during the past century, one of its notable manifestations being the scholarly, critical, and editorial attention given to his work by southerners or persons associated with southern colleges and universities. Nor did he alter his view of the compelling need for all of America to transform itself into "something higher, ampler, more gracious," as he made unmistakably plain in the final essay he published, "Civilisation in the United States." There he provided an appropriate conclusion to his comments on the American South, returning to the idea adumbrated years before at the end of *A French Eton* and closing on the note with which we began—the renovation and perfection of human society (*CPW*, 11:369).

NOTES

1. Later, in *St. Paul and Protestantism*, Arnold employed a related image to illustrate expiation: "Fire and the knife, cautery and amputation, are often necessary to induce a vital action, which, if it were not for our corrupting past, we might have obtained from the natural, healthful vigour of our moral organs" (*CPW*, 6:66).

2. Mary Custis Lee to Mrs. Francis Asbury Dickens, n.d. [1864]; Dickens Papers, catalog 2447, Manuscript Collection, Arlington House, Robert E. Lee Memorial. I am indebted to my wife, Mary P. Coulling, for this reference.

3. Arnold's sympathy with the South is pointed out by C. H. Leonard, *Arnold in America: A Study of Matthew Arnold's Literary Relations with America and of His Visits to This Country in 1883 and 1886* (Ann Arbor: University Microfilms, 1965), pp. 6–7.

4. *Letters of Matthew Arnold, 1848–1888*, ed. George W. E. Russell, 2 vols. (New York: Macmillan, 1895), 1:150 (hereafter cited in the text as *L*). Later, in dealing with the Irish question, Arnold used the analogy of the American South to argue against secession (see *CPW*, 11:68, 84, 132–33).

5. Hugh Kingsmill, *Matthew Arnold* (New York: Dial Press, 1928), pp. 199–200. Here, as throughout the book, Kingsmill presses his Freudian thesis: "[Arnold] was especially warped in his attitude to the Civil War by his unconscious distaste for everything and everyone that reminded him of Dr. Arnold. . . . The Puritan North . . . repelled Matt."

6. Jay B. Hubbell writes, "The Civil War had in large measure cut [the cultivated southerner] off from current Northern and British literature. He had thus missed reading Matthew Arnold, for example" (*The South in American Literature, 1607–1900* [Durham, N.C.: Duke University Press, 1954], p. 722).

7. The passage was deleted by Russell from the letter of Dec. 22, 1883 to Mrs. Forster.

8. *Recollections of Alexander H. Stephens,* ed. Myrta Lockett Avary (New York: Doubleday, Page, 1910), p. 483.

9. *Charleston Courier,* May 23, 1866, as quoted by Edd Winfield Parks, *William Gilmore Simms as Literary Critic,* University of Georgia Monographs, 7 (Athens: University of Georgia Press, 1961), p. 141 n. 53.

10. Hubbell, *South in American Literature,* p. 176, quotes Browne's comment on Methodist preachers: "For one man of general culture among them interested in Science, Art, Literature, there are ten that see, hear, eat, drink, breathe nothing but Methodism with its narrow formularies and pietistic vocabulary."

11. "Derby's and Bryant's Iliad," *Southern Review* 8 (July 1870): 39, 47.

12. "Dogma and Literature," *Southern Review* 14 (Apr. 1874): 245–46.

13. Burton J. Hendrick, *The Training of an American: The Earlier Life and Letters of Walter H. Page, 1855–1913* (Boston: Houghton Mifflin, 1928), pp. 55–56, 109.

14. *Southern Presbyterian Review* 27 (Oct. 1876):697–718; 28 (Apr. 1877):411; 30 (Apr. 1879):429; 35 (July 1884):577–78.

15. Ellen Glasgow, *A Certain Measure: An Interpretation of Prose Fiction* (New York: Harcourt, Brace, 1938), p. 12.

16. Apr. 4, 1876, as quoted by C. Vann Woodward, *Origins of the New South, 1877–1913* (Baton Rouge: Louisiana State University Press, 1971), p. 151. Woodward discusses "the divided mind of the New South" on pages 142–74.

17. Louis Rubin, "Two in Richmond: Ellen Glasgow and James Branch Cabell," in *South: Modern Southern Literature in Its Cultural Setting,* ed. Louis D. Rubin, Jr., and Robert D. Jacobs (Garden City,

N.Y.: Doubleday, 1961), pp. 115, 133; Glasgow, *A Certain Measure,* p. 27.

18. *Mary Chesnut's Civil War,* ed. C. Vann Woodward (New Haven: Yale University Press, 1981), p. 508 (entry of Dec. 18, 1863); Glasgow, *A Certain Measure,* p. 11. According to Hubbell (*South in American Literature,* p. 361), John P. Little wrote in his *History of Richmond* (first published in 1851–52) that the city library was "one of the most insignificant ones that could be collected in any place as large and prosperous as Richmond; it may be classed among the curiosities of the city, as it scarcely deserves mention as any thing else."

19. *Selected Letters: John Garland James to Paul Hamilton Hayne and Mary Middleton Michel Hayne,* ed. Daniel Morley McKeithan (Austin: University of Texas Press, 1946), pp. 411, 422; Harris in *Atlanta Constitution,* quoted in *Harper's Weekly* 24 (1880):19, as quoted by Woodward, *Origins of the New South,* p. 166.

20. Lewis P. Simpson writes, "In his highly influential history of the Civil War from the Southern point of view (1866) Edwin A. Pollard, editor of the Richmond *Examiner* during the war years, warns against the South's concentrating upon 'recovering the mere *material* prosperity' and admonishes Southerners to assert their well-known superiority in civilization" (*The Man of Letters in New England and the South: Essays on the History of the Literary Vocation in America* [Baton Rouge: Louisiana State University Press, 1973], p. 222).

21. The judgment of the *Dictionary of American Biography,* 3:495.

22. *Washington Post,* Dec. 18, 1883.

23. Leonard (*Arnold in America,* pp. 47–48) points out the friendship between Arnold and Sylvester, who had tried to get him to take the professorship of English literature at Johns Hopkins.

24. *Baltimore Sun,* Dec. 24, 21, 1883.

25. *Daily Dispatch* (Richmond), Dec. 27, 1883, which predicted: "Each night will see a full house." Leonard (*Arnold in America,* p. 170) mistakenly says that Mrs. Langtry was performing in Richmond on the evening of Arnold's lecture.

26. *State* (Richmond), Dec. 19, 1883.

27. Ellen Glasgow, *Barren Ground* (Garden City, N.Y.: Doubleday, 1925), p. 5.

28. *Daily Dispatch* (Richmond), Dec. 27, 1883.

29. Leonard (*Arnold in America,* p. 170) mistakenly identifies Arnold's host as Colonel Archer Anderson, General Anderson's son. The fullest account of Anderson is by Charles B. Dew, *Ironmaker to the Confederacy: Joseph R. Anderson and the Tredegar Iron Works* (New Haven: Yale University Press, 1966).

30. T. C. DeLeon, *Belles, Beaux and Brains of the Sixties* (New York: G. W. Dillingham, 1909), p. 125.

31. Douglas Southall Freeman, *Lee's Lieutenants: A Study in Command*, 4 vols. (New York: Scribner's, 1942–44), 1:27, 34, 596, 649–51; 2:279, 450; 3:238, 351, 582, 629, 632, 672–73.

32. The identification is made by Arthur Kyle Davis, Jr., in "Matthew Arnold Comes to America" (Manuscripts Department, University of Virginia Library, Accession no. 9829, Box 19), p. 28, on the basis of a marginal comment by McCabe in his copy of Arnold's *Letters*. The essay, originally entitled "Matthew Arnold Comes to Virginia," was brought to my attention by Park Honan, *Matthew Arnold: A Life* (New York: McGraw-Hill, 1981), p. 479, n. 48.

33. Armistead C. Gordon, *Memories and Memorials of William Gordon McCabe* (Richmond: Old Dominion Press, 1925), 1:92, 171. After the war McCabe, whose favorite book was *Tom Brown's Schooldays*, established a school in Petersburg, Virginia, which was patterned after Rugby. When he visited Rugby in 1866 and identified himself as a southerner, one of the boys replied, "You will find almost everybody 'Southern' in England" (1:195, 276).

34. Davis, "Matthew Arnold Comes to America," p. 32. The visit is briefly recorded by Elizabeth Gray Valentine, *Dawn to Twilight: Work of Edward V. Valentine* (Richmond: William Byrd Press, 1929), p. 175.

35. Leonard (*Arnold in America*, p. 171) quotes Arnold's remark to William Forster that "Americans should get done with the Civil War as a topic; it was a bore" (Thomas Beer, *Stephen Crane: A Study in American Letters* [London, 1924], p. 45), a comment inconsistent with Arnold's expressed interest in the subject.

36. David J. DeLaura, "Matthew Arnold and the American 'Literary Class': Unpublished Correspondence and Some Further Reasons," *Bulletin of the New York Public Library* 70 (1966):242; Gordon, *Memories*, 2:342.

37. Arnold's view of Falkland is at the heart of John P. Farrell's "Matthew Arnold's Tragic Vision," *PMLA* 85 (Jan. 1970):107–17.

38. Andrew Carnegie, *Autobiography of Andrew Carnegie* (Boston: Houghton Mifflin, 1920), p. 298.

39. *Daily Dispatch* (Richmond), Dec. 19, 1883; *The Letters of Henry Adams*, ed. J. C. Levenson et al. (Cambridge, Mass.: Belknap Press of Harvard University Press, 1982–), 2:527.

40. Michael B. Chesson, *Richmond after the War, 1865–1890* (Richmond: Virginia State Library, 1981), pp. 204, 210.

41. Robert B. Munford, Jr., *Richmond Homes and Memories* (Richmond: Garrett and Massie, 1936), p. 35.

42. Howard Mumford Jones, "Arnold, Aristocracy, and America," *American Historical Review* 49 (Apr. 1944):400. Arnold disarmingly confessed to Carnegie, "We are all snobs. Hundreds of years have made us so, all snobs. We can't help it. It is in the blood" (Carnegie, *Autobiography,* p. 301).

43. Mrs. Burton Harrison, *Recollections Grave and Gay* (London: Smith, Elder, 1912), pp. 351–52.

44. Henry James, *The American Scene* (London: Rupert Hart-Davis, 1968), p. 394.

MARY G. MCBRIDE

Matthew Arnold and Andrew Carnegie: The Religion of Culture and the Gospel of Wealth

In his examination of Matthew Arnold's influence on American culture, John Henry Raleigh writes that "like all lengthy historical evolutions, the direct American tradition of Matthew Arnold is not without its ironies, those strange anomalies in the courses of events by which history defies logic."[1] Although Raleigh does not include Andrew Carnegie in his study, I believe that the relationship between Arnold and Carnegie illustrates one of the most interesting of the apparent anomalies of Arnoldian influence on American civilization. Given their differences in educational background and temperament, friendship between the British man of letters and the self-educated Pittsburgh millionaire would, at first glance, seem to be impossible. Park Honan notes that before his first visit to the United States, Arnold knew few Americans of the 'Mr. Bottles' type" and that "Carnegie almost symbolized an unrefined, middle-class America—which might listen to critics."[2] The American steel baron did indeed listen to the English critic, and his "Gospel of Wealth" was profoundly influenced by the social idealism of Matthew Arnold.

Andrew Carnegie first met Matthew Arnold at a dinner

given by Mr. and Mrs. Henry Yates Thompson (of the *Pall Mall Gazette*) in London on June 21, 1883. Carnegie was eager for Arnold to visit America on a lecture tour and, to further that goal, entertained him for dinner at the Grand Hotel on July 17, 1883. Arnold, who had been contemplating such a trip for several years, told the American he might have difficulty obtaining a leave from his school inspection duties.[3] Difficulties finally overcome in October of that year, Arnold, his wife, and his daughter Lucy sailed on the Cunarder *Servia* to the United States for a tour of some seventy speaking engagements. The Arnolds stayed with Carnegie and his mother at the Hotel Windsor in New York, and the Carnegies entertained them lavishly. When Arnold had problems projecting his voice during the inaugural lecture in New York (General Grant walked out on this lecture because he could not hear the British lion roar), Carnegie arranged for some coaching from his own elocution teacher, Professor John Wesley Churchill of Andover. No account of Arnold's first American lecture is complete without Mrs. Carnegie's perceptive description of his style. When Arnold asked her opinion of his performance, Margaret Carnegie slowly replied in a phrase that delighted Arnold: "Too meenisteerial, Mr. Arnold, too meenisteerial." Arnold frequently quoted the remark, saying that Mrs. Carnegie "hit the nail on the head."[4]

Despite Arnold's limitations as a public lecturer and the hostility of many American newspapers, Carnegie considered Arnold's visit to be a major triumph of his life. His most recent biographer describes their relationship during the first American visit in energetic terms: "Like a mother hen showing off her only chick, Carnegie clucked and hovered over the bewildered poet throughout his visit, arranging elocution lessons for him in Boston, leading him through the frightening smells and sounds of the Chicago stockyards, and proudly displaying him to the bemused steelworkers at Braddock. Curiously enough, Arnold was fascinated by all of it, amused by Carnegie's enthusiasms, delighted by his intellectual naiveté, and almost hypnotized by his solicitous care. The two became close friends, and their friendship endured until Arnold's death four years later."[5] This listing of incidents, while colorfully conveying the hectic nature of Arnold's trip, illustrates some of the inaccuracies found in accounts of the American tour. Carnegie indeed wanted Arnold to see the wonders of the Chicago stockyards, where, the claim went, a living hog could be driven into a machine at one end and a ham emerge at the other before its squeal was out of the spectator's ears. Arnold quietly declined: "Why should I see pigs killed! Why should I hear pigs squeal!" Carnegie did not press the invitation. (Arnold was amused, however, when Carnegie repeated Chicago's boast that "when she went in for culture she would make it hum.") Furthermore, Arnold did not tour the steel mills until his 1886 stay with Carnegie during the second American visit.[6]

The highlights of the five-year friendship encompass both civic and personal activities. In the spring of 1884, Carnegie invited the Arnolds and Lucy to join a group of prominent Englishmen on a coaching tour from London through southern England.[7] Arnold stayed for three days with Carnegie at Braemar Cottage in 1886 and accompanied him to sites of interest around Pittsburgh, Holidaysburg, and Loretto. He also visited Carnegie's Kilgraston house in Scotland in 1887. Each year the American millionaire sent the English critic the traditional gift of a Christmas turkey, which Arnold said was the best he had ever tasted. When Arnold died in 1888, Carnegie considered it a deep privilege to be thought worthy to spearhead contributions to his memorial fund in the United States. Ramifications of their friendship touched each man's life in unexpectedly intimate ways: Lucy Arnold met her future American husband at one of Carnegie's parties in 1883, and Arnold introduced Carnegie to John Morley, who was to become his closest friend and adviser until Carnegie's death in 1919. Carnegie begins the chapter of his *Autobiography* that he devotes to Arnold with the statement that he and Morley considered him the most charming man they ever knew: "He had, indeed, 'a charm'—that is the only word which expresses the effect of his presence and his conversation. Even his look and grave silences charmed."[8]

The friendship of Arnold and Carnegie was thus affectionate and strong. But the intellectual and moral influence was to survive Arnold's death and become an important source of Carnegie's mature philanthropic philosophy. Recent studies of

Carnegie reveal a flexibility and complexity in his thought that challenge earlier stereotypes of him as a Gilded Age robber baron and Social Darwinist. Largely self-educated, Carnegie was nevertheless widely read and traveled. He valued the friendship of the eminent men of his time—particularly poets, statesmen, and men of letters. Devoted to the world of ideas and a prolific writer who took more pride in his books and numerous articles in the *Nineteenth Century,* the *Fortnightly,* the *North American Review,* and the *Pall Mall Gazette* than in his great steel works, Carnegie is the culmination of the tradition of American success stories that begins with Benjamin Franklin. Although he drew his social and spiritual values from several sources, evidence of Arnold's influence can be traced throughout his long career. If Joseph Wall and Richard M. Huber are correct in their contention that Carnegie's great need was for moral and humanitarian justification of his life,[9] and I think they are, Arnold provided him with an ethical vocabulary, a spiritual orientation, and an intellectual stance that facilitated that self-justification in several important ways.

Lionel Trilling notes the satisfaction that Arnold felt about his growing influence in the 1880s, pointing out that "while his name might be dangerous among some sects and among the most rigorously orthodox of the church . . . a man like Andrew Carnegie [made] him his guide in religion." Arnold, however, did not guide the formation of Carnegie's beliefs so much as he legitimized, humanized, and broadened them. Carnegie was, in his own words, "not much hampered" by traditional teaching in religion. He writes that even before the family emigrated to Pennsylvania from Scotland, there was "not one orthodox Presbyterian in our family circle." His mother, passively reticent upon religious matters, did not attend church, although his father participated in Swedenborgian Society services and took young Andrew and his brother with him. As a young adult, Carnegie solemnly debated theological issues with his Pittsburgh friends and determined to follow Carlyle's resolve: "'If it be incredible, in God's name let it be discredited.'" Traditional religious dogmas were discussed and voted down one by one by the youthful Carnegie and his friends as "the mistaken ideas of men of a less enlightened age." Rejecting the Calvinistic theology of his Scottish heritage and the Swedenborgian faith of his father, Carnegie found in evolutionary theory and the writings of Herbert Spencer a belief in the progress of humanity toward perfection that he embodied in the motto: "All is well since all grows better and better." [10]

He credits the exposure to other civilizations in his around-the-world voyage of 1878 with giving him the belief that man's religions were equally valuable and that Buddha, Confucius, Zoroaster, and Christ were all great teachers. Carnegie explains that "the teachings of all these I found ethically akin so that I could say with Matthew Arnold, one I was so proud to call friend":

> "Children of men! the unseen power, whose eye
> For ever doth accompany mankind,
> Hath looked on no religion scornfully
>   That men did ever find.
>
> Which has not taught weak wills how much they can?
> Which has not fall'n in the dry heart like rain?
> Which has not cried to sunk, self-weary man,
>   *Thou must be born again.*" [11]

Yet Carnegie, as Joseph Wall points out, "would qualify Arnold's poetic universalism by insisting that the Supreme Ruler would certainly scorn many of the religious practices that were performed by men everywhere in the name of the Deity whom they would honor." [12] Carnegie was convinced that the dogmatic intransigence of any creed—Christian as well as Hindu—was equally degrading to the nature of man. In *Round the World,* the account of his 1878 journey, he is scathingly critical of the Christian dogma of salvation, using the negative language that Arnold found so destructive in contemporary religious debate.

Although he alludes to spiritual unrest and even chaos in his *Autobiography,* Carnegie's life gives little evidence of the deep spiritual anguish that characterizes so many Victorians. The influence of his mother's religious attitude was surely an important factor in his comparative serenity. But Arnold brought him to a more respectful understanding of traditional belief and an insight into the sorrow that liberal theological ideas could cause religiously conservative family and friends. He describes a conversation on this subject when he and Arnold visited the grave of Bishop John Keble in Hursley Churchyard during the coaching tour of 1884, succinctly summarizing Arnold's influence on his own thought: "If ever there was a seriously religious man it was Matthew Arnold. No irreverent word ever escaped his lips. In this he and Gladstone were equally above reproach and yet he had in one short sentence slain the supernatural. 'The case against miracles is closed. They do not happen.'" [13] If Arnold had slain the supernatural, he nevertheless provided Carnegie with a mature confidence in the truth of Christian teaching and the vital relevance of its ethics as well as an appreciation of the beauty of its traditional forms. In marked contrast to the language of *Round the World,* he describes religion in Arnoldian terms in "The Gospel of Wealth" as a "beautiful and enchanting realm," a "magic circle" that nourishes "an inner life more precious than the external." [14] The Arnoldian distinction between dogma and religion was especially appealing to Carnegie. It is the key concept of an address written for his installation as rector of St. Andrew's University in 1902, although he was dissuaded from delivering it because of the supposed unsuitability of its ideas for students. In this speech, first published in 1933, he credits Spencer, Darwin, and Arnold with helping him to understand that theology is of man, whereas religion is in man, stressing the deep obligation of "'improving our fellow-man'" and "'obeying the judge within.'" [15] Carnegie concludes this confession of his personal religious philosophy with a plea for social justice.

Carnegie translated his spiritual and psychological need for self-justification and his concern for social justice into a philanthropic philosophy based on the idea of stewardship. He wrote the essay known as "The Gospel of Wealth" in 1889, but the genesis of the idea came twenty years earlier. In late December of 1868, when Matthew Arnold was composing the preface to *Culture and Anarchy,* Andrew Carnegie was writing an introspective analysis of his own life. The memorandum to himself begins with a blunt accounting of his age and financial worth: "Thirty three and an income of 50,000$ per annum!" Carnegie notes that if he can secure this annual income, he will make no effort to earn more but will give the surplus each year to benevolent purposes, will go to Oxford for three years and make the acquaintance of literary men, and will then settle in London as the publisher of a newspaper or review, taking part in discussions on such public issues as education and the condition of the poor. The memorandum concludes: "Man must have an idol—the amassing of wealth is one of the worst species of idolatry—no idol more debasing than the worship of money. Whatever I engage in I must push inordinately; therefore should I be careful to choose that life which will be the most elevating in its character. To continue much longer overwhelmed by business cares and with most of my thoughts wholly upon the way to make more money in the shortest time, must degrade me beyond hope of permanent recovery. I will resign business at thirty-five, but during the ensuing two years I wish to spend the afternoons in receiving instruction and in reading systematically."[16]

Carnegie's admonition to himself is remarkably akin to Arnold's warning to the Philistines in *Culture and Anarchy* that only the idea of culture can help men to perceive that wealth is simply machinery, that no amount of money is worth the price of giving all life and thought to its possession. Carnegie feared that single-minded concentration upon wealth would degrade him beyond hope of recovery; Arnold warned that such devotion would mean the sacrifice of a generation of industrialists, contending that "culture admits the necessity of the movement towards fortune-making and exaggerated industrialism, readily allows that the future may derive benefit from it; but insists, at the same time, that the passing generations of industrialists,—forming, for the most part, the stout main body of Philistinism,—are sacrificed to it" (*CPW,* 5:105). Carnegie did not reach his goal of retirement at thirty-five, nor did he stop earning money when his income reached $50,000 per year, but neither did he allow himself to be sacrificed to a degrading Philistinism.

The social idealism of Matthew Arnold informs the essence of "The Gospel of Wealth," the title given Carnegie's

1889 *North American Review* essay "Wealth" when W. T. Stead reprinted it in the *Pall Mall Gazette*. Carnegie's thesis is that the proper administration of wealth is the key to the harmonious relationship of all classes in a spirit of brotherhood. He contends that industrialism creates a dangerous spirit of competition that leads to the loss of societal homogeneity and inevitably puts wealth and resources in the hands of a few. Carnegie believes that the man who dies rich dies disgraced. The wealthy man thus has the obligation to spend his fortune for the public good: "To set an example of modest, unostentatious living, shunning display or extravagance; to provide moderately for the legitimate wants of those dependent upon him; and, after doing so, to consider all surplus revenues which come to him simply as trust funds, which he is called upon to administer in the manner which, in his judgment, is best calculated to produce the most beneficial results for the community."[17] Carnegie, in effect, translates Arnold's concept of the best self as the basis of authority within the state into the idea that the best minds must dispose of surplus wealth by administering it for the community and bringing rich and poor together in a harmonious whole. He takes literally the Arnoldian injunction that culture means the passion for making sweetness and light prevail, and, in the essay that follows "Wealth," he describes his concept of the most deserving objects of philanthropy.

Carnegie's analysis of the proper use of surplus wealth in "Best Fields for Philanthropy" includes a hierarchical listing of human needs that corresponds to the powers Arnold believed constituted the harmonious development of human nature and that he lists in "Equality" (1878), "A Word about America" (1882), "Literature and Science" (1882), and "Civilisation in the United States" (1888). Carnegie places chief emphasis on what Arnold calls the power of intellect and knowledge, declaring that the creation and support of universities, free libraries, and hospitals, medical colleges, and laboratories are the three most important areas of philanthropy. Carnegie next advocates the support of parks and concert halls so that the masses of men "can feed their love for the beautiful." The power of social life and manners is addressed in Carnegie's sixth recommendation of beneficence for community swimming pools. Bequests to church buildings (not their activities) come seventh and last in Carnegie's list, and he includes churches not so much because of their influence on conduct as because they are often the "center of social life and source of neighborly feeling," and their beauty, enhanced by the colors of stained glass and the music of the organ, will inspire the young to an intuition of a higher, spiritual realm.[18]

Carnegie's philanthropic philosophy was startling to many because it ignored the usual objects of charity in the nineteenth century. Focusing on Arnoldian objectives, Carnegie believed that great wealth must be used to stamp out ignorance and to reconstruct society through the improvement of human knowledge, broadly defined. He praised Leland Stanford for providing $10 million for a new university in California and later criticized John Jacob Astor for willing $150 million to one descendant, while the Astor library lacked funds to purchase the books required of a first-class institution. In a long article in the *Nineteenth Century* in 1900, Gladstone approved Carnegie's solution for the newly urgent problem of the disposition of riches but expressed dismay at his neglect of religious institutions and his denigration of hereditary wealth. Gladstone realized that Carnegie's ideas represented a practical solution to what he considered to be the irresponsible use of wealth recently acquired by businessmen and financial speculators with no real foundation in civic obligation or the traditions of landed estates.[19]

Shortly after the publication of *The Gospel of Wealth* in book form in 1900, Carnegie was able to realize the dream that he had first formulated in the memorandum of 1868: he retired from business and devoted himself completely to the implementation of his philanthropic philosophy. In *Culture and Anarchy,* Arnold had written that "all the love of our neighbor, the impulses towards action, help, and beneficence, the desire for removing human error, clearing human confusion, and diminishing human misery, the noble aspiration to leave the world better and happier than we found it,—motives eminently such as are called social,—come in as part of the grounds of culture, and the main and preeminent part" (*CPW,* 5:91). These goals, the grounds of culture, became the motivating principle of Carnegie's great bequests of the early twentieth century. As Gladstone had perceived, Carnegie became the founder of modern philanthropy. He consciously assumed Arnold's language and made his understanding of sweetness and light the foundation of his philanthropic policy.

Arnold's concept of culture is informed by the scientific passion of seeing clearly as well as by the passion of doing good. Combining the two Arnoldian goals, Carnegie declared himself to be a "scientific philanthropist" whose gifts were marked by the careful analysis and forethought described in *The Gospel of Wealth*. In 1903, when he set up a $2.5 million trust for his native town of Dunfermline, Scotland, Carnegie explained that he wished to test "'by experiment'" the advantages that might come to a community from "'funds dedicated to the purpose of providing the means of introducing into the daily lives of the masses, such privileges and enjoyments as are under present circumstances considered beyond their reach, but if which brought within their reach are calculated to carry into their homes and their conduct sweetness and light.'" In the original draft of the bequest, Carnegie noted his intention of bringing the same gifts of sweetness and light into the lives of the citizens of a town of equal size in the United States and of comparing the effects in the old country and the new. The concept of such a comparative experiment in sweetness and light was deleted from the final draft of the deed, but as Joseph Wall points out, "it was an interesting idea, and sociologists might well have been provided with material for fascinating comparative studies between the two cultures had the experiment been carried out."[20]

In the earlier drafts of the Dunfermline bequest, Carnegie listed the specific areas of sweetness and light that he wished to support; they included "public gardens, parks, golf links, art galleries, public exhibitions of art, lectures, public entertainment such as theatrical and musical events, musical societies, field trips for school children to historic and scenic spots in Scotland, the restoration of the Abbey and the palace of the Stuarts, medical clinics, even model housing for the poor." In 1911 he wrote to the chairman of the Dunfermline Trust insisting that he look into the issue of model housing at once, especially the inclusion of indoor plumbing and a bathroom in each house. "'I consider this the most important feature,'" Carnegie wrote, "'I know of no way of diffusing sweetness and light more easily and practically than by improving housing conditions among the poor.'" Carnegie was persuaded to leave such specific projects in the hands of the trustees who were on the scene, and the final draft of the deed called only for the general goal of bringing "some charm, some happiness, some elevating conditions of life" into the lives of the young people of his native town. He insisted that all classes be represented on the board of the Trust: a miner, a union officer, and a dyer were duly named to represent the Populace and joined the town's Barbarians and Philistines in administering the funds. Wall comments that these trustees actually "did a remarkable job over the years in dispensing 'sweetness and light' to the fortunate citizens of Dunfermline. The endowment, originally $2,500,000 but soon raised to $4,000,000, yielded an interest amounting to $200,000 annually, making Dunfermline, a town of only 27,000, the community with the largest private endowment in the world."[21]

The Dunfermline experiment in sweetness and light is, of course, only one example of Carnegie's philanthropic endeavor to make reason and the will of God prevail. It is estimated that he gave away $350 million in his own lifetime to libraries, museums, art institutes, research centers, and educational institutions. The only stipulation that he placed on the bequests to municipal libraries was that the inscription "Let There Be Light" be placed over the entranceway (these words probably have an Arnoldian as much as a biblical reference). He was devoted to technology and science and believed that scientific study should be given the central emphasis in modern universities. John Morley wrote to Carnegie in 1901 to protest his heavy support of scientific and technical subjects: "'True, literary education has had an excessive share—very excessive—but that is no reason at all why a man like you should now like Luther's drunken man on horseback having swayed violently to one side sway violently to the other. We expect you to show that you have not been the friend of M. Arnold for nothing.'"[22]

Carnegie, however, did not yield, insisting that he was only attempting to redress a balance in education essential for the modern world. On most issues, however, the views of Carnegie and Arnold were complementary. They shared the belief that the state must regulate unrestricted competition and provide for social change. They admired the excellence of America's federal system of government, considered the United States Senate to be the most effective governing body in the world, and deplored inequality and aristocracy. Neither had confidence in the ability of those at universities to regulate themselves.

Arnold's chief criticism of American life was that it ignored the human problem, that it was uninteresting. In a letter to Grant Duff in 1886, he discusses Carnegie's *Triumphant Democracy* as an example of America's inability to understand this great defect: "The facts he has collected as to the material progress of this country are valuable, and I am told the book is having a great sale. . . . He and most Americans are simply unaware that nothing in the book touches the capital defect of life over here: namely, that compared with life in England it is so uninteresting, so without savour and without depth. Do they think to prove that it must have savour and depth by pointing to the number of public libraries, schools, and places of worship?"[23] Arnold repeats this basic criticism in "Civilisation in the United States," arguing that Americans have solved the political and social problem but have not even recognized the human problem that creates such a void in American civilization: "In what concerns the solving of the political and social problem they see clear and think straight; in what concerns the higher civilisation they live in a fool's paradise" (*CPW,* 11:367). Although Carnegie was devoted to statistical demonstrations of progress in the United States, he understood Arnold's concern about the quality of life in the young country.

The diffusion of sweetness and light became Carnegie's mission in life. His friendship with Matthew Arnold is an apt illustration of Trilling's description of Arnold as "one of the many foreigners who, dropped into the uneasy brew of American culture, could make it boil and seethe and precipitate strange things."[24] It is certain, however, that Carnegie saw nothing strange or anomalous in providing the material means to Arnoldian ends. The "gospel of wealth" is a philanthropic philosophy that attempted to provide the savor, the depth, and the higher civilization that Arnold found so lacking in American life. Carnegie's grand experiment in sweetness and light, which lives on with each performance at Carnegie Hall, with each report of the Carnegie Foundation for the Advancement of Teaching, and with each pension payment from TIAA-CREF, is thus a vital part of the American Arnoldian tradition.

NOTES

1. John Henry Raleigh, *Matthew Arnold and American Culture* (Berkeley and Los Angeles: University of California Press, 1961), p. 253.

2. Park Honan, *Matthew Arnold: A Life* (New York: McGraw-Hill, 1981), p. 394.

3. Howard Bernard Leichman, "Matthew Arnold's Correspondence: The American Visits, May 21, 1882, to September 19, 1886" (Ph.D. dissertation, University of Washington, 1972), p. 18.

4. Lionel Trilling, *Matthew Arnold* (1939; rpt. Cleveland: World, 1955), p. 362; Honan, *Arnold,* pp. 398–99.

5. Joseph F. Wall, *Andrew Carnegie* (New York: Oxford University Press, 1970), p. 426.

6. See Andrew Carnegie, *Autobiography of Andrew Carnegie* (Boston: Houghton Mifflin, 1920), p. 294; Honan, *Arnold,* p. 405; Leichman, "Arnold's Correspondence," p. 288; and Chilson Hathaway Leonard, "Arnold in America: A Study of Matthew Arnold's Literary Relations with America and of His Visits to This Country in 1883 and 1886" (Ph.D. dissertation, Yale University, 1932), p. 341. Carnegie tells of Arnold's reaction to the invitation to the Chicago stockyards in *Triumphant Democracy or Fifty Years March of the Republic,* ed. Martin L. Fausold, 2 vols. (1886; rpt. New York, 1971), 2:216–17. The Chicago story is also found in Burton J. Hendrick, *The Life of Andrew Carnegie,* 2 vols. (1932; rpt. New York, 1969), 1:244.

7. In his *Autobiography,* Carnegie gives the date of this coaching tour as 1880, but Arnold and Carnegie did not meet until 1883, and the coaching tour was in 1884. See Wall, *Carnegie,* p. 435.

8. Leichman, "Arnold's Correspondence," pp. 288, 227; Carne-

gie, *Autobiography*, pp. 289, 296, 286 (quotation); Honan, *Arnold*, p. 416.

9. Richard M. Huber, *The American Idea of Success* (New York: McGraw-Hill, 1971), p. 67; Wall, *Carnegie*, p. 813.

10. Trilling, *Arnold*, pp. 355–56; Carnegie, *Autobiography*, pp. 21, 48, 72, 327.

11. Carnegie, *Autobiography*, p. 199; the quotation is from Arnold's poem "Progress" (1852).

12. Wall, *Carnegie*, 368.

13. Carnegie, *Autobiography*, pp. 286–87. Regarding this incident, Honan writes that Arnold "found a dramatic, amusing appeal in Andrew Carnegie's own personality at this time and later 'performed' for that friend, as when M.A. impressed him with a speech at Keble's grave" (*Arnold*, 478). There is no hint in Carnegie's account, however, that Arnold was anything but sincere in his remarks at Keble's grave.

14. Andrew Carnegie, *The Gospel of Wealth*, ed. Edward C. Kirkland (1900; rpt. Cambridge, Mass.: Harvard University Press, 1962), p. 47.

15. Quoted in George Swetnam, *Andrew Carnegie* (New York: Twayne, 1980), pp. 113–14. Swetnam perpetuates another of the inaccuracies of detail in the Arnold-Carnegie relationship noted above by identifying Edwin Arnold as Matthew Arnold's brother (p. 36). This misidentification was common in nineteenth-century America. Arnold, who considered Edwin Arnold's most famous poem, "The Light of Asia," unintelligible, was annoyed by the confusion of the two in the popular press. Carnegie, however, admired Edwin Arnold's poetry almost as much as he did that of Matthew Arnold. He considered the original manuscript of "The Light of Asia" one of his most valuable possessions (*Autobiography*, p. 200).

16. Carnegie, *Autobiography*, pp. 152–53.

17. Carnegie, *Gospel of Wealth*, p. 25.

18. Ibid., pp. 44–46.

19. Hendrick, *Carnegie*, 1:343–44.

20. Quoted in Wall, *Carnegie*, p. 849; see also pp. 850–51.

21. Quoted in ibid., p. 851; see also p. 854.

22. Quoted in ibid., p. 838.

23. Leichman, "Arnold's Correspondence," p. 294.

24. Trilling, *Arnold*, p. 357.

Laurence W. Mazzeno and Allan Lefcowitz

SIX

Arnold and Bryce: The Problem of American Democracy and Culture

The modern reader of James Bryce's *The American Common-wealth* may be struck with the Arnoldian tone and substance of much of Bryce's discussion of American cultural patterns, while at the same time, he rebuts Arnold's writings about America, particularly "Civilisation in the United States."[1] Bryce's study, of course—insofar as it had a political subtext— was intended to change British attitudes about America, and Arnold's public statements could be taken as simply reflecting what other observers were saying. Still, it appeared to us more than fortuitous that Bryce was composing the latter portions of the *The American Commonwealth* during 1888. Arnold's "Civilisation in the United States" had just been published, and much of those final sections of *The American Commonwealth* did appear to take Arnold to task.

Bryce had a simple explanation for the situation. In a letter to Sarah Wyman Whitman, an American friend, written shortly after he finished his study, Bryce wrote: "When I read Mr. Arnold's articles I feel how much better he would have done it if he had been longer over there and taken even half the pains I have taken. He in fact errs; but he errs from ignorance, not from any defect in handling."[2]

It is doubtful if Arnold would have changed his point of view had he been more informed. Even with *The American Commonwealth* before him, Arnold may still have said to Bryce: "Yes, yes! my good Bryce, you are quite right, but, you see, my view of the matter is different, and I have little doubt it is the true one!"[3]

The differences in their outlook on American society resulted from deep philosophical differences in their attitudes toward democracy. Their reactions to American newspapers provide a vivid example. Arnold found American newspapers to be one measure of the nation's lack of "distinction": "I should say that if one were searching for the best means to efface and kill in a whole nation the discipline of respect, the feeling for what is elevated, one could not do better than take the American newspapers. The absence of truth and soberness in them, the poverty in serious interest, the personality and sensation-mongering, are beyond belief" (*CPW,* 11:361). Bryce says of the newspapers: "[Their] vigour and brightness . . . are surprising. Nothing escapes them: everything is set in the sharpest, clearest light. Their want of reticence and delicacy is regretfully admitted by all educated Americans—the editors, I think, included."[4] For him, the phenomenon was not a symptom of the American lack of discipline but was more universal: "Most of the reasons I have hazarded to account for a phenomenon surprising to one who recognizes the quality of intellect current in America, and the diffusion, far more general than in any other country, of intellectual curiousity, are reasons valid in the Europe of to-day as compared with the Europe of last century, and still more true of the modern world as compared with the best periods of the ancient" (*AC,* 2:646–47).

Why two men who believed equally in the values of the great Western tradition should so radically disagree about how to read the facts they essentially agreed on evidences something about the intellectual problem that American democracy presented to Arnold and reveals more starkly Arnold's tendency to mask beneath his rhetoric essentially a priori thinking habits. Reading Arnold's work against *The American Commonwealth* shows that Arnold is less flexible about and accepting of democracy and equality than he appears when read out of the context of the Victorian debate about democracy. In brief, Bryce is a touchstone to measure Arnold's taste for what America represented.

Selecting Bryce and his work for comparison with Arnold has considerable merit. Both Britishers and Americans in the nineteenth century considered Bryce a man of note. Born in Belfast in May 1838, the son of a schoolmaster and geologist, Bryce enrolled in Glasgow University in 1854 and three years later entered Oxford. There he distinguished himself as a writer and orator and made important contacts—including one with Matthew Arnold. He won the Thomas Arnold prize for history in 1863 with his essay on the Holy Roman Empire, which became a standard work on the period.[5]

An inveterate traveler, Bryce journeyed to the Americas, all across Europe, to Africa, Asia, and Australia. By far his most frequent stop was the United States, to which he had considered emigrating in 1870 on his first visit. From that visit and subsequent ones during the next two decades, he developed an impression of the country that he fleshed out in the volumes of *The American Commonwealth*. The work, which sold more than a quarter of a million copies, made him the most popular Englishman of his generation in America. His friends included Theodore Roosevelt, William Howard Taft, Oliver Wendell Holmes (Senior and Junior), Henry James, and Woodrow Wilson, who reviewed *The American Commonwealth* in 1889.

Bryce was by no means uncritical, yet Americans sensed that he had a genuine understanding of the virtues of their country and their culture. Arnold, too, claimed to appreciate America and to be on the side of democracy and equality; however, most Americans sensed that Arnold did not like America, democracy, or equality.

No single quotation provides a distillation of Arnold's views, but it appears safe to say that the "equality" and "democracy" he envisioned and wrote about are not, as in Bryce, processes but states of being—an equality and a democracy of intellectual equals whose goals should be to pursue both goodness and beauty. To Arnold, America had not achieved that desired culture, and everything he says indicates his belief that it never could. America had not solved the "human problem" because it could not be led to grace by its remnant, of whom there were too few and too few in potential. The dominant mode of thought in the United States was the product of dissenters, the seed of Philistinism. Arnold's praise of America was strategic, serving as a rhetorical opportunity to goad English society—Americans, he tells his countrymen, have solved the "political and social problem" (*CPW*, 10:202). But American democracy was forever flawed when it came to creating a race of ideal gentlemen. Arnold's pessimism, even his visceral dislike of the structure of the American experiment, is revealed when compared to Bryce's words on these same matters.

Arnold's leitmotif in both "A Word More about America" and "Civilisation in the United States" is Sir Lepel Griffin's statement that the United States is "of all countries calling themselves civilized, except Russia, the country where one would least like to live" (*CPW*, 10:216). Chapter 111 in *The American Commonwealth* is an extended answer to Arnold's claim. Using Arnold's technique of dramatizing his main points by placing the thesis in the mouth of a composite observer, Bryce offers this rejoinder: "I have never met a European of the upper or middle classes who did not express astonishment when told that America was a more agreeable place than Europe to live in. 'For working men,' he would answer, 'yes; but for men of education or property, how can a new rough country, where nothing but business is talked and the refinements of life are only just beginning to appear, how can such a country be compared with England, or France, or Italy?' It is nevertheless true that there are elements in the life of the United States which may well make a European of any class prefer to dwell there rather than in the land of his birth" (*AC*, 2:676).

For Bryce this pleasantness is the function of American material well-being compared to English squalor. Bryce continues: "I doubt if any European can realize till he has been in America how much difference it makes to the happiness of any one not wholly devoid of sympathy with his fellow-beings, to feel that all round him . . . there exist in such ample measure so many of the external conditions of happiness: abundance of the necessaries of life, easy command of education and books, amusements and leisure to enjoy them, comparatively few temptations to intemperance and vice" (*AC*, 2:678).

Arnold, of course, mentions Americans' general well-being, symbolized in his noting that they have fruit aplenty, although they do not have the Marie Louise pear. One feels that Arnold's praise of this abundance of fruit is halfhearted if the price is inferior fruit. This is a terrible burden of argument to lay on the poor pear, but shortly after praising Americans for their abundance of fruit he observes that happiness does not consist "merely or mainly, in being plentifully supplied with the comforts and conveniences of life" (*CPW*, 11:355).

For Arnold, what America lacks is the "interesting." "Do not tell me only, says human nature, of the magnitude of your industry and commerce; of the beneficence of your institutions, your freedom, your equality; of the great and growing number of your churches and schools, libraries and newspapers; tell me also if your civilisation—which is the grand name you give to all this development—tell me if your civilisation is *interesting*" (*CPW*, 11:357). A list of his examples of America's lack of "distinction and beauty," which lead to its being uninteresting, include its landscape; its climate; the names of its towns; its undistinguished architecture; its newspapers; its addiction to that "national misfortune," the "funny man"; its boasting; and its lack of criticism.

Bryce, too, says, "Life is not as interesting in America, except as regards commercial speculation, as it is in Europe; because society and the environment of man are too uniform" (*AC*, 2:641). That condition is simply a matter of rawness. Storied association will come with time and with leisure. To Arnold, however, everything suggests that this rawness will persist, and beauty remain unattainable, because America was founded by "that great class in English society amongst whom the sense for conduct and business is much more strongly developed than the sense for beauty" (*CPW*, 11:359). Born Philistines, Americans lack the capability to acquire the "discipline of awe and respect" (*CPW*, 11:360).

To Arnold, social equality achieved from below is impossible: "The glorification of 'the average man,'" he observes, "'is

. . . against [distinction]" (*CPW,* 11:360). Bryce's response is markedly different in tone from Arnold's:

> To many Europeans . . . the word [social equality] has an odious sound. It suggests a dirty fellow in a blouse elbowing his betters in a crowd. . . . Or, at any rate, it suggests obtrusiveness and bad manners. The exact contrary is the truth. Equality improves manners, for it strengthens the basis of all good manners, respect for other men and women simply as men and women, irrespective of their station in life. . . . The naturalness of intercourse is a distinct addition to the pleasure of social life. . . . It raises the humbler classes without lowering the upper; indeed, it improves the upper no less than the lower by expunging that latent insolence which deforms the manners of so many of the European rich or great.   (*AC,* 2:678–79)

Dozens of other such contrasts exist. For example, at the end of "Civilisation in the United States," just before his reassertion of the doctrine of the saving remnant, Arnold reveals his true concern—English democracy. To his countrymen he says:

> Already we feel [American] influence much, and we shall feel it more. We have a good deal to learn from them; we shall find in them, also, many things to beware of, many points in which it is to be hoped our democracy may not be like theirs. As our country becomes more democratic, the malady here may no longer be that we have an upper class materialised, a middle class vulgarised, and a lower class brutalised. But the predominance of the common and ignoble, born of the predominance of the average man, is a malady too.   (*CPW,* 11:368)

The "ill-condition" in the body politic is a function of democracy leveling down to the average.

Bryce, in his chapter "The Influence of Democracy on Thought," challenges all such preconceptions about the relationship between democracy and culture. He finds two opposing attitudes: first, that democracy leads to higher culture by stimulating people, and second, that democracy leads to "dulness and conceit" (*AC,* 2:625). Both are a priori, and America "furnish[es] little support to either. . . . To ascribe the deficiencies, such as they are, of art and culture in America, solely or even mainly to her form of government, is not less absurd than to ascribe . . . her marvelous material progress to the same cause" (*AC*, 11:625). And surely he is referring to Arnold when he says:

> If some one, starting from the current conception of democracy, were to say that in a democratic nation we should find a disposition to bold and unbridled speculations, sparing neither theology nor morals, a total absence of rule, tradition, and precedent, each man thinking and writing as responsible to no criticism, "every poet his own Aristotle," a taste for strong effects and garish colours, valuing force rather than fitness, grandeur rather than beauty, a vigorous, hasty, impetuous style of speaking and writing, a grandiose, and perhaps sensational art: he would say what would be quite as natural and reasonable *a priori* as most of the pictures given us of democratic societies. Yet many of the suggested features would be the opposite of those which America presents.
>
> Every such picture must be fanciful. . . . Let any one study the portrait of the democratic man and democratic city which the first and greatest of hostile critics of democracy left us [Plato], and compare it with the very different descriptions of life and culture under a popular government in which European speculation has disported itself since De Tocqueville's time. He will find each theory plausible in the abstract, and each equally unlike the facts which contemporary America sets before us.

The "salient intellectual features" which Bryce discovers in his analysis of America sound familiar: "A desire to be abreast of the best thought and work of the world everywhere, to have every form of literature and art adequately represented, and excellent of its kind, so that America shall be felt to hold her own among the nations" (*AC*, 2:630).

Thus, though Bryce does criticize the present state of American intellectual life, he has no fear, as Arnold does, that democracy and equality are inherently resistant to sweetness and light. In ways that Arnold could not, Bryce understands that the laws under which one lives are, somehow, different from the life of a people. Reading Bryce while reading Arnold reveals that, stripped of his rhetorical positioning, Arnold is pessimistic about democracy and equality.

Though the parallels appear clear, scholars have not seen this relationship—even those writing about Arnold and America. Not once in *The American Commonwealth* does Bryce refer to Arnold by name. He did not have to. Bryce was aware of what Arnold had written, and he could depend on his readers being aware of Arnold's writings. Bryce, Arnold, and the other writers of the age shared with their readership a community of awareness that allowed them to address their subjects without a great deal of clutter and with great authority and subtlety because they could trust their readers. This community of awareness has been lost, partly because of specialization. The loss makes writing difficult and reading tedious, and scholarly writing becomes clotted, requiring an excess of evidence and example to bring us up to awareness. Communication becomes a specialized, hermetic affair on any level but news and gossip. Yet the great Victorians—Arnold, Ruskin, John Stuart Mill, T. H. Huxley, and Bryce—all wrote without trivializing their arguments, for journals with circulations of a hundred thousand or more in a country of 32 million people. That is equivalent to the *American Scholar* having a circulation of eight hundred thousand. What writer today who wishes to communicate about a serious, complex subject can hope to command such a broad and aware audience?

Arnoldians feel the loss of a cultured audience. But there is another side to the story. Inheritors of the Arnoldian task— to preserve and disseminate the best that has been thought and said and to bring the light from above—often have a warm feeling about themselves. They comfort themselves by assuming that the campaign to reject the Arnoldian prescription for righting what is wrong in America is spearheaded by Philistines. As they remind themselves from time to time, those who have adhered to the Arnoldian principle of inflexibility in matters of taste and conduct really are the saving remnant—aren't they?

Americans, however, are committed to democracy and equality. This creates certain tensions in them because their attitude, their profession, is founded on the Arnoldian base, which contains only two positions—the remnant and the majority. Reading Bryce both reveals that tension more clearly and offers another way to read the tenets of democracy and equality without the pessimism of the Arnoldian point of view. May we not, like Bryce, come from an Arnoldian point of view and yet have hope that our society can achieve the quality of life we would want without the light from above?

A final question about Arnold in his time and ours is whether, if Arnold were alive today, he would like what he would find in America. Of course, he would not be expected to have present attitudes about democratic education, and any speculation would have to give proper credit to his ability to grow. Perhaps he could come to appreciate the openness of the society and understand the particular quality of the inner discipline that characterizes social life in the United States. Yet the atmosphere in the country has not created in the population as a whole an appreciation of the best that has been thought and said. Finally, the increasing tendency of academics to treat popular fashion as if it had the ability to raise men to their higher selves would leave Arnold even more disillusioned because it would appear to him that the remnant had abandoned hope and was joining the ranks of the Philistine majority. This portrait may not be Arnold as his followers like to see him, but it seems to be a fairly accurate portrayal of him as he reveals himself when engaged in debate with a fellow countryman who had a genuine appreciation for democracy as it was growing, and continues to grow, in the United States.

NOTES

1. The sense that Bryce was having a conversation with Arnold about America may result, in part, as much from our awareness of the Victorian community of discourse as from the existence of any real debate between them. The Victorians shared a community of awareness that extended far beyond the limits of any such community today.

2. Bryce to Whitman, Apr. 25, 1889, Misc. Papers, Bryce Collection, Bodleian Library, Oxford.

3. Such a statement was characteristically Arnoldian, according to Max Muller, who writes of Arnold's penchant not to be swayed by facts once his mind was made up on an issue (*Auld Lang Syne* [New York: Scribner's, 1898], p. 135).

4. James Bryce, *The American Commonwealth*, 3d ed., 2 vols. (New York: Macmillan, 1888), 2:645 (hereafter cited in the text as *AC*).

5. Details of Bryce's life can be found in H. A. L. Fisher, *James Bryce*, 2 vols. (London: Macmillan, 1928). A brief account of his life and friendship with Arnold is in Allan B. Lefcowitz and Laurence W. Mazzeno, "Matthew Arnold and James Bryce," *The Arnoldian* 10 (Winter 1982):28–41.

LINDA RAY PRATT

SEVEN

Matthew Arnold and the Modernist Image

The modern poets grudgingly acknowledged their debts to the Victorians, though every major modern poet grew up reading Browning, Arnold, and Tennyson. In Blake, Shelley, and Keats, the moderns saw a romantic legacy they could esteem, but they pretended that the Victorians were useless to their work. Yeats called himself one of the "last Romantics," but none came forward as the "last Victorian." To see oneself as the "last" of any literary period implies the clear sense of an end of that era. Perhaps the moderns did not claim their Victorian heritage because it was not yet digested as the literary past. Unlike the Victorians, who had to confront the ways that the romantic world was largely dead, the moderns were sufficiently unclear about definitions of "Victorians" to be confident of how they were different or secure that they were. In discussing the periods, critics have usually preferred to praise the moderns for their romanticism and the Victorians for their modernism.[1] No Victorian has been more often noted for his modernism than Matthew Arnold, who did admit to wandering between two worlds and who suppressed one of his finest poems because it was, alas, unrelievedly "modern." Arnold defined the modern condition as characterized by "depression and ennui" "in which the suffering finds no vent in action" (*CPW,* 1:32,1,2). Though Arnold repudiated in 1853 the "dialogue of the mind with itself" as an adequate basis for poetry, later readers valued it and learned to read the Victorian discourse of despair as the proverbial hymn to doubt instead of to faith. The familiar irony is our appreciation of the very poems Arnold rejected.

For Arnold "modern" meant isolation and enervation in response to the furnace of the urban world. His transitional world was not nihilistic, but the ebbing tide of religious faith, societal coherence, heroic individualism, and connection to nature left the Victorians "gasping on the strand."[2] When the romantic landscape of the nineteenth century disappeared into the wasteland of the twentieth century, the term *modern* denoted a world beyond transition, a world where nihilism had settled all questions except how one was to survive at all. When this definition of *modern* becomes a tool of criticism, it obscures both the dialectical nature of modernism in art and the continuity between Victorian and modern periods. With at least twenty-five years of revisionist Victorian studies behind us, scholars now read nineteenth-century literature in the sometimes contradictory context of values we have learned to call the "Victorian frame of mind."[3] A thoroughgoing revisionist study of modernism is, however, still incomplete.

Stephen Spender defines modernism as a pattern of hope that the world may be transformed through art so that inner and outer realities achieve a balance that can preserve our sanity.[4] Genuine despair does not product art, and modern art is more properly seen as the result of the imaginative effort to control and transform despair. Spender's definition is bolstered by the recent scholarship studying the artistic history of the fin-de-siècle period from a comparative perspective. Books such as Carl E. Schorske's *Fin-de-Siècle Vienna* (New York: Knopf, 1980), Robert Delevoy's *Symbolists and Symbolism* (New York: Rizzoli International Publications, 1978; English ed. 1982), and Anna Balakian's edition of essays, *The Symbolist Movement in the Literature of European Languages* (Budapest: Akademiai Kiado, 1982), provide a rich picture of the depth and breadth of Symbolism as a key part of European modernism. From the vantage point of postmodernism, figures such as Ezra Pound and T. S. Eliot belong near the end of the modernist era and seem less central and less original than when taken in the isolation of a British tradition that frequently dismissed fin-de-siècle art as a "decadent" aberration. New importance has accrued to the Symbolists, including their forerunners, the Pre-Raphaelites, as part of a European artistic movement extending almost from the mid-nineteenth century to World War I. An essential similarity in technique and purpose links the Symbolist image and the modernist image as a moral, emotional, and spiritual solution to the perceived emptiness of positivist philosophy and social and industrial materialism.[5]

Revisions of the definition of modernism which emphasize the pattern of hope and locate it in time between the 1880s and 1920s raise the question of continuities between Victorian and modern poetry with renewed urgency. Arnold and Tennyson do not parallel Yeats, Wallace Stevens, and William Carlos Williams, but we may want to recall that Yeats published his first major poem as early as 1889, that "The Love Song of J. Alfred Prufrock" was in draft as early as 1911,[6] and that Stevens and Williams had seriously begun their poetic careers by the time of the 1913 Armory Show. The idea of an extreme disjunction between Victorian and modern is now intellectually bankrupt, but the problem remains of recognizing the legitimate continuities while distinguishing artistic strategies and philosophical perspectives that separate the two periods.

In Arnold's case, we are familiar with the modern anguish in the poetry and the Victorian remedies in the prose. The question at hand is whether Arnold's poetry also embodies the dialectic of hope and despair which Spender describes. Arnold shares with the modernists the belief that poetry must address the traditional roles of philosophy and religion. For Arnold good poetry should offer "a criticism of life" "under the conditions fixed for such criticism by the laws of poetic truth and poetic beauty (*CPW,* 9:163). For the moderns, however, poetry was not a criticism of life but, in Yeats's words, "a vision of reality." The "conditions fixed" for the modernist were the power of the self-born image to transform "the world of outward materialism back into inner tragic values."[7] The belief was that the image could create an alternative vision of reality that would comfort and sustain because it invented a new order of meaning to replace an old order that was shattered, corrupted, or lost in the past. Unlike the romantic image, which is discovered or "perceived,"[8] the modernist image must be self-consciously *made.* Such images are always beauty born of despair and betray by their artifice the artist's struggle to invent and sustain them: Yeats's "masterful images" that consumed his time and energies but seemed to some mere "silliness"; Stevens's exotic vocabulary with which he pieced together a world that some considered "dandified"; Eliot's elaborate structure of literary allusion, which some thought merely "pedantic"; and Williams's fierce exaltation of the commonplace, which some dismissed as American provincialism.

The malady of the modern mind which Arnold acutely analyzed drove the modernist poets to their artistic refuge in the image, and it is here that we may measure the ways in which Arnold is a Victorian poet while seeing his connection with the moderns. Arnold's poetry contains several images that momentarily sustain a self-consciously created alternative to reality, but these images are characteristically tentative and frequently appear to be a secondary focus or even an afterthought. Unlike the moderns, who believed the image should make the poem, Arnold distrusted his images to accomplish what he thought poetry must do for its audience. Whatever comfort he personally found in the images, Arnold felt that poetry relying on "the richness of images" was, like that of Shelley and Keats, "on a false track."[9] In the 1853 Preface to his *Poems,* Arnold says that he turns to the ancients for "what is sound and true in poetical art" because "they, at any rate, knew what they wanted in Art, and we do not. It is this uncertainty which is disheartening, and not hostile criticism" (*CPW,* 1:14). In his uncertainty about his poetry, Arnold clung to the clarity of action in classical art and thus valued "Sohrab and Rustum" and the critic's chair over his own best poetry. The paradox that stopped him as a poet is that the poetic images that perhaps helped him preserve his sanity were not those he was schooled to value in poetry.

A. Dwight Culler describes the central problem in Arnold's poetry as "How are we to live on the darkling plain?"[10] In such poems as "Empedocles on Etna," "Dover Beach," "Stanzas from the Grande Chartreuse," or "Resignation" Arnold looks for an answer to that question. Arnold's problem as a poet is not just that he is on a darkling plain but that he was reared on

romantic expectations. In "Stanzas from the Grande Chartreuse" he tells us that he has learned too well the lore of his
romantic "fathers." Arnold recognizes that the romantic dream
has exploded and that the noble sorrow of Heine or Goethe or
Etienne Pivert de Senancour is "a past mode, an outworn
theme." His plight is to inherit unfulfilled romantic aspirations
in an industrial age that rejected the belief that romanticism's
failure was essentially tragic. Unlike Shelley and Byron, Arnold
perceived no sympathetic audience for his bleeding heart and
no field for noble action. The stature of his grief was reduced
to melancholy, action to mere "fret." Since his "iron time" was
inexorable, Arnold's only alternative was, to paraphrase Yeats,
himself to remake. In his poetry he creates a series of images
that simultaneously acknowledge the age's denial of heroic suffering and reject that denial through the creation in art of images of such emotion. At least momentarily Arnold creates in
these images a transformation of self which achieves heroic
courage by admitting the impossibility of that experience to
exist outside the boundaries of art. In short, he creates an Empedocles who must choose to die so that Arnold can choose to
live.[11]

The earliest of these saving images appears in "Mycerinus." Mycerinus has also learned too well a law higher than
his world allows, and he has been gulled by his belief that the
gods are just. Disabused of such illusions by his death sentence,
he withdraws "to the cool region of the groves he loves," the
first of Arnold's noted forest glades. The grove is an image of
revelry and joy designed to ease the mind and give pleasure to
the senses. The imagery of lamps in the gloom, golden goblets,
burnished foliage, and silver arrows of the moon resembles the
symbolic world of the three islands of Yeats's "The Wanderings
of Oisin." Mycerinus's celebration of joy as the alternative to
despair is also like the chant that "joy is God and God is joy"
which Oisin sings on the Island of the Living, where he seeks
refuge from the tragic defeat of the Fenians at Gabhra. The
revelry of the forest glade does not in the end shut out death,
but its creation allows Mycerinus to live out his six years
"calmed, ennobled, comforted, sustained."[12] With his rule as
king a declared exercise in futility and his life under sentence,

Mycerinus has two problems: what to do with himself for six years (action) and how to compose himself while awaiting death (emotion). Alan Roper sees Mycerinus's "hectic lack of purpose" as a substitute for "quiet work" and his mirth in the face of the "mild reproof" of "winter's sad tranquility" as the evidence of his moral failure and the poem's "explicit condemnation of Mycerinus."[13] But Mycerinus could not attain the prescribed Arnoldian solutions. He could not become a poet or a critic because, "though something would [he] say—/ Something—," he never knew what it should be, and he is barred from civic duties. His choice is closer to that of later Yeatsian heroes: he puts on his mask in an effort to achieve emotional harmony. Culler observes that if Mycerinus's "Epicureanism was merely apparent, the appearance of that Epicureanism was just as important to him as was the fact of his Stoical endurance" and that "a mask was necessary to preserve his soul from hurt."[14] The purpose of the mask was to restore imaginative unity to the self, whose wholeness was divided between an idealizing imagination and a hostile material world. In creating the forest glade in which he could take measure of his soul, Mycerinus sought the interior calm and nobility of the true Stoic. Though this poem is marred by some of its rhetoric, "Mycerinus" is Arnold's first exploration of the possibility central to symbolism—that the only place one may live is in the palace of art.

Even Arnold's domesticated glades function as modernist images. The forest glade in "Lines Written in Kensington Gardens" (published in 1852) illustrates both the comfort such images offered Arnold and his insecurity in letting them sustain the poem. The image of Kensington Gardens has the potential to do for Arnold what the island of Innisfree does for Yeats. Yeats's image creates an alternative reality that eliminates the need for a material Innisfree. Yeats will not actually go to Innisfree as a result of the poem because "always night and day" he goes there in "the deep heart's core." This imaginative retreat comforts Yeats when he is furthest from what it evokes: he hears lake water lapping while he stands on the gray pavements. Yeats's "bee-loud glade" offers "peace" to a sensibility jangled by the dissonant urban world. Arnold, too, seeks "peace" amid the "city's jar." Unlike Yeats, who seizes the immediacy of his image and keeps its imaginative reality a constant present—"I will arise and go *now* . . ."—Arnold abandons the image to worry the problem it has emotionally solved. Before he deserts it, Arnold cultivates in his Kensington glade a place where "peace comes dropping slow." The birds, the boughs, the sheep, and the child enrich the image in the way the cabin, bean-rows, cricket, and linnet do in Yeats's poem. Even the awareness of the urban roar surrounding the glade deepens the charm of the imagined seclusion. Only after he surrenders his concentration on the image of the glade so as to analyze and entreat does it lose its power to calm the emotions and content the mind.[15] Arnold's belief that one retreats from the world so as to return usefully to it divides the strategies of the poem between imagistic intensity and discursive thought. The result is that the poem fails in modernist terms because the image is diffused. More important, the poem fails in Arnold's terms because the dialogue of the mind moves back to the unrest that sent him to Kensington Gardens. He loses the feeling of calm when he leaves the image and instead asks at the end of the poem

> To feel, amid the city's jar,
> That there abides a piece of thine,
> Man did not make, and cannot mar.   (ll. 38–40)

The difference between feeling calm and feeling "that there abides" a calm is critical to Arnold's emotional state. In the last stanza his impassioned plea is for *more* calm: "Calm, calm me more! nor let me die / Before I have begun to live" (ll. 43–44).

In contrast to "Lines Written in Kensington Gardens" Arnold finds in his images of the Grande Chartreuse a powerful emotional resolution. To borrow Eliot's terms, Arnold found an adequate "objective correlative" in the remote home of the Carthusians. Arnold climbs the mountain in search of an image, hoping for no less than "to possess [his] soul again." He imagines that he shares with the monks a devotion to an exploded dream, though their dream presumably was in Christianity and his in romanticism.

Arnold's image of the Grande Chartreuse provides a setting and a rationale to explore his loss, to give tragic dignity to his tears, and to reaffirm the inevitability of his alienation from the modern world. Neither the call to action of the soldiers nor the laughter of the hunters can lure him from the shadowed nave, and he cannot think how he could "grow" or "flower" in any other world. In Culler's reading, the vision quickly crumbles and leaves Arnold back in the desert of the modern world. The "desert" is, however, that of the abbey graveyard, and the call of the modern world passes and fades, leaving Arnold the "peace" of his "living tomb." Culler says that one cannot go back to the forest glade because "it does not exist; it is an illusion."[16] But the power of Arnold's image of the Grande Chartreuse reverses this and gives the glade such sustained imaginative reality that the poet can shut out the "Sons of the world." The image of the Grande Chartreuse parallels in function Yeats's city of Byzantium, the Tower, or the wild swans at Coole. Both poets use images to create moments of emotional release under aesthetic control, moments that synthesize the material world with the inner life. At the Grande Chartreuse Arnold finds a revelation of his buried life, an epiphany in which "the eye sinks inward, and the heart lies plain, / And what we mean, we say, and what we would, we know" (ll. 86–87).

Many of Arnold's poems give us what Stevens calls life as a bitter aspic, but it is at Dover Beach that Arnold, like Crispin in Stevens's "The Comedian as the Letter C," is stripped of "the last distortion of romance."[17] Arnold hears in the "melancholy, long, withdrawing roar" of the ocean the "eternal note of sadness" and the ebbing of faith. At Dover Arnold momentarily confronts the nihilistic vision Irving Howe says is "at the Heart of modern literature."[18] Culler believes that the central, and most modern, statement of the poem is "We are here as on a darkling plain."[19] That statement of the condition seems to me the most Victorian line in the poem. The most modern is "Ah, love, let us be true to one another" because that line casts up an alternative image designed to counter the reality of the darkling plain. At the end of the poem Arnold lists all the values the world does not possess: joy, love, light, certitude, peace, and help for pain. The speaker here learns what Empedocles knew when he cast himself into the crater: that the only alternative to the void was an image of oneself in opposition to its inviolable emptiness. Unlike Stevens in "Le Monocle de Mon Oncle" Arnold will not say directly of love that "It comes, it blooms, it bears its fruit and dies." Yet he implies—whether we read "love" as a providential order or as a personal devotion—that love has at least momentarily disappeared from the world because one's hold on the personal becomes, for a Victorian, utterly tenuous in the absence of a divine source. Stevens tells us in "Sunday Morning" that what lasts is our need for love. Nothing endures like our remembrance of awakened birds and our desire for June. The purpose of Arnold's image of faithful love is to lighten the darkling plain and counter the ignorant armies. Despite the popularity of the poem, Joseph Carroll thinks "it is not a fully coherent statement; a personal devotion devoid of 'love,' 'joy,' or 'light' is scarcely imaginable. It is, at best, a bleakly subintellective form of mutual commiseration. If, as Arnold rather melodramatically declares, the world is so completely empty, individuals would possess very little to which others might be true."[20] Carroll's reading misses the authentic nihilism which Arnold repudiates in "Dover Beach" and his courage and imagination in opposing it. In short, Carroll's reading of the poem is a romantic one. Unable to speak as a visionary and unwilling to speak as a bard, Arnold does all that a man without assurances can do: he casts up the highest value he can claim to understand and clings to it in good faith. Perhaps the poem is popular with modern readers because they recognize in it the only "fully coherent" response that preserves tragic dignity. Arnold's sense that the plain is darkening reveals just how menaced he is by despair, a condition that deepens the poignancy of his courage to assert love among his "fictive things."

Lacking a traditional dramatic narrative, "Tristram and Iseult" (1852) relies almost solely on a set of images to achieve a resolution in art that is denied in the actual lives of the characters. Tristram and Iseult of Ireland wear out life in an endlessly frustrating fever of love and desire. In contrast, Iseult of Brittany's calm is almost deathlike. Though Tristram retreats to the "green wood," his "endless reveries" only briefly calm him, and he is quickly consumed in "musing fits" (l. 47). Iseult of Ireland has drained her vitality by burying her inner life in the "furnace" of the court. Iseult of Brittany is "fatigued," her voice languid, her cheeks "sunk and pale" (l. 32). Her youth has been absorbed in the "waning" dark life of Tristram (l. 70). The point is that all three are damaged by suffering and sorrow and all three are images of beauty.

Thus interpretations of the poem that set up a choice between the romantic but miserable Tristram and the realistic but enervated Iseult of Brittany cannot resolve the issues. All the characters are beautiful, noble, and unhappy, and all are fragmented so that their lives are but "shadow and dream." The resolutions in the poem lie not in the choices individual characters make but in the symbolic function of the images each life illustrates as a part of a poem.[21] Two images are the key to the poem's meaning. In the first the narrator poses Tristram and the first Iseult in a timeless image of passionate love. Self-consciously pointing to the deathbed tableau the narrator says, "You see them clear" (l. 101), and then proceeds to describe the scene with all the exotic imagery that Kenneth Allott said was "a subject for a Pre-Raphaelite painting."[22] Death anneals the ravages of their lives and grants the lovers the tranquil loveliness and tragic dignity that drive the myth. The power of the image moves even the huntsman in the tapestry, himself an image in art, out of his own timeless stillness and into their silent chamber. The lovers are passion perfected in stillness.

The other image in art is that of Merlin and Vivien, the story Iseult tells to forget her suffering. In this version Vivien is the "spirit of the woods" "so witching fair," and Merlin the enraptured lover whose passion subdues his craft and wits (ll. 180–81). "No fairer resting-place" (l. 210) could be found than the "open glen" where they pause (l. 191). In this paradisical forest glade a sleep "like death" falls on Merlin, and Vivien's magic imprisons him "till the judgment-day" (l. 222). Though his little plot of magic ground resembles the grave, as did the Grande Chartreuse, it is for Arnold a "daised circle" in which passion and peace, commitment and detachment, dream and reality, life and death are artistically reconciled (l. 221).

The stories of Merlin and Vivien and Tristram and Iseult are, of course, pieces of literature, images in art. Like Arnold,

Iseult of Brittany has learned that art allows what life denies, that is, the experience of passion and the release from it, the dream and the end of the dream, Tristram tortured and Tristram transfigured. What cannot be endured in life can be endured in its transformation in art. The story of Merlin and Vivien enables Iseult to fathom the passion that transfigured her husband's suffering but touched her only as blight. Earlier in the poem she had wept at his bedside as one "who can divine a grief, and sympathise" (ll. 323–24). In modernist terms, Iseult's material reality and her inner being are reshaped through an experience of the image. Moreover, the experience in art yields meaning without confusion. The layering of one image over another—Arnold's poem, Iseult's tale, Tristram's mythic transfiguration, and the huntsman in the arras—leaves moot any question about which experience is "real" or "true." William Buckler concludes that the poem fails to offer any reconciliatory insights because "we can hardly opt for Iseult's alternative of an isolated fantasy life."[23] Iseult's refuge in Breton tales is not a fantasy life because the tales are themselves poetic renderings from history and experience. Iseult tells stories to order reality so that she may learn its meaning and thus restore a sensibility that might otherwise be broken by loneliness and pain. Iseult schools her children with these stories so that they can possess what poetry can offer, which is more than just the ability to distance themselves from their experience, achieve control over it, and transform it into a thing of beauty, as Culler describes it.[24] Art becomes experience.

A poem such as "Tristram and Iseult" shares with such diverse poems as Yeats's "The Wanderings of Oisin," Stevens's "The Comedian as the Letter C," and Eliot's *Four Quartets* the pursuit of an aesthetic wholeness in art that can give meaning outside the material reality that is beyond our control or understanding except as it enters into the artistic transformation. In Eliot's words,

> We had the experience but missed the meaning,
> And approach to the meaning restores the experience
> In a different form.

Experience without meaning lacks emotional or intellectual significance, and the power of art to devise meaning gives it its supreme importance in modern life. When Arnold says that poetry will assume the function of religion, he is thinking of a "criticism of life" that can reveal the moral values by which we should live and not of the image's power to invest a meaningless world with an imagined order. Arnold's design was never to create the symbolic "vision" Yeats sought, and he did not suffer with Eliot the ambition to make words reach the stillness. His poems do, however, derive their meaning and intensity from the dynamics of his involvement with the images. The romantic poet's posture toward the image was usually that of an observer inspired to make metaphors: Wordsworth at Tintern Abbey, Shelley scanning Mont Blanc, Keats listening to the nightingale. The modern poet's imagination was no eolian harp, and the process of image-making in modern poetry is an active struggle demanding all one's creative energy to invent a momentary experience that exists only within the elaborately conjured imaginative expression. To return to the metaphor of the eolian harp, the modern poet must invent the harp, the wind, the belief that the wind can produce music when striking the harp, and finally, the song itself. Unlike the images of a high modernist, Arnold's images do not presume to be the whole of the poem, but they are the center on which the whole rests. The images Arnold creates in these poems are for him moments of emotional immediacy which plunge him into a self-born order of experience that counters the material world by replacing it with an aesthetic one whose meaning can sustain its creator.

Despite the indifference of the moderns to the Victorian poets, the Victorians left them a usable intellectual analysis of modern problems and the outlines of artistic forms with which to treat them. Arnold and many other Victorians felt that their place in history was unique, by which they meant uniquely alone. Their romantic legacy only underscored their historical isolation and made more painful by contrast their lack of confidence about the function of artists and the usefulness of the poetic expression they struggled to devise. Unlike the moderns, who developed a contempt for poetic traditions and could shout to "make it new," the Victorian poets felt a passion for the past. They believed that the old poetry and the world it expressed were nobler than their own, but their artistic dilemma was that touchstones from the past could no longer serve them as models. In the dialogue of *Hic* and *Ille* in Yeats's poem "Ego Dominus Tuus," *Hic* advised *Ille* to abandon his search for symbols and work on a style by imitating the great masters. *Ille* responds, "I seek an image, not a book." In a sense Arnold sought a "book" instead of an image in that he wanted a poetry that offered a criticism of life instead of one that created "a vision of reality." He distrusted the image and failed to appreciate that what was most subjective in his poetry might also be what was best. In an 1852 letter to Arthur Hugh Clough, Arnold expressed his belief that because modern poetry must include the functions of religion, it had to reach beyond "parts and episodes and ornamental work":

> More and more I feel that the difference between a mature and youthful age of the world compels the poetry of the former to use great plainness of speech as compared with that of the latter: and that Keats and Shelley were on a false track when they set themselves to reproduce the exuberance of expression, the charm, the richness of images, and the felicity, of the Elizabethan poets. Yet critics cannot get to learn this, because the Elizabethan poets are our greatest, and our canons of poetry are founded on their works. They still think that the object of poetry is to produce exquisite bits and images—such as Shelley's *clouds shepherded by the slow unwilling wind*, and Keats passim: whereas modern poetry can only subsist by its *contents*: by becoming a complete magister vitae as the poetry of the ancients did: by including, as theirs did, religion with poetry, instead of existing as poetry only, and leaving religious wants to be supplied by the Christian religion, as a power existing independent of the poetical power. But the language, style and general proceedings of a poetry which has such an immense task to perform, must be very plain direct and severe: and it must not lose itself in parts and episodes and ornamental work, but must press forwards to the whole.[25]

Seeking a *magister vitae* that pressed "forwards to the whole," Arnold passed severe judgment on the accomplishment of much of his own poetry. Arnold realized that the dialogue of the mind with itself produced no clear prescriptions

for the age. He undervalued the power of the image of Empedocles at the edge of the crater or himself at the Grande Chartreuse to achieve what the best poetry has always done:
console, criticize, sustain, complete.[26] Arnold would probably
be shocked to know how modern readers linger in his forest
glade, how many have heard the eternal note of sadness at
Dover Beach and taken courage from his courage, how many
scholar gypsies there are among us, how many have felt the
chill of the Carthusians and known ourselves better in the
morning. Unfortunately for the future of his own poetry, he
was too close to the dead world of one poetic tradition and too
far from another not yet wholly born. Arnold relied on the
argument or the dramatic action of his poems for the "something to be done" to relieve modern distress, unaware that the
emotional power of the image to create an alternative reality
might indeed be a crucial "vent in action."

NOTES

1. Gerald L. Bruns wittily notes, "Among the New Critics, nothing could be more abominable than a received idea. Regularly, that
which was received was said to be 'romantic': in utterly disreputable
cases it was 'Victorian'—a term that even at this date is sometimes
used to refer to *decaying* romanticism" (Review of George Bornstein,
Transformations of Romanticism in Yeats, Eliot, and Stevens and Helen
Regueiro, *The Limits of Imagination: Wordsworth, Yeats, and Stevens,*
Criticism 10 [1978]: 76).

2. The phrase is from W. B. Yeats's short poem of literary history,
"Three Movements."

3. I date the revisionist view of the Victorians from Walter E.
Houghton's *The Victorian Frame of Mind* (New Haven: Yale University
Press, 1957).

4. Stephen Spender's six major characteristics of modernism appear in *The Struggle of the Modern* (Berkeley and Los Angeles: University of California Press, 1963), p. 83. They are as follows: (1)
realization through new art of the modern experience; (2) the inven-
tion through art of a *pattern of hope,* influencing society; (3) the idea
of an art that will fuse past with present into the modern symbolism

of a *shared life;* (4) the *alternate life of art;* (5) *distortion;* and (6) the *revolutionary concept of tradition.*

5. Though most critics of Arnold's poetry remark on the modern sensibility, few have placed Arnold in the currents of Symbolist art. One exception is Ruth apRoberts, whose *Arnold and God* (Berkeley and Los Angeles: University of California Press, 1983) contains a brief but suggestive discussion of Arnold's "theory and practice as being in the symbolist mode" (p. 8). David DeLaura in *Victorian Poetry* (New York: Edward Arnold, 1972), sees Arnold's influence "on the self-indulgent melancholy of late Victorian England" in both the "aesthetic" "line from Pater through Wilde to the 1890's" and in figures such as Thomas Hardy (p. 55). He also notes that Arnold "provided the English imagination with the terms and images by which to apprehend its own emerging experience, and in the process to control it" (p. 54). In addition to the help provided by his published scholarship, Professor DeLaura's thoughtful critique of this essay was extremely useful to me, especially in his challenge to my assumptions about romanticism.

6. Lyndall Gordon, *Eliot's Early Years* (Oxford: Oxford University Press, 1977), p. 45.

7. Spender, *Struggle of the Modern,* p. 87.

8. Frank Kermode, *Romantic Image* (New York: Vintage, 1964), p. 2.

9. *Letters of Matthew Arnold to Arthur Hugh Clough,* ed. Howard Foster Lowry (London: Oxford University Press, 1932), p. 124.

10. A. Dwight Culler, *Imaginative Reason* (1966; rpt. Westport, Conn.: Greenwood Press, 1976), pp. 44–45.

11. Stressing the romantic dialogue of Callicles and Empedocles, Kermode sees Arnold's rejection of "Empedocles on Etna" as "in a sense a personal consequence of the suicide of Empedocles; the poem wrote off Arnold's main topic. It contains his solution—Empedocles is Arnold's Leech Gatherer. But there seemed no prospect of indefinitely repeating this victory (Pyrrhic, because suicide is the least useful of answers in *life*) and so Arnold rejects it in favour of another solution which involves not death but merely poetic extinction, or rather a curiously effective compromise which keeps the poet in a state of suspended animation" (p. 13). I am arguing that the symbolic victory in the poem leads Arnold to the self-awareness that permits him to explore other solutions.

12. Alan Grob, "Arnold's 'Mycerinus': The Fate of Pleasure," *Victorian Poetry* 20 (1982):1–20, argues that the groves in "Mycerinus" are "functionally similar to those verdant regions in the poetry of

Wallace Stevens that seem islands of earthly abundance in the void that surrounds them" (p. 6).

13. Alan Roper, *Arnold's Poetic Landscapes* (Baltimore: Johns Hopkins Press, 1969), p. 97.

14. Culler, *Imaginative Reason*, p. 61.

15. Culler notes that the poem, "though a pleasant one, does not really create the true Wordsworthian feeling, and one may say that it stands to the poetry of Wordsworth as Kensington Gardens stands to the Lake country. It is an imitation created in the city" (ibid., p. 26). It is precisely as a self-conscious "imitation created in the city" that the poem is like its modernist counterparts. Pauline Fletcher, *Gardens and Grim Ravines: The Language of Landscape in Victorian Poetry* (Princeton: Princeton University Press, 1983), observes that "Arnold does not have to go to the banks of the Wye, or to the Cumberland hills in order to experience the soothing power of nature. Indeed, Kensington Gardens may be more soothing than the Lake District, as the harsh landscape of 'Resignation' suggests" (p. 98). She dismisses the poetic importance of this point, however, in her conclusion: "The forest glade, or protected green hollow, remains for Arnold a *locus amoenus* where a man may retire temporarily from the busy world, but it is not a place where one may live permanently. Nor does it function as in any sense an image of the world, either as it is, or as it should be. For this reason, it is a more limited symbol than Tennyson's gardens. It is also more limited in that, unlike Tennyson's gardens, the glade remains a fairly constant symbol in Arnold's poetry, almost always being associated with youth, innocence, and freshness. It represents an escape from duty, even, one might say, a place where one may hide from the stern father" (pp. 99–100).

16. Culler, *Imaginative Reason*, p. 28.

17. Wallace Stevens, *The Palm at the End of the Mind* (1971: rpt. New York: Vintage Books, 1972), p. 60.

18. Irving Howe, *The Decline of the New* (New York: Harcourt, Brace, 1970), p. 36.

19. Culler, *Imaginative Reason*, pp. 44–45.

20. Joseph Carroll, *The Cultural Theory of Matthew Arnold* (Berkeley and Los Angeles: University of California Press, 1982), p. 23.

21. See Beverly Taylor, "Imagination and Art in Arnold's 'Tristram and Iseult': The Importance of 'Making,'" *Studies in English Literature, 1500–1900* 22 (1982):633–45. Taylor's interpretation of the poem is similar to mine: "'Tristram and Iseult' furnishes both an explicit ethical message about consuming passions and an implicit

aesthetic indication of the importance of 'making,' of exercising imagination to re-create experience in art. The created form—whether tapestry, poem, or dream—can be accepted and interpreted precisely because it is art rather than life. Extrapolated from experience, art gives enjoyment and truth, both of which are too often destroyed in the 'gradual furnace of the world'" (p. 634). See also M. G. Sundell, "The Intellectual Background and Structure of Arnold's 'Tristram and Iseult,'" *Victorian Poetry* 1 (1963):272–83: "In effect, Iseult enables herself to live with her experience by making it into mythology, as she organizes it into art" (p. 279).

22. *The Poems of Matthew Arnold*, ed. Kenneth Allott, 2d ed., ed. Miriam Allott (London: Longman, 1979), p. 224.

23. William E. Buckler, *On the Poetry of Matthew Arnold: Essays in Critical Reconstruction* (New York: New York University Press, 1982), p. 128.

24. Culler, *Imaginative Reason*, p. 150.

25. *Letters of Arnold to Clough*, ed. Lowry, p. 124.

26. Kermode laments not only the cost to Arnold's work of his rejection of his poetry but also the implications for the next generation of poets. Kermode observes, "Arnold was a very influential transmitter of Romantic thought, and no one was more fully aware of our problem, under all its aspects, than he. Unhappily, he himself rejected "Empedocles on Etna," in this connexion his most important poem; and consequently it is not much read. If it were, we should be less prone to think of the poets of the nineties as merely wayward young men who picked up bad habits from the French" (*Romantic Image*, p. 12).

PATRICK J. McCARTHY

EIGHT

Matthew Arnold, the Novel, and the World Without

In an unpublished letter of 1862, Matthew Arnold recommended to his mother that she read Mary Elizabeth Braddon's *Lady Audley's Secret,* a best seller second in popularity only to Mrs. Henry Wood's *East Lynne* of the year before. He had found Braddon's novel readable, and, hearing next about her *Aurora Floyd,* he read it three months later. He went on to her next novel, *Henry Dunbar, the Story of an Outcast,* when it came out the following year. These bursts of self-indulgence among works not readily classifiable as "the best that has been thought and said" were not for Arnold isolated falls from grace. He read Ouida and others whose names have not the limited currency of hers, including Carolyn Archer Clive, Dinah Maria Mulock, Jemima Montgomery Tautphoeus, and J. M. Hooper Winnard. Can this be the same Arnold who warned us that "of the contemporary rubbish which is shot so plentifully all round us, we can, indeed, hardly read too little" (*CPW,* 9:273)?

Once alerted to Arnold's reading of second-rate novelists, we begin to notice the novelists, good and bad, he mentions in letters and notebooks. We take seriously his admission in a letter to having "a weakness for novels," a remark that had passed as politeness to a would-be writer.[1] We discover that he read, for example, all the ranking British novelists of his century; only Mrs. Gaskell and George Meredith do not appear on his lists. He read the French from Le Sage and Prevost to Zola. Except for a long slack period in the 1860s, he read most of George Sand's many novels as well as her letters and journals as they became available. He read an occasional Scandinavian or Russian or German novelist, too, and picked up along the way the major eighteenth-century British novelists.

In all, we can count at least sixty novelists whose work he knew at first hand, and though the number is not overwhelming it comes as a gentle surprise. When we think that he made very little critical use of this material, wrote no essay specifically about British novelists, and only the pieces on Sand and Tolstoy for the Europeans, we may find it useful to look further into his sense of the form and try to account for it. It is not, I will suggest, an accident of biography or a matter of literary imperceptivity. Arnold's attitudes toward the novel follow from his full sense of himself as a literary artist.

By way of preliminary summary we may say that by turns Arnold expresses two basic attitudes toward novels, first, the casual interest of a reader who enjoys them and sees their value, and second, the disregard of a person with more serious concerns than the novel addresses. Both of these attitudes have roots in the cultural and intellectual life of Fox How, his family home. But there is another and more interesting relationship to the novel, to its literary form, in which Arnold is implicated for reasons largely personal and individual. The novel form as we have come to think of it in the twentieth century, which finds its conclusions in the dynamics of time, particular circumstance, and every kind of contingency, does not accord with Arnold's artistic constructions of meaning and reality. He might be called a Platonist in a world increasingly distant from the ideal, but although this is true it does not entirely state the matter. More is involved. The personal place in which Arnold as poet and literary artist locates himself in the grainy, interacting, distracting world of things and other people is closer to the point.

As Arnold's letter to his mother suggests, novels were read regularly at Fox How; the family did not fear them as did devout Evangelicals or dismiss them as low and unworthy as did Thomas DeQuincey.[2] As happened in many a clergyman's family, the exemplary tales of Mrs. Sarah Trimmer and the practical pieties of Hannah More made their way there. Sir Walter Scott also found a welcome at Fox How as he had at Haworth and throughout Britain; Arnold's later references to him are so ready and frequent that he was surely an early reader. His mother admired that lively Irishwoman Maria Edgeworth and the Cockney upstart Charles Dickens.[3] Closer at hand the Arnolds had Hariett Martineau, near neighbor and frequent visitor, who had written a readable middle-class novel of her own and would have opinions on all kinds of fiction. She was a friend of the author of *Jane Eyre,* the book William Delafield Arnold remembered that the family "were all talking about" when he left home for India in 1848.[4] Charlotte Brontë visited the Lake District, coming twice in 1850. During the visits she saw the Arnolds several times, including Matthew, who had kept up with the work of this shy literary lion and had read her latest novel, *Shirley.*[5] In short, the novel was a familiar genre at Fox How. In 1853, when his younger brother William wished to publicize his experiences with the Indian Civil Service, he chose the novel as his vehicle and wrote *Oakfield.* Even doubting and troubled Thomas, the second oldest brother, had read and thought about novels sufficiently over the years to publish a piece on the subject in the 1860s and to give prescriptive advice to lesser novelists of the day.[6]

Yet though the novel had its place in the family's interests, we can well believe that Dr. Arnold's influence would be to keep that place from becoming too high. With his own reading time well occupied with the classics and history, he judged what novels he read by high standards. He disliked Maria Edgeworth and found in Dickens "nothing very good or inspiring." He read Scott but considered historical novels only accidentally truthful because, he said, "the writer's object is merely to amuse."[7] Matthew Arnold later quoted Coleridge's complaint against novels, which he may have heard first from the headmaster of Rugby: "Novel reading spares the reader the trouble of thinking, it saves him from the boredom of vacancy, and establishes a habit of indolence."[8]

These views mirror the judgment passed on novels by a large and, to a degree, surviving segment of educated Western opinion. In the serious world, a diverting, undemanding, light-weight literary form would never do, or rather would do only if kept in its modest place. Matthew Arnold accepted this view, and all his life he expressed the familiar litany of dismissal, often uttered under his breath as he dealt with other concerns. Thus he associated novel readers with novelty hunters, con-nected people who feed their minds on novels with those who feed their stomachs on opium, and noted the penchant of the tired and bored to fall back on these least profitable of works. Novels, he observed, blur the real world into phantasmagoria; only young ladies who want their heroes to have all per-fections read novels. Worse, readers who go to novels for information may be consulting a medium that spreads "presumptuous ignorance" (*CPW,* 3:21, 380; 6:379; 7:83; 9:4, 125; 11:149).

Here of course Arnold had in mind lesser novels, the easily digestible fare craved by ordinary appetites. But he knew that there were others as well, novels from which one can learn. "All people," he wrote in his sixties, "want to know *life,* above all the life which surrounds them and concerns them; and we come to the novel . . . to help us to what we want." He had found novels useful in imagining France, and before he went to America he read that country's novelists (Adams, James, Hawthorne, Howells) to prepare himself for what he would find.[9]

But the novel's representations of the life that surrounds and concerns people gave Arnold continuing cause for con-cern. As an artist, he early observed that in novels "the matter is uncontrollable," but he did not insist on this aesthetic objec-tion.[10] Instead, the issue of what is included in a novel's matter deepened into questions of the entire function and purpose of literature. Here the problem arose with French novelists, so ready, as he notes in his seriocomic phrase, to pay allegiance to "the great goddess Lubricity." We know that by his forties he had made acquaintance with Balzac, Hugo, and Rousseau, was able to refer to writers such as Belot and the novels that French schoolboys read, and adored George Sand. Later he read Ed-mond de Goncourt, Alphonse Daudet, much more Balzac, and Zola. Essentially, his reaction to them was against their portrayal of ugliness in the absence of the ideal. In 1863, he quoted with approval Joseph Joubert's condemnation of novelists who "harrow our hearts" by giving us, instead of the beautiful, which is "the one aim of art," "the mere frightful reality." I would stress here the word "mere," for Arnold specifically excludes from his criticism Rabelais, Sand, and Rousseau. It is the "mere" frightfulness especially of Balzac, Zola, and Daudet that Arnold refused to accept, even under the rubric of the "disinterested curiosity" he had been wont to praise. His objection is that such writers hurt our souls, that they have not the thought "Let the good prevail" as "the master-pressure upon their spirit" (*CPW*, 3:202; 10:96, 135–36, 155, 187–89).

Arnold's animadversions against the French naturalists and realists are fully consistent with his earlier critical views. They do not constitute a late aberration in behalf of Mrs. Grundy. And they, too, like my earlier citations, are uttered almost by the way, mostly as he writes in praise of other writers.

His more interesting relationship to the novel is suggested by what he does not say as well as by what he says. It may be an accident of survival, but we hear nothing from him about his brother William's novel, *Oakfield*, or the two novels written by his close friend James Anthony Froude. And he makes few favorable mentions of the great novelists. Thackeray, whom he read, knew personally, and liked, he dismissed as a first-rate journeyman. Dickens, whom he read, met, but said nothing of personally, came in for strong praise for *David Copperfield* in the 1880s essay "The Incompatibles," but the praise, besides being openly compensatory—*Copperfield* being, as he wrote, a book to which "we are in danger of perhaps not paying respect enough"—is also carefully limited in scope and must be matched against Arnold's general ignoring of the famed writer and his penchant for using the novels in joking references (*CPW*, 9:273; see also 3:538; 5:350, 353).[11] Trollope he read but spoke of not at all though Arnold may be including him, in 1887, as among "the famous English novelists who have passed away" (*CPW*, 11:282). Similarly, there is only a casual mention of George Eliot and none of Jane Austen, though he read both and the latter was a favorite of his wife, Fanny Lucy.

Part of his attitude toward novels surely follows from the conviction, stated even as he writes of European novelists in the 1880s, that "the crown of literature is poetry" (*CPW,* 11:284). We may well agree, but as an explanation of his lack of responsiveness to the form as one worthy of consideration, and his consequent treatment of British novelists with silence or faint praise, his dictum does not go very far. Something more basic is involved.

Clough, in the course of his 1853 review of the poems of Arnold and Alexander Smith, gives the clue to what it is. He makes two pertinent distinctions, noting first of all, "that people much prefer Vanity Fair and Bleak House" to "poems after classical models, poems from Oriental sources," because "the novelist does try to build us a real house to be lived in." What the novelist makes "is thrown away indeed tomorrow, but is devoured today." Second, focusing particularly on the differences between Smith and Arnold, Clough sees the former "going forth to battle in the armor of a righteous purpose," and Arnold, wandering by night, "reflecting, pondering, hesitating, musing, complaining." One acts with courage and optimism; the other cautiously reflects and delays. Where, Clough asks, should one look, inward to the self to resolve doubt and find assurance or outward to action and self-assertion? [12]

In the review, Clough makes a connection between the Arnold of the poems and the Arnold who five years earlier had written a letter to him expressing an "almost bitter feeling" against Clough's poem *The Bothie of Tober-Na-Vuolich,* its admirers, and Clough himself. Arnold had heard their mutual friend William Sellar praise *The Bothie,* which deals with a summer reading party of Oxford undergraduates and the contemporary social realities they face. "Yes," Arnold had written, "I can, if need be, at last dispense with them all, even with him: better that, than be sucked for an hour even into the Time Stream in which they and he plunge and bellow. I became calm in spirit, but uncompromising, almost stern. More English than European, I said finally, more American than English: and took up Obermann, and refuged myself with him in his forest against your Zeit Geist." [13]

Arnold thus explicitly refuses to be involved with time,

change, other people, and the turbulent changes of his own emotions. He abjures energetic confrontation with the moment. He desires timelessness, fixity, solitude, and quietness. Like Senancour's *Obermann* he would locate himself in a landscape in which he is a solitary figure, meditative, inward-looking, infinitely sad, but calm and measured in thought and expression. He wishes to join Obermann, who for him had taken a place beside the heroine of George Sand's early novel *Lélia* as ravaged, desolate idealists thrown back upon themselves. In the two French writers he had found fellow idealists bereft of traditional religion by rationalism, of social hopes by political reaction, and of human society by "the reign of stupidity" (*CPW,* 8:223).[14] Although the works in question take a form between novel, essay, and philosophical discourse, their orientation to experience is set from the beginning. A loss has been suffered, and the recourse from it is not excitement and more experience but inwardness, solitude, and the beauty of the natural world.

Arnold's letter dates from late 1848; Clough's review covers the poetry Arnold wrote over approximately ⊿n eight-year period, 1843 to 1851. In the years just before and after his letter Arnold wrote poems directly referring to *Lélia* and Obermann. Early on, the tentative, wary narrator of "The New Sirens" draws back, as had Lélia, from alternating periods of excitement and ennui. In "Stagirius" a young monk for a time lives as a hermit and struggles desperately when "torn between faith and atheism," both experiences of Sand's heroine.[15] Later, Arnold's speaker in the valedictory "Stanzas in Memory of the Author of 'Obermann'" consciously bids farewell to the French solitary and turns to "the world without," but he still feels Obermann's "spell" and leaves "half of his life" with him. Thus a complete break is neither desirable nor possible. As many of the other poems of the 1849 and 1852 volumes attest, besides the ones cited above, Arnold was attracted to Obermann and to the George Sand of *Lélia* in part because they share a commonality of belief and ideal but more centrally because they are temperamentally akin and react similarly to the experience of loss.

Time and again, the principal figure comes to us already

deeply marked by a past he must confront and deal with. He survives into "late days" and needs support. The merman is already forsaken, the reveler has strayed, the king of Bokhara is already sick, and Mycerinus has been told that he will die young. Even in the Marguerite poem "Meeting," as the hopeful lover springs forward to the beloved, he is counseled by the gods to retire. For comfort and the power to go on, he must look inward. "Sink in thyself," he is told, and again, "Sink, O youth, in thy soul!" His central self is buried; the "gulph of himself" is unlit. He must make an effort to bring it to the light and, as another poem observes, create in himself "some order" ("Empedocles on Etna," II, l. 146; "The Youth of Man," l. 116; "The Youth of Nature," l. 102; "A Modern Sappho," l. 7).

These relationships between Arnold's self, time, and experience are not easily traced to a particular trauma, say, to the loss of his father or the challenges to his faith. In his earliest writings, past, present, and future slip into a dim campagna of regret and loss. The protagonists of his prize poems, "Alaric at Rome" and "Cromwell," look on an evanescent past in tears and sorrow; then the one looks forward to a glory that is never realized, and the other envisions a future encompassing victory and death, but even as he dreams he is fixed permanently in the past: the coda strips him of his dream and leaves him standing as if forever "once more alone beside the gleaming flood" (l. 240). The juvenilia repeat the same tale. "Mary Queen of Scotts on her departure from France" fears that she is bidding "adieu for aye to human happiness" (l. 10). One of the more ebullient of his youthful efforts, "The First Sight of Italy," conjures up scenes of Italian valleys but discovers that they are "too bright for such a world as ours" (l. 49). "Restore our hearts once more," he cries; restore them, that is, to "stern reality." His unbelieving side imagines frozen Russia as "more congenial": there one may pitch a "retreat afar from human kind" (ll. 57–64). The poem does not end there, but something in Arnold, then only thirteen, embraced thoughtless joys reluctantly.

A whole set of consequences follows from the way the Arnoldian protagonist sets himself to deal with his life. Together, they totally deny the validity of the novelist's engagement with reality. By the time he is ready to speak, the Arnoldian figure, sitting "alone, / Centered in a majestic unity," hears no voices save his own ("Written in Butler's Sermons," ll. 7–8). He may recall the voices of fools and false counselors, but only to reject them.[16] When ghostly presences appear in his poems and pass on acceptable warnings and encouragements, we note that they have vocal profiles identical to the poet's. When, too, a specific auditor is present in a poem and we expect the speaker to react and adapt to the auditor's presence, no such interchange takes place. It would appear that the power of others to influence has been assessed and discounted before it can be exercised. In "Resignation" Fausta draws out the poet to further revelations by her smiles and glances, but his resignation and anti-Faustianism have been present from the start and remain unchanged. The strayed reveler learns nothing from Ulysses and Circe save the cause of his magical sleep. The auditors in "Philomela" and "Dover Beach" exist only to give occasion and point to the "sad lucidity" of the speaker's words.[17] To use terms we are familiar with in the criticism of Mikhail Bakhtin, Arnold dismisses the "dialogic imagination" as irrelevant. "Aliens" who might embody a genuine otherness do appear in the poems as "Oxford hunters," "passing troops," and "the merry Grecian coaster," but they are sent off and given no hearing.

They must be sent off, for no interaction is possible when change and the time in which it may take place have had a stop. The Arnold figure looks backward, existing in the present principally to reconcile himself to the past. He is, as Sainte-Beuve said of Obermann, a seeker after permanence and therefore an enemy of time. For time only distracts him, "the empire of facts" may dominate him, and the waters of the timestream may swamp him. Nor does he look to the future. Something in him has "foreknown the vanity of hope" and "foreseen [his] harvest," and he judges "vain beforehand" ordinary human cares and concerns.[18] Dispossessed in the past, he lives to recover some fragments of his ruin and to give them permanence.

Places as the loci of change also threaten him so that he dwells preferably in quiet, empty landscapes. As Dwight Culler has taught us, he creates a private geography that subsumes change and return within a metaphor of permanence.[19] At his most remote, as the scholar gypsy, he becomes part of the natural world and flees human paths and feverish contacts. Even at his most sociable, he seeks to avoid cityscapes and their special points of interchange, the drawing room and parlor. We smile that the lover of Marguerite never stays long indoors and that Arnold's walker in the city, when assailed by the "impious uproar" of the Kensington Road or High Street, escapes into Kensington Gardens. Nevertheless, it is there as a solitary onlooker that he feels the calm of past days and "peace for ever new" ("Lines . . . Kensington Gardens," ll. 25, 29).

In its relations, then, to place, time, change, otherness, interaction, and self, the Arnoldian figure here outlined has a certain schematic overconsistency. But the point made by it is not, I would suggest, inaccurate. As it represents itself in the poems, its imagination is a priori rather than dialogic. Its utterances are made to itself rather than to others and seek to enact a changed or changing relation of the self to the a priori situation. It would be absurd to deny that there is conflict or that the poems are always proleptic to the extent that in their beginnings are their ends, though this is sometimes the case. But we have only to think of his poems as against literary works that find meanings in the clash of temporal, local, multiple, and unpredictable forces to see radical differences.

By August 1853 Arnold had received Clough's review of his poems and was preparing a third volume for the press. His preface to that volume responds to Clough in the two regards I stressed earlier, Arnold's subjectivism and preference for Ionic porticoes to the modern structures of Tennyson and Dickens. Much more is involved, of course, but on the first matter Arnold acknowledges his subjectivism but restricts the charge to one poem. For modern readers, however, his brilliant phrase "the dialogue of the mind with itself," which he used to describe modern poetry and his own "Empedocles on Etna," applies to a wide range of his work. On the second point, however, he has no doubts as to the necessity of avoiding contemporaneity and staying apart from the whirligig of time. The "elementary feelings" most important to us exist "independent

of time" and never change. Great actions that bear on our ele-
mental selves are "grand, detached, and self-subsistent." We
must be wary of "familiar manners" and "contemporary allu-
sions" and of the attractions of "the details of modern life
which pass daily under our eyes." The disciplined writer, he
says, goes so far as to repress hostility toward "the false pretensions of his age; he will content himself with not being overwhelmed with them" (*CPW,* 1:1, 4, 7, 14). He will stand in
effect outside history, and he will therefore shun merely modern subjects and, what hardly needs stating, he will not favor
the novel, the daughter of time, circumstance, and change.

Within the year following the 1853 preface Arnold had
written "Balder Dead" and, within three years more, *Merope.* It
may fairly be said of these works, whatever one thinks of their
value, that they do not strike Arnold's characteristic note. He
appears in them to have striven too hard for the "character of
Fixity," as he put it,[20] and taken too literally his own strictures
against the subjective and the contemporary. To us they appear
to be aberrations because they sacrifice Arnold's sense of the
present and hope for the future to an antiquarian's sense of the
past. In later poems his special sense of time and himself survives, particularly in "Thyrsis," which so marvelously confronts
change and affirms the values that overcome it.

But Arnold also did not take his own advice to repress
hostility toward the "false pretensions of his age." The Arnold
who was withdrawing to *Merope* was at the same time creating
for himself a new persona as professor of poetry and then as
literary, social, and religious critic to confront the age which as
a poet he had almost turned his back on. Arnold had in effect
turned from the world within to the world without, determined to resist rather than be overcome by its contemporaneity, determined to make his conception of the good prevail
in it.

In doing so, Arnold surely felt himself faithful to the early
shapers of his mind, among them the French novelist George
Sand. She had revered Senancour and edited *Obermann* and
then turned from him as Arnold was to do. Her early heroines
Lélia and Indiana had withdrawn from European civilization,
but, after uttering "the cry of agony and revolt," she returned

to the world she knew to seek "consolation from nature and poetry" and to tend "the aspiration toward a purged and renewed human society." The phrasing here is Arnold's and reflects their shared sense of past loss and of present need and future hope for social and religious change. Certainly he knew her work as he knew the work of few of his contemporaries. The many entries from her writing in his *Note-Books* show that he read even her potboilers with attention and gleaned extracts from her pages with care. He read her books not so much as novels but as ways of seeing the ideal in contemporary France and even as shadowing forth renewed religious truths. In the two pieces he was to devote to her he recommended six of her works as "characteristic and representative," works extolling on one hand the pastoral life, on the other ideals of marriage and love (*CPW,* 10:189).[21] From *Spiridion,* a mystical work of hers which Thackeray dismissed with a jeer, Arnold copied thirty-two citations into his *Note-Books,* the most from one book in a single year. This he did in 1882, six years after her death and late in the development of his own ideas.

With this in mind, we read with different eyes his attack on Charlotte Brontë's *Villette* thirty years earlier, not just because he called it "a hideous undelightful convulsed constricted novel," but that he had gone on to say, "Religion or devotion or whatever it is to be called may be impossible for such people now: but they have at any rate not found a substitute for it and it was better for the world when they comforted themselves with it."[22]

Religious considerations, this time favorable, also lie behind Arnold's remarkable essay entitled "Count Leo Tolstoi," completed only five months before his death. It is an astonishing performance, for although the essay formally turns on the conversion of Levin in *Anna Karenina* and then engages Tolstoy's nonfictional writings, the novel and its heroine particularly charm Arnold into a fresh, warmly responsive critical appraisal. Before beginning, he deals with the question of genre so that he can consider Tolstoy's work on its own terms. He reminds us that its form is that of a novel, a popular form, and though "the crown of literature is poetry," the Russians do not have a great poet, and we therefore read what they do have, great novelists. This much said, he introduces criteria of judgment that delight us with their appropriateness and his flexibility. In *Anna Karenina,* he observes, "things and characters go as nature takes them," its author deals "with the life which he knows from having lived it," and "what his novel . . . loses in art it gains in reality" (*CPW,* 11:283–85). He does not trouble to remind us that he is setting to one side his 1853 counsels in behalf of noncontemporary subjects and softening his old complaint against the novel's lack of architectonic shaping.

Clearly, the reality of Anna has touched his heart, and he willingly forgives her errors as he earlier had forgiven the un-English extravagances of George Sand. He even acknowledges that he may be taking her too seriously, but he does not stop himself. A few years earlier he had said that a work that faithfully represents actual life needs a special quality to make it acceptable reading. *Madame Bovary* does not have that quality; it is "a work of *petrified feeling*" (*CPW,* 10:136; 11:288, 293). But *Anna Karenina* has that quality, genuine feeling together with a profound moral ideal that informs and justifies the whole.

The tensions between art and life, the ideal and the real, the world within and the world without, however much we disconstruct them in these late days into meaningless distinctions, mark Arnold's sense of life and work from beginning to end. He loved the reality of the contingent, passing world. He loved it to the extent of reading, as we all do, second-rate novelists who mirror it inaccurately. In George Sand he found a fellow disciple of Senancour seeking to shape a world out of materials of modern deprivation. In Tolstoy he was able late in life to respond warmly to a great representation of contemporary Russian life in which feeling and a sense of the ideal mingled. But as poet he was early disposed to turn from outward show to inmost heart, and his impulse from the beginning was to grieve and to seek consolation within himself. Once confirmed by the "rigorous teachers" of his youth in his ravaged idealism, he was not to be charmed into mistaking the evanescent for the lasting or contemporary fictions for serious art. However dominant a form the novel became, and perhaps still remains, the Arnoldian temperament will not be content with it.

NOTES

1. Iris Esther Sells, *Matthew Arnold and France: The Poet* (Cambridge: Cambridge University Press, 1935), p. 271. Joan P. Campbell's essay "Matthew Arnold and the Novel," *Jackson State College Review* 5 (Summer 1973):6–21, focuses on Arnold's influence on foreign, British, and American novelists. Park Honan's biography, *Matthew Arnold: A Life* (New York: McGraw-Hill, 1981), mentions novelists Arnold read, and Ruth apRoberts's *Arnold and God* (Berkeley and Los Angeles: University of California Press, 1983), p. 277, lists many more. By checking all the titles in Arnold's *Note-Books*, ed. H. F. Lowry, K. Young, and W. H. Dunn (London: Oxford University Press, 1952), published letters, and (some years ago) those in the University of Virginia collection, I have been able to double Professor apRoberts's list.

2. Kathleen Tillotson, *Novels of the Eighteen-Forties* (Oxford: Clarendon Press, 1954), p. 15; Richard Stang, *The Theory of the Novel in England, 1850–1870* (New York: Columbia University Press, 1959), pp. 3–4.

3. Honan, *Arnold*, pp. 22, 25, 32; *Letters of Matthew Arnold to Arthur Hugh Clough*, ed. Howard Foster Lowry (London: Oxford University Press, 1932), pp. 59, 133.

4. *Poems of Matthew Arnold*, ed. Kenneth Allott, 2d ed., ed. Miriam Allott (London: Longman, 1979), p. 423 n.

5. Kathleen Tillotson, "'Haworth Churchyard': The Making of Arnold's Elegy," *Brontë Society Transactions* 15, no. 2 (1967):114.

6. Thomas Arnold, "Recent Novel Writing," *Macmillan's Magazine* 13 (Jan. 1866): 202–9.

7. Honan, *Arnold*, p. 22; Thomas Arnold, *Introductory Lectures on Modern History* (London: B. Fellowes, 1845), p. 285.

8. Stephen Coleridge, *Famous Victorians I Have Known* (London: Simkin, Marshall, 1928), p. 33.

9. See, for example, *CPW,* 3:16; 9:130; 10:135, 175–76, 180; *Note-Books*, pp. 595, 601, 604.

10. *Unpublished Letters of Matthew Arnold*, ed. Arnold Whitridge (New Haven: Yale University Press), p. 11.

11. From Taine, Arnold copied strictures on Dickens into his *Note-Books*, pp. 361–62.

12. Arthur Hugh Clough, "Recent English Poetry," *North American Review* 77 (July 1853), in *Selected Prose Works of Arthur Hugh Clough*, ed. B. B. Trawick (University, Ala.: University of Alabama Press, 1964), pp. 144–45, 161.

13. *Letters of Arnold to Clough*, p. 95. Arnold may be reacting to Clough's seeming defection. The latter had earlier written in *Ambarvalia* of "excitements" that cannot "reach / the buried world below" but appeared now to have opted for them.

14. For Arnold's relationship with Senancour and Sand, see Sells, *Arnold and France*; F. J. W. Harding, *Matthew Arnold, the Critic, and France* (Geneva: Librairie Droz, 1964); and esp. Patricia Thomson, *George Sand and the Victorians* (London: Macmillan, 1977), pp. 90–120.

15. George Sand, *Lélia*, trans. Maria Espinosa (Bloomington: Indiana University Press, 1978), p. 116.

16. Besides "In Harmony with Nature," "The Voice," and "The World and the Quietish," see "Rude Orator."

17. On the use of auditors in Arnold and others, see Dorothy Merwin, *The Audience in the Poem: Five Victorian Poets* (New Brunswick: Rutgers University Press, 1983).

18. "To a Gipsy Child by the Sea-shore," ll. 39–40; "Resignation," l. 232.

19. See A. Dwight Culler, *Imaginative Reason: The Poetry of Matthew Arnold* (New Haven: Yale University Press, 1966), esp. pp. 2–16.

20. *Letters of Matthew Arnold, 1848–1888*, ed. G. W. E. Russell, 2 vols. (New York: Macmillan, 1895), 1:57 (July 25, 1857).

21. The six works are *Lettres d'un Voyageur, Mauprat, François Le Champi, La Petite Fadette, Jean de La Roche, Valvêdre*.

22. *Letters of Arnold To Clough*, p. 132 (Mar. 21, 1853).

ALLAN C. DOOLEY

NINE

Literature and the Pleasure Principle: An Arnoldian Antidote for Critical Confusion

The idea that novelty in art and its interpretation constitutes progress or improvement in art and in criticism is an illusion that does not die easily. Despite our veneration of Samuel Johnson, despite our citations of Aristotle and the rediscovery of Vico, many current literary critics would concede to even their most illustrious predecessors only limited importance and waning influence. This essay argues that Arnold the critic should be more directly influential today than he appears to be. Arnold's seeming role today is often as a sort of critical Jonah: not the major prophet he thought himself but one who has to be thrown overboard. He also has a latent importance as the father who must be overthrown. But where Arnold should be influential is in the arena of our ongoing debates about the nature of literature and literary criticism. I am convinced that if we do not apply an Arnoldian corrective in these debates, we will put our profession and its usefulness at risk by raising up a generation of critical projectors whose considerations of literature will be as removed from reality as the experiments in the Grand Academy of Lagado.

A clear manifestation of the dangers in current theoretical

criticism appeared in the centennial issue of *PMLA,* in which
Geoffrey Hartman, in a bewildering tour de force, argued
essentially that the object of criticism is now criticism itself.
Hartman tells us that "in Barthes's *Lover's Discourse,* the meta-
languages of scholarship and theory are already being resyn-
thesized into art."[1] This art is what serious critics are to
consider, study, and presumably teach; criticism has replaced
literature. This struck me as such nonsense that I had to wonder if I were radically misreading Hartman and his intention.
But Hartman is hardly alone in making this proposition, and I
am not alone in my view of its meaning. Wendell Harris, reviewing Elizabeth Bruss's recent book *Beautiful Theories,* finds
Bruss arguing that "theory about literature . . . performs (or
should perform . . .) much the same function as literature, and
might as well be written as literature."[2] I cannot help but remember Carlyle's prediction in "Characteristics": "By and by,
it will be found that all Literature has become one boundless
self-devouring Review."[3] It may be that, for the mandarins of
the new schools of criticism, critical writing itself has become
the corpus to be examined, dissected, theorized about—but
this can hardly be true for the undergraduate English major,
puzzling out a conceit of John Donne's and enjoying doing it.
It can hardly be true, or if it is true it cannot be desirable, for
the graduate student whom we thought was taking pleasure in
sorting out the shifting voices and shaded tonalities of *The Ring
and the Book.* Experienced, well-read critics—and such our
leading theorists are—can find value in exploring theoretical
possibilities, but for most readers the important, exciting encounter remains that with a great poem, a great novel, a great
play. My first Arnoldian corrective, then, is to recall his comment in "The Function of Criticism at the Present Time" on the
relation of the critical intellect to the creative imagination:
"The critical power is of lower rank than the creative" (*CPW,*
3:260). Even though Arnold qualifies and augments this view,
arguing that artistic creation is nourished by criticism, nothing
he or any later critic has said diminishes the lasting force of
that sound principle: "The critical power is of lower rank than
the creative."

One also finds in current advanced criticism a fairly widespread view that an author's intended meaning is a snare and a delusion, or is unknowable, or is nonexistent. Terry Eagleton contends that "there is no more reason in principle why the author's meaning should be preferred than there is for preferring the reading offered by the critic with the shortest hair or the largest feet."[4] I will let E. D. Hirsch, the critic Eagleton is attacking, answer for himself in terms Arnold would endorse: "To treat an author's words as grist for one's own mill is ethically analogous to using another man merely for one's own purposes."[5] And I will add that the critic who said that "the greatness of a poet lies in his powerful and beautiful application of ideas to life,—to the question: How to live?" (*CPW*, 9:46) was describing that profound interest in an author's intended meaning which characterizes the efforts of most readers. Specialists in formal criticism and theory may legitimately take an interest in many other aspects of a work, but literature has always been made for other readers than specialists.

Much current criticism is executed in a style I find irritating and opaque; indeed, if I understand Jacques Derrida at all, his style is designed to be opaque because clarity might suggest an authority and accuracy which, it is alleged, criticism cannot rightly claim. Beyond this, and behind much of the effort of literary theorists, lies a more provocative matter: the pursuit of a general theory of literature. Whether we need a general theory of literature is one question; whether such a theory is possible is another. I doubt that we will see a useful general theory of literature (at least as I comprehend the nature of a theory) because literature as a subject of inquiry is different from those subjects for which general theories have been developed. Literature, like other arts, but unlike fossils, molecules, and stars, is not given in nature. We cannot be observers of literary works in the sense that a geneticist is an observer of molecular processes because we, as critics and interpreters, participate in literature in more intimate and direct ways that the geneticist participates in the phenomena she observes and considers. We can theorize, but we cannot predict what literature will be. We can speculate more freely than the physical scientist, but we cannot experiment; we cannot repeat the conditions and the chain of events that brought a particular work of art into existence. Yet we can predict, with fair accuracy, what is likely to happen to an attentive reader in an encounter with a given work of literature; *King Lear* will break your heart. It takes no general theory, no rarefied style, to understand this; a great artist can affect vast numbers of very different people in a consistent way because the emotional nature of human beings does not alter in its elements. Human authors write, and human readers read, and criticism's task is not to supplant either of these but to understand the methods of the one and the responses of the other.

Where does Arnold fit into the current debates and spec- ulations about literature and criticism? In the books and ar- ticles I have been reading, Arnold has a place as universal whipping boy. He is read unsympathetically or with malice aforethought. He is blamed for many of the faults of Anglo- American criticism over the last hundred years. He is an elitist, deceiving us with the guise of a democrat. He is a rigid ideo- logue but not a systematic one. Hartman tells us that for Ar- nold, "the idea that [culture] might oppress rather than enlighten the uncultured classes . . . was not an issue."[6] But we can remember the end of the first chapter of *Culture and Anar- chy,* which warns: "Plenty of people will try to give the masses, as they call them, an intellectual food prepared and adapted in the way they think proper for the actual condition of the masses; . . . but culture works differently" (*CPW,* 5:112–13). Elsewhere, however, Arnold is portrayed as conniving with the ruling class, "distracting the masses from their immediate com- mitments, nurturing in them a spirit of tolerance and generos- ity, and so ensuring the survival of private property."[7] Certainly the concepts of "the author" and "the author's intention" are alive on those particular pages of modern literary theory.

The hostility that generates such distortion is not baseless. Arnold indeed stands against many principles and practices common in current criticism. Fundamentally, Arnold dis- trusted criticism based on theory. In "A French Critic on Goethe" he categorizes some sources of critical error: "There is the judgment of ignorance, the judgment of incompatibility, the judgment of envy and jealousy. Finally, there is the system- atic judgment, and this judgment is the most worthless of all. . . . The systematic judgment is altogether unprofitable. Its author has not really his eye upon the professed object of his criticism at all, but upon something else which he wants to prove by means of that object. . . . He is no genuine critic, but a man with a system, an advocate" (*CPW,* 8:254–55). A modern critic, trying to work toward an internally consistent theory of authorship or of semiotic representation, must find the Arnold of that passage a powerfully anxiety-inducing influence.

Yet Arnold himself is not a theoryless critic. Though he was unsystematic, eclectic, and sometimes self-contradictory, one of his most memorable and valuable essays is primarily a statement of literary theory. I mean, of course, the 1853 Preface to *Poems,* whose propositions about literature are powerful and provocative to this day. Arnold's theory seems simple because he states it so baldly and so briefly. But this apparent simplicity masks the real radicalism of his position.[8] By taking a radical view, which simultaneously accepts both the historicity of literature's content and style and the timelessness of its effects on readers, Arnold brilliantly eludes the traps of circularity and indeterminacy that mar several current critical methods. Furthermore, Arnold's radical simplicity, based as it is on actual works and plausible readers, makes possible a practical criticism which late twentieth-century attempts at theory have endangered or discarded.

Arnold's first and all-ruling principle is that the aim of literature, the purpose of literature, the rationale for the existence of literature, is the pleasure of the reader. I must quickly add that his definition of pleasure is suitably broad, including the pleasure gained from knowing, even when what we come to know from a work is somber, tragic, or painful: "In presence of the most tragic circumstances, represented in a work of art, the feeling of enjoyment, as is well known, may still subsist; the representation of the most utter calamity, of the liveliest anguish, is not sufficient to destroy it; the more tragic the situation, the deeper becomes the enjoyment." In support of this principle Arnold cites Schiller in the preceding paragraph: "'The right art is that alone, which creates the highest enjoyment.'" This enjoyment or pleasure, though created and perceived by means of the intellect, is essentially emotional; the greatest works of art are those that "most powerfully appeal to the great primary affections: to those elementary feelings which . . . are independent of time. . . . To the elementary part of our nature, to our passions, that which is great and passionate is eternally interesting" (*CPW,* 1:2).

At the same time, this pleasure is much more than sensation, as Arnold suggests in a later essay, "A French Critic on Milton": "Human progress consists in a continual increase in the number of those who, ceasing to live by the animal life alone and to feel the pleasures of sense only, come to participate in the intellectual life also, and to find enjoyment in the things of the mind" (*CPW,* 8:196). Furthermore, and contra Derrida and Roland Barthes, the effect such pleasure has on us is not narcissistic or hedonistic; Arnold describes it, rather, in moral terms: "The right function of poetry is to animate, to console, to rejoice—in one word, to *strengthen*" (*CPW,* 8:1). This is Arnold's equivalent to modern "reader-response" analysis, but with the strong, empirically based conviction that some works have a more powerful and more salutary effect than others.

From these principles and convictions Arnold derives a view of the critic's role that might surprise those who are familiar only with the prescriptive terms of the 1853 Preface and "The Function of Criticism at the Present Time." The modern reader, Arnold says, expects the critic to assist him: "Does the work you praise, he asks, affect me with high pleasure and do me good, when I try it as fairly as I can? The critic who helps such a questioner is one who has sincerely asked himself, also, this same question; who has answered it in a way which agrees, in the main, with what the questioner finds to be his own honest experience in the matter, and shows the reasons for this common experience" (*CPW,* 8:171–72). Our encounters with literature, then, are governed by the pleasure principle, and we want to understand that pleasure and the artistic means that give rise to it for the simplest of reasons: so we can find it and experience it further. The useful critic is, in Virgil Thompson's phrase, "someone who tells you what it was like to be there." The critic serves as a representative responder who, though skilled, articulate, and specially trained, does not differ in "common experience" from the rest of a work's potential audience. We need critics not because they can supply us with a coherent theory of art (though we can understand why they might work toward one), but because, as Walter Pater tells us, "a counted number of pulses only is given to us."[9] We would prefer not to waste our allotted time on the second-rate, and the valuable critic will help us, not deracinate us with self-immolating theory.

Arnold's insistence on the primacy of the reader's pleasure—complex as that is—is important and bracing for criticism because his view is not ideological. It is not the application of a historically determined value system, but a series of empirical observations about human nature and the art that humans have made for themselves. Arnold takes literature as a given, a wonderfully diverse set of artifacts whose precise categorizations and psychic origins he is usually content to leave unexamined. I suppose this makes him the original New Critic, even to the point of bearing in very closely on the relations of words in a single line, as in his much mentioned but seldom analyzed touchstones. As a species of positivist, Arnold accepts the plainest of definitions of author, reader, and critic; one is not simultaneously all three. We cannot overlook the real limitations on Arnold's critical stance, but neither should criticism ignore the Arnoldian outlook because of its limitations or because it is a century old.

The influence of Arnold on our time that I would like to see consists of a reassertion, in the realm of criticism, of several Arnoldian assumptions and principles. First, we must recognize as Arnold did that true and useful criticism functions by judgments about the quality of actual works of literature; our critical acts, in the classroom or on the page, cannot be and should not attempt to be purely theoretical or value-free. Second, our criticism must restrain its tendencies to become abstract and overly speculative by applying to itself the tests of probability and relevance to the task—the task of the critic as a skilled and representative common reader. Like Arnold, we must try to learn and remember what the common reader is likely to experience and what the common reader wants and needs from criticism. Finally, we must reassert for our students, our colleagues, and ourselves the primary importance of literature as a source of pleasure and, yes, truth. Too many students of literature, professional and amateur, do not find enjoyment in reading literature because they feel obligated to get more out of it than that—and they feel guilty if they don't. Too many teachers take pleasure in leading students into the deep, centerless waters of speculative theory and leaving them there.

I do not wish to see an end to theorizing about the manifold relations among authors, works, and readers. Much valuable, stimulating criticism, such as that of Harold Bloom, Lawrence Lipking, and E. D. Hirsch, to list a few famous names, has come from the pursuit of literary theories. Yet what a sad commentary it is to have heard my colleagues say, "Well, I don't understand his theories in that book, but he does come up with some interesting readings along the way." I might mention also the rueful comment of a friend who teaches comparative literature and the history of criticism. She said that she looked forward to being known as a "neo-revisionist-post-deconstructionist," whose position would be that every detail of a literary work is a direct and intentional reflection of the author's own experience. Still, I take a Bloomian view of the relation between the English romantics and the Victorians, and I recently came close to a deconstruction by insisting that my class follow out the possibilities of Telemachus's savage observation that he was not sure Odysseus really was his father.

I also do not wish to see speculation and glib terminology passing for or replacing the hard work and broad learning on which literary scholarship and criticism have always rested. Hartman, Paul DeMan, J. Hillis Miller, Stanley Fish, all are immensely learned critics. But will their followers be? Will they feel the need to be learned, when with a system and vocabulary at hand, any text will serve as a starting point for the critic's own dance before the mirror? At the centennial Modern Language Association convention, George Ford complained a little about the terminology he encounters in current articles. "They speak," he said, "of intertextuality. We used to call that literary allusion." But to take Professor Ford's joke seriously, there is a crucial difference. An allusion is a complex transaction among human beings: one author makes direct or slanting reference to another; the reader completes the transaction only if he knows both those people's works. Intertextual relations, on the other hand, seem to be carried on by texts themselves, the only human agency being the critic who overhears them. If a passage in Browning seems to me to echo a passage in Donne, I can say that Browning alludes to Donne only if I can find out whether Browning read Donne, and if so, whether he had read the relevant work by the time he wrote his poem— presuming that I am satisfied with the dating of Browning's poem. If, on the other hand, I assert an intertextuality between "'Childe Roland to the Dark Tower Came'" and "A Valediction: Forbidding Weeping," the historical question, Did Browning read Donne, and when? becomes blissfully irrelevant. I do not have to look it up.

Perhaps our situation in literary studies will evoke an application of the wisdom of Candide, who responded to the last idiotic inductions of Pangloss by stating, exhaustedly: "It is very well said, but we must cultivate our gardens." Our gardens, for the most part, are our classrooms, our departments, our organizations, and our journals. Whether we will see ever more of our colleagues, and worse, our students, enchanted by abstract and speculative criticism, or whether we will see a reaffirmation of humanist principles like Arnold's, I do not know. But I do know that all of us, as readers, teachers, scholars, and critics, will decide. We are the people who get to vote.

NOTES

1. Geoffrey Hartman, "The Culture of Criticism," *PMLA* 99 (1984):390. In a sense so obvious that Hartman cannot intend it, criticism has always taken other criticism as its object; Aristotle scrutinized Plato, and Coleridge evaluated Lessing.

2. Wendell V. Harris, review of Elizabeth Bruss, *Beautiful Theories, Modern Language Quarterly* 44 (1983):220–21.

3. Thomas Carlyle, "Characteristics," in *English Prose of the Victorian Era*, ed. C. F. Harrold and W. D. Templeman (New York: Oxford University Press, 1938), p. 17.

4. Terry Eagleton, *Literary Theory* (Minneapolis: University of Minnesota Press, 1983), p. 69.

5. E. D. Hirsch, *The Aims of Interpretation* (Chicago: University of Chicago Press, 1976), p. 91.

6. Hartman, "Culture of Criticism," 380.

7. Eagleton, *Literary Theory,* p. 26.

8. Though he does not discuss the matter, Morris Dickstein notes in his contribution to a recent discussion of Arnold's criticism that "it was more truly radical . . . than the work of the deconstructionists themselves" ("Arnold Then and Now," *Critical Inquiry* 9 [1983]:492).

9. Walter Pater, "Conclusion" to *The Renaissance,* in *Criticism: The Major Texts,* ed. W. J. Bate (New York: Harcourt Brace Jovanovich, 1970), p. 511.

JOHN P. FARRELL

―――

TEN

―――

"What I Want the Reader to See": Action and Performance in Arnold's Prose

The most influential part of Arnold's work, according to Raymond Williams, is "his effort to give his revaluation a practical bearing in society."[1] Williams completely rejects the notion that Arnold devalued social action and subordinated it to the inward operations of culture. Clearly, Williams's point has not always been taken to heart. Peter Allen Dale, for example, though accepting a social purpose in Arnold's work, claims that Arnold shifted decisively toward an inward concern with moral being or "'the right ordering of the soul.'" Dale acknowledges that Arnold does not deny "the need for virtuous action in the world," but Arnold seems at the outset to have raised significant questions "about the meaningfulness of action; and in face of what looked like the inability of the human will to change the course of history, [he] redirected [action] toward the reformation of . . . man's . . . own inner nature."[2] Critics such as Dale have a crucial case, but they make it by collapsing what Williams astutely says about Arnold's continuing engagement with the social environment.

My purpose here is to urge the point that Arnold was fundamentally concerned with the problem of connecting action in the world of practice with the inward drives of personal growth and self-culture. The clearest ground in Arnold's work for discovering how he linked these areas of experience is in the nature of performance that he exhibits as a writer and that he elicits from his audience. Crudely put, my thesis is that Arnold grasped and deliberately exploited the dynamics of performance, the putting on and acting out of roles, as a way to mediate between social practice and personal process. He saw, in other words, that our very capacity for performative roles, including the role of reader, arises from our own social being and profoundly influences all inward forms of self-culture. The quoted phrase in my title is from "The Literary Influence of Academies." This essay, together with its companion piece, "The Function of Criticism at the Present Time," I will eventually use to illustrate briefly what I mean by performance in Arnold, and more to the point, what Arnold means.

It makes sense to look at Arnold's prose in this light because the nature of action and performance became for him a decisive question in the formation of his critical discourse. Writing to his mother in 1864, the year the essays I have mentioned were published, Arnold said, in response to one of the perplexing events of the day, that it "makes me fix all my care upon a spiritual action, to tell upon people's minds, which is after all the great thing, hard as it is to make oneself fully believe it so" (*CPW,* 4:345). How could action be "spiritual"? Arnold, of course, means an action not calculatedly political or in the loosest sense pragmatic. But telling upon people's minds does not occur through some mystic medium. Arnold's oxymoronic phrase "spiritual action" is a revealing indication of his feeling that discourse is performative, that it *does* something. He is in this sense like Carlyle from whom he undoubtedly learned a great deal about the performative relations of author and reader, even though he needed, for the sake of his own instincts and values, almost exactly to reverse Carlyle's come-on. But the nature of performance, of course, is much more than a matter of literary style. It involves the writer's attitudes about social identity and social being. Arnold's assumptions about men as social agents seem to me to anticipate Emile Durkheim's and an even later line of phenomenological sociology that branched off from Durkheim. In one of his lectures Durkheim summarized the key orientation of his work when he said that "the human personality is a sacred thing; one dare not violate it or infringe its bounds, while at the same time the greatest good is in communion with others."[3] This fraught and urgent condition underlies both Durkheim's discussion of the "collective conscience" and Arnold's discussion of culture. Arnold put the point this way: "By our everyday selves . . . we are separate, personal, at war. . . . But by our *best self* we are united, impersonal, at harmony. . . . This is the very self which culture, or the study of perfection, seeks to develop in us" (*CPW,* 5:134). What I am interested in is how Arnold creates an image of the best self by evoking the action of the performative self.

To gain some purchase on this relationship we can take at least a grainy glimpse of Arnold at Oxford, the significant site where he tended to locate the ideal of the best self and where his own performances, both as poet and critic, were initially tested. Oxford served as a stage for Arnold, and the intersection there of his two careers is dramaturgical in nature since it vivifies for us—and may well have for Arnold himself—the confrontation of roles that is so strikingly played out in his transformation from poet to critic. As an external sign of the confrontation we might remember that the poetic Arnold deliberately cultivated a self-absorbed, dandified persona and the critical Arnold returned to Oxford in the guise of a professor of poetry who had a quite unacademic conception of his office.

More to the point, of course, is the symbolic performance Arnold develops in the forms of communication he ventures with an audience. When Arnold wrote in "Democracy" about the achievement of the British aristocracy, he identified the source of its efficacy as its "bond of common culture" (*CPW,* 2:5). An analogous bond is evidently what Arnold sought when, as professor of poetry, he addressed his audiences at Oxford. As we well know, he openly solicited solidarity with them and proposed, in gorgeous rhetoric, that a bond of common culture formed the inspiriting relationship uniting himself and his auditors. "I am all in the faith and tradition of Oxford," he told them (*CPW,* 5:106). Yet looking out among his fellow Oxonians, as he delivered his lectures, Arnold must have seen a shadow of himself as a student when he was writing a poetry filled with directions for withdrawal, isolation, and inwardness:

> Where I stand the grass is glowing;
> Doubtless you are passing fair!
> But I hear the north wind blowing
> And I feel the cold night air.
> Can I look on your sweet faces,
> And your proud heads backward thrown,
> From this dusk of leaf-strewn places
> With the dumb woods and the night alone?
>
> ("New Sirens," ll. 187–94)

The lines typify the disbanded or disbonded world of Arnold's poetry and remind us of the poetic identity he so instinctively assumed. Arnold belongs, as Frank Kermode has written, to a line of romantic poets for whom the poet is as a limb torn off from society and whose destiny is to be "lonely, haunted, victimized, devoted to suffering rather than action."[4]

The Arnold who returned as lecturer to Oxford had clearly changed his mind about the priority of suffering and action. But it must be remembered that the image of the poet in isolation is continuous with Arnold's whole sense of the self as mystery. "Weary of myself, and sick of asking / What I am," he says in "Self-Dependence," ll. 1–2, adding in "The Buried Life" that we have, nevertheless,

> A longing to inquire
> Into the mystery of this heart which beats
> So wild.   (ll. 51–53)

And so, if it is true that Arnold found the burden of the poet to be isolation, he saw the same burden weighing, at last, on the human personality. To remember this theme is to sharpen the drama at the site of intersection. Arnold, delivering his critical discourse to his audience at Oxford and avowing his bond of common culture with them, might well have wondered at the opposing figure of himself just beyond the horizon of his discourse, sealed in some "leaf-strewn place." Yet the figure would be not only the poetic self he had abandoned but the ineffable self who was, in fact, speaking. Once again Durkheim's plangent remark is appropriate: "The human personality is a sacred thing; one dare not violate it or infringe its bounds, while at the same time the greatest good is in communion with others."

The consequence of the doubleness I am describing, the *homo duplex* Arnold sees, is that when Arnold cast off the estrangements of the poet's life and "plunged into action, into other people's business," as Kermode puts it,[5] he certainly did not lose his intimate sense of the self enisled. It can only be a reification of Arnold to claim that he left the leaf-strewn places of his isolation behind him in the counterdiscourse of his prose. Nevertheless, Raymond Williams rightly says that Arnold's commitment is to social practice. The point to be made, of course, is that Arnold is always advancing a process of inner personal transformation, but one that begins to take its motive power from the inherent and irreducible social agency that marks even the muddiest human discourse and that comes potently to life when discourse is shaped not only by its dialectical drives but by its performative possibilities. The best self, as Arnold knew, cannot simply be legislated or advocated or even cultivated. It has to be enacted.

Arnold himself is largely responsible for the impression that his prose discourse puts a wall between the ideal of the best self and the mysterious phenomenon of subjectivity. He disowned Empedocles for looking too much into subjectivity. And then he wrote criticism dedicated to guarding against any further Empedoclean outbursts. Arnold remains all against the extrusions of the self, the personal estimate, and in favor of the submerging of subjectivity beneath the shadow of that colossal imperative, the best that has been thought and said in the world. Geoffrey Hartman rightly attributes the idealization of impersonality in Arnold's criticism to the anti-self-consciousness principle in Victorian literature. Arnold invokes this principle as a condition of criticism.[6]

And yet there is something farfetched and fantastical in this Arnoldian account of Arnold. Hartman has everything right about Arnold's critical orientation except for what readers actually experience when they read him. There is an impressive polarization in Arnold's critical discourse between the impersonality he recommends and the personality he exhibits. In John Holloway's view, Arnold *is* what he advocates, and what he conveys "in the whole experience of reading him [is] not a view of the world, but a habit of mind." This helps to explain, Holloway goes on, "why he is so prominent himself in his writings."[7] What Holloway is saying was already said by some of Arnold's own contemporaries, and the point is always being rediscovered. William Buckler and George Levine are the latest proponents of the same thesis. Levine argues that "in a way, Arnold's criticism is an autobiographical fiction, a set of inventions of the self."[8] It would seem, then, that the human personality, the mirroring surface of the self's mysteries, is the secret sharer of a critical discourse that celebrates impersonality. The area of identity Arnold once traced in the "leaf-strewn" places of his poetry is thrust forward in the prose as the ground of his own performing self.

This process accounts for Arnold's highly successful negotiation of the distance between the buried self and the best self. Mask or persona draws its alluring inventiveness from the personal self, but it also opens a social space, as all roles do, by intrinsically defining an audience. Arnold understood that his discourse on high culture had to be folded within a bond of common culture uniting him in fellowship with his readers. What he once said about the relations of culture to society is exactly true of the dramatistic quality in his own prose: "For us—who believe in right reason, in the duty and possibility of extricating and elevating our best self, in the progress of humanity towards perfection,—for us the framework of society, that theatre on which this august drama has to enroll itself, is sacred" (*CPW,* 5:222–23).

The drama that enrolls itself in Arnold's critical discourse is openly staged around the author's effort to form a bond with the reader that is exemplary of the larger, more complex system of relationships that Arnold called culture. What Arnold practices in his prose is just the opposite of what happens in his poem "The Scholar-Gipsy." There, a reader has reached such intimate communion with a figure in a text that he attains virtual identity with him; but a point comes when the illusion of identity cannot be sustained, and a complicated meditative process overwhelms a simple narrative one so that the reader *in* the poem loses all contact with the scholar-gipsy while the reader *of* the poem becomes increasingly confused and in the final stanza nearly dispossessed.

In the prose, the reader is repossessed. The principal means by which Arnold effects the responsiveness and interplay in the criticism's drama of relationship is through his pervasive account of numerous distinctively defined qualities of sensibility that ultimately constitute the basis both of Arnold's reflexive presence in his prose and his reader's sense of a mutual bond with him. Arnold's prose is saturated with a language of motives for right action that are the insignia of the best self: disinterestedness; sweetness and light; sincerity and strength; flexibility; curiosity; imaginative reason; energy and honesty; resignation; mildness and sweet reasonableness; high seriousness; and many others. Considered thematically, these are important topics in themselves. But the pattern adds up to a modeling of the human personality around a new account of the virtues. All of Arnold's critical ideas are extensions of these personal traits, and the key to the social bond Arnold establishes with his audience is to be found in the symbolic density of personal traits that can be simultaneously understood as the collective endowment of an epoch, a nation, or a class. Arnold can thus conceive his audience at the richly subjective level of personal temperament, and, what is more, being a personal agent himself, he can enact what he defines. The virtues discussed in Arnold's prose are precepts of cultural identity, the nodal points through which the uninfringeable self and social being connect. Such qualities are the collective representations of *homo duplex.* They inhere *in* the self, but *for* the other.

"The Function of Criticism" and "The Literary Influence of Academies" provide some illustrations of the point I have been pursuing. Both essays make a peculiar claim on their readers for they seem, notoriously, to be doing the opposite of what they are advocating. In "The Function of Criticism," Arnold seems forever to be engaging in the world of practice while repeating again and again the principle that "criticism must maintain its independence of the practical spirit and its aims" (*CPW,* 3:280). In "The Literary Influence" he never does recommend the British academy that he appears to be proposing. These discordances vanish, however, when we attend to what actually happens in the essays. In "The Function of Criticism" Arnold is giving his reader practice in the ideal of criticism, whereas in "The Literary Influence" he is effectively turning his implied readers into the academy that Britain officially lacks.

The ideal of disinterested criticism, Arnold says, in the former essay, is "obedience to an instinct for trying to know the best that has been thought and said in the world, irrespectively of practice, politics, and everything of the kind." He follows this declaration immediately by saying, "This is an instinct for which there is, I think, little original sympathy in the practical English nature" (*CPW,* 3:268). The elementary but still crucial point to be made about this passage, as well as the many others like it in the essay, is that it signifies Arnold's attribution to his readers of a Burkean return upon themselves. Their ability to transcend an ingrained national habit and rise to the cultural virtues of the best self is everywhere projected in the essay as the critical role of Arnold's readers. Moreover, the social contract of the essay depends on the reader's ability to make a disinterested appreciation of the decisive difference between the author and the tainted practitioners of criticism, who are held up not only as bad examples but as the scandalous source of criticism's disrepute. All the instances of "practice" in the negative sense that Arnold cites in the essay exist in a category entirely different from the practice Arnold himself undertakes for the sake of his reader. Practice as exhibited by the Philistines is a politicizing of criticism; but practice as exhibited by Arnold is the performance of criticism. To the degree that Arnold's reader responds to his implicit role in the essay, he undertakes a performance that mirrors the best self of the discriminating, disinterested critic. Notice the similarity in the way Arnold described criticism as a function with what could be said about the critic as a person: "It must be patient, and know how to wait; and flexible, and know how to attach itself to things, and how to withdraw from them. It must be apt to study and praise elements that [are wanted] for the fulness of spiritual perfection" (*CPW,* 3:288). This is a fair description of what we must do to read "The Function of Criticism" and not find it, dialectically speaking, in violation of its own thesis.

Our performance is guided in more complex ways as well. Much the most important of these is the way Arnold creates an ensemble of voices playing off one another. The first is a textual voice, that is, the voice of various quoted texts, which by tone, style, or other textual gesture seems aimed at a reader of such monstrous insensitivity that Arnold's readers can only gape. The second voice is mimic. Arnold imitates the voice of Philistine critics so that their shrillness is plainly heard, but it is heard riding the graceful rhythms of Arnold's own prose. Here is just one instance: "Let us organise and combine a party to pursue truth and new thought; let us call it *the liberal party,* and let us all stick to each other, and back each other up. Let us have no nonsense about independent criticism [and] don't let us trouble ourselves about foreign thought; we shall invent the whole thing for ourselves as we go along" (*CPW,* 3:276). The mingled measure of Philistine inanity and Arnoldian wit prompts the reader to an act of discrimination that is itself an initiation into disinterested criticism. Finally, there is an oracular voice, often speaking in a foreign tongue, which is dramatized as the very language of the best self. The supreme significance of this voice is that it occasions the display of Arnold's own responses as a reader, which are, in turn, cues to ours. The single most important oracular voice in the essay is Edmund Burke's. Burke, of course, does not speak in a foreign tongue, but he does speak in italics, which is almost as good.

The dramatic manipulation of all these voices has the same effect as multiple narration, which is not a disguising of the implied narrator but his elevation to a privileged position— or, in this case, the situating of a critical dialectician at some point beyond the logomachies of critical discourse. The act of reading the discourse carries the same effect—as author and reader jointly discover the best self instanced in the social bond their performance elicits. Arnold gives in the essay a marvelously illuminating reflection of how he approached the construction of this bond: "It is by communicating fresh knowledge and letting his own judgment pass along with it,—but insensibly and in the second place, not the first, as a sort of *companion and clue, not as an abstract lawgiver,*—that the critic will generally do most good to his readers" (*CPW,* 3:283; emphasis added).

"The Literary Influence of Academies" is an even more extraordinary manifestation of Arnold's virtuosity since what it is basically accomplishing with its reader is the symbolic construction of a British academy. Arnold's interest in the Academie Française is limited to its operation as "a force of educated opinion," which establishes and guards standards of clearness, correctness, and propriety in thinking and speaking (*CPW,* 3:241). Obviously, this is a focus that has much more relevance to the prose literature of France than to its poetry. Arnold is quite open about this point; his essay, in fact, becomes a critique of English and French prose. An academy may not preside well over the genius of poetry, but it does superbly in presiding over "intelligence, the ruling divinity of prose" (*CPW,* 3: 243).

It cannot escape Arnold's audience that his discussion, in effect, offers for judgment the degree to which his own prose measures up to the standards of taste and clarity that he believes an academy can promote. And this is all the more evident when Arnold forthrightly declares that the true prose is Attic prose, which is to say prose like his own.

"How much greater," Arnold contends, "is our nation in poetry than prose" (*CPW,* 3:240). His essay pursues this proposition by detailed and subtle discussion of what he calls the note of provinciality in English prose. Such a note is altogether extirpated in Arnold's style. What Arnold wants his reader to see, of course, is just what the reader is reading. The reader has only to internalize as personal virtue what is inscribed as rhetorical decorum in the text on the page. Arnold comes very close to outrageous self-congratulation in the design of the essay, especially because he cites some of his own contemporaries, including Ruskin, for their sins. But the essay wins the risky game it is playing because it accords to its readers the power of "lucidity, measure and propriety" (*CPW,* 3:248) that it associates with the influence of academies. Arnold turns deliberately and severely to his readers at the end and tells them: "Every one amongst us with any turn for literature will do well to remember to what shortcomings and excesses, which [an] academy tends to correct, we are liable. . . . He will do well constantly to try himself in respect of these, steadily to widen his culture, severely to check in himself the provincial spirit" (*CPW,* 3:257).

We can see the academy being built in these remarks, but it is an academy quite different in spirit from the rather forbidding enterprise of the French. If its task is the development of high culture, its basis is a bond of common culture. Arnold identified the best self with the social self, and his prose is an effort to turn the author-reader relationship into an image of the perfected social bonding that becomes available in culture. Arnold enters into a performative space with his reader in which he becomes not an abstract lawgiver but a companion. There in that space the cultural virtues appear in action. It is true that they appear, in the first instance, as the contingencies of a role, a mask put on in partial fulfillment of that incredibly subtle process by which discourse is distributed between author and audience. But as Hamlet says, we may assume a virtue if we have it not and by the use of action fair and good become what we play. Raymond Williams has it right: Arnold's achievement was to give his revaluation a practical bearing in society.

NOTES

1. Raymond Williams, *Culture and Society, 1780–1950* (London: Chatto & Windus, 1958), p. 118.

2. Peter Alan Dale, *The Victorian Critic and the Idea of History: Carlyle, Arnold, and Pater* (Cambridge, Mass.: Harvard University Press, 1977), p. 119.

3. Emile Durkheim, *Sociology and Philosophy,* trans. D. F. Pocock (Glencoe, Ill.: Free Press, 1953), p. 37.

4. Frank Kermode, *Romantic Image* (1957; rpt. New York: Vintage Books, 1964), pp. 6–7.

5. Ibid., p. 18.

6. Geoffrey Hartman, *Criticism in the Wilderness: The Study of Literature Today* (New Haven: Yale University Press, 1980), p. 174.

7. John Holloway, *The Victorian Sage: Studies in Argument* (London: Macmillan, 1953), pp. 207–9.

8. For the contemporary view of Arnold in his art, see my "Homeward Bound: Arnold's Late Criticism," *Victorian Studies* 17 (1973):193. Buckler's blustery but occasionally illuminating views are offered in *Matthew Arnold's Prose: Three Essays in Literary Enlargement* (New York: AMS Press, 1983), pp. 29–66. And see George Levine's "Matthew Arnold: The Artist in the Wilderness," *Critical Inquiry* 9 (1983):476.

LEONARD ORR

ELEVEN

The Mid-Nineteenth-Century Irish Context of Arnold's Essay on Celtic Literature

Arnold's essay on Celtic literature is one of the most complex documents on an Irish subject by an Englishman (*CPW,* 3:291–395). Study of this document has been narrowly focused, almost completely from the British viewpoint, on Arnold's sources and his many mistakes in Celtic scholarship, his racial and social theories, and the influence of the essay on the later Celtic Twilight movement. Surprisingly, the Irish context of Arnold's Celtic literature essay appears to have been neglected.

Arnold's connections with Ireland are long and deep; they are emotional rather than scholarly, however, so much of the error-counting among his early commentators is beside the point. Arnold's viewpoint is certainly unusual for England, or even Ireland, with the exception of an important group of Irishmen. His ideas, arguments, methods, inclinations, and sources perfectly match the ideas of Celtic literature put forth by the Protestant Ascendancy in its scholarly review, the *Dublin University Magazine,* during the mid-nineteenth century and in the book publications by this magazine's contributors. This is not to say that these writers were sources for Arnold, for they probably were not; but I believe that Arnold came to the same conclusions that they did and read the same sources as the Irish Protestant intellectuals.

Celtic literature could not have been merely a convenient essay topic for Arnold, one that he could ruin through last-minute research or rushed writing. Park Honan's recent biography of Arnold indicates his revulsion, at age twenty-five, when he worked as Lord Lansdowne's secretary, at Lansdowne's prediction that one million people would die before the Irish famine of 1847 was over. Despite this belief, and even though he was one of the largest landowners in Ireland with 121,000 acres, Lansdowne, along with other conservative Whigs, actively campaigned in Parliament to reduce the amount of famine aid to Ireland and to leave it to private charities to undertake relief work. Arnold wrote poems and letters, but he knew of no other way to deal with Lansdowne.[1] In one of his last essays, almost thirty-five years later, he notes that the best way to achieve justice and peace in Ireland "is not to confer boons on all tenants, but to execute justice on bad landlords" (*CPW,* 9:251).

Of course, Arnold had numerous, less horrific ties to the Celts. First, he clearly loved James Macpherson's *Ossian.* He read the *Revue Celtique* and such important foreign scholars as Renan, Ernest Martin, Charles Vallancey, and Hersart de la Villemarque (all of whom have frequently been mentioned in connection with Arnold's essay). Arnold read some specific Irish sources also, the *Dublin Review* and the *Transactions of the Royal Irish Academy,* but these have not received much attention from Arnold scholars.[2] His brother Thomas, after his first conversion to Catholicism, taught at the new but disorganized Catholic University of Dublin from 1856 to 1862 and again, after his second conversion, he taught in Dublin from 1877 until his death in 1900; in 1882 Thomas Arnold was elected a Fellow of the Royal University and became an English professor at University College, St. Stephen's Green. Thomas Arnold's Catholic University colleague Eugene O'Curry was one of Matthew Arnold's most scholarly and accurate sources in his Celtic literature essays, and he praises O'Curry lavishly.[3]

More important, Arnold imagined, because of his Cornish

ancestry, a connection between himself and Celtic culture. Honan notes,

> A year before going to Italy, he had walked in Wales with the easy, reflective Tom Arnold. "All interests are here," Matthew wrote happily of Wales, "—Celts, Romans, Saxons, Druidism, Middle Age. . . ." His paradoxical longing for faith and the "Middle Age," and rational dislike of that yearning, are explored in . . . *On the Study of Celtic Literature*. For pages in this delightful work, with its racial theories occasionally mocked by its author, there is nothing very logical. We might be reading a psychoanalytic transcript by a relaxed Matthew, dreamily telling us what he *sees* when we say to him such words as "German," "Celt," or "Englishman."[4]

Honan's metaphor here, as well as R. H. Super's observation that all of Arnold's major essays (*Essays in Criticism, Culture and Anarchy,* and, one "of the most sensitive of Arnold's works of literary criticism, *On the Study of Celtic Literature*"[5]) are first of all political and social essays, are much to the point here and explain the strange way Arnold's essay has been treated by literary critics. James Simpson also points to the increasing social and political interest in Arnold's essays beginning in the 1860s and notes that Arnold's literary criticism "is so often concerned with aspects of English civilization that the distinction between literary and social criticism seems arbitrary."[6]

As early as 1897 Andrew Lang had pigeonholed and ridiculed Arnold's essay as the basis for the Celtic Twilight and Celtic Renaissance movement. One of Arnold's editors, Alfred Nutt, "recorded in 1910, that in judging Eisteddfod essays dealing with the Celtic influence on English literature, he found most of the papers to be a mere elaboration of Arnold's ideas."[7] More recently, John V. Kelleher, in one of the major essays on Arnold's Celtic studies, makes Arnold's sponsorship of the Celtic Renaissance his thesis.[8] In other words, twentieth-century critics have been content to work backward, from the Celtic literature essay to Arnold's French and German sources, or forward, from the essay to the Celtic Renaissance. Celtic scholars such as Nutt and Kelleher wished to show that Arnold was unqualified to write on his subject and that, through his influence, the Celtic Renaissance, under the equally benighted Yeats and AE (George Russell), was made ridiculous and un-Celtic. Arnold has had very few defenders for his essay, though Rachel Bromwich, in her 1965 lecture as the holder of the chair at Oxford in Celtic languages and literature, does go a long way toward demonstrating that Arnold was basically correct in his critical intuitions and judgments about Celtic literature even though his actual knowledge of the subject was extremely scanty and his sources were unreliable.[9]

But if we see Arnold's Celtic literature study as primarily personal and political, as Super and Simpson have suggested, it is easier to see that Arnold's views are congruent with those of contributors to the Protestant journal the *Dublin University Magazine.*

Arnold did not wholly approve of his brother's conversions, and he certainly did not approve of the Fenian violence. At the same time, he had a great sympathy for Ireland and a fear of more widespread violence unless accommodation was reached. He was not, as some chose to think in the late 1860s, a rabid Celtophile. He did not wish to encourage, as he was called upon to do in the Welsh Eisteddfod, the Welsh language movement, or the study of Scots Gael or Irish Gaelic. He did not wish Ireland to be independent of England, just treated fairly. He believed that it was necessary for the Irish to make their case known in England to those in power who might sympathize with them, and to do so, to be treated properly as a country that was part of the British Empire, required communicating in powerful English, the language of those to whom Arnold refers as "the Saxon invaders." The Irish had not made their case known, Arnold believed, because they were not listened to by the English. So Arnold, ignorant of Celtic literature, as he cheerfully admits, would try to speak for them at Oxford University, from his position as professor of poetry. Arnold presents the case for the study of Celtic literature for the same reasons he accepted an invitation to the Bardic Congress of Wales. Arnold says, "I, whose circus days are over, I who have a professional interest in poetry, and who, also, hating all one-sidedness and oppression, wish nothing better than the Celtic genius should be able to show itself to the world and make its voice heard," and so he accepted the invitation with delight (*CPW,* 3:294). But the Eisteddfod that year was a failure; such devices would not work because it was a school exercise, a show for the "Saxon philistines." Instead of writing new pieces in an old, and to Arnold, archaic and useless language, Arnold believed that the Celtic peoples should devote themselves to English and the scholarly study of the old Celtic texts. Arnold was not arguing from the point of view of a Celtic scholar but instead calling for people to become Celtic scholars to show the Celtic genius to the English and the world to avoid "one-sidedness and oppression." The English stereotype of the Irishman was that of the drunken bumpkin of the stage or the violent, unlettered ruffian. Arnold, whose faith in the powers of literature was greater than most, believed that by properly translating, editing, and publishing the thousands of manuscripts described by O'Curry and others the Irish would make the point abroad, but especially in England, that they were worthy of respect and deserved social and political justice. This brings us to Samuel Ferguson and Macpherson.

Let us look at Ferguson first. He was a lawyer of the Protestant Ascendancy; he was terrified of Irish Catholics, hated Catholicism generally, and strongly desired that the Protestants should remain the ruling power in Ireland. He wrote anti-Catholic poems·and satires for years under pseudonyms in various Protestant journals. At the same time, he hated the oppressive rules and arbitrary acts of the English, considered himself to be thoroughly Irish and a patriotic Irishman, and wished to raise the stature of Ireland in the world. Ferguson realized that he had to form an alliance with Irish Catholic intellectuals, and he became associated with John O'Donovan, Eugene O'Curry, and other antiquaries and philological scholars who could read the Celtic manuscripts and who had vast collections of material. He became well known for defending some Irish Catholics charged with sedition, and, although he abhorred the journal, he wrote an elegy on the death of Thomas Davis, editor of the radical publication the *Nation.*[10]

Ferguson's early poetry, like that of most Irish Protestant intellectuals, was imitation English poetry: the subject matter was the glory of Greece or Rome, Oriental fantasy, or in praise of industry and commerce. Early in the 1830s, Ferguson, like many Irish Protestants in response to the rise of Daniel O'Connell, turned to the study of Irish and "Celtic" materials in an effort to join Protestant Ascendant Irish to Catholic Irish and to demonstrate the Irish patriotism of the Protestants; it also served to separate Irish Protestant interests from those of English Protestant landowners and authorities. To learn what Celticism was, Ferguson and his fellow contributors used many of the same French sources Arnold was to exploit thirty years later, such as Vallancey.[11] Ferguson and his friends began at this time the necessary communication between Protestant and Catholic Irishmen and laid the groundwork for the flourishing of Irish antiquarian scholarship of the 1840s, the decade of Eugene O'Curry's gathering of manuscripts, the publications of John O'Donovan's *The Annals of the Four Masters* and *The Banquet of Dun Na N-Gedh and the Battle of Magh Rath,* George Petrie's *Ecclesiastical Architecture of Ireland,* and many other works.

In his desire for the Irish Protestant intellectuals to lay claim to the materials of medieval Ireland, Ferguson was thwarted by the publication, in 1831, of James Hardiman's *Irish Minstrelsy; or, Bardic Remains of Ireland, with English Poetical Translations.*[12] Hardiman, a Catholic Celtic scholar, with a team of collaborators, had published the first substantial collection of translated Irish poetry since Charlotte Brooke's 1798 *Reliques of Irish Poetry.* It took Ferguson almost three years to respond, but when he did, it was in a series of four articles in the *Dublin University Magazine* between April and November 1834 (altogether, eighty-five closely printed double-column pages). He mainly attacked the lack of Celtic qualities in the English translations; Hardiman's group used traditional English meters and forms, censored the poems (for example, they removed references to women having drinks), and otherwise produced unsatisfactory poetry. As Malcolm Brown has noted, "Ferguson was so full of his subject that the excited eloquence of his first paragraph ran to fourteen hundred words before he drew breath."[13]

Ferguson constantly praises the idea and the dedication of the translators, but the praise is mixed, at best: "These are the songs before us—songs such as the speakers of the English language at large have never heard before, and which they could not see and hear now but for the pious labours of a man who, however politically malignant and religiously fanatical, has yet done good service to his country in their collection and preservation."[14] As is well known, both Renan and Villemarque, sources for Arnold, had found a certain "Celtic melancholy." Renan, according to Bromwich, assigns "to the Celts the characteristics of fatalism, unprogressiveness, and a fondness for defending lost causes"; the Celtic voice "laments defeat more often than it celebrates victory"; and Renan's analysis, which was certainly important for Arnold, was equally influential for the mid-nineteenth-century Protestant Irish writers who preceded Arnold. They were, for the most part, reliant upon the same sources he was and therefore came to the same conclusions; few of the Protestant intellectuals in Ireland could read Gaelic or any Celtic language. It may be that the Irish simply borrowed a romantically attractive trait from Welsh literature. Bromwich points out that, in fact, resigned pessimism and fatalism are indeed characteristic of the older Welsh poems, such as the Llywarch Hen *englynion* and the older sections of the *Goddodin,* and that Arnold was essentially correct in intuiting that fatalism was a characteristic of Celtic medieval literature.[15] What is difficult for scholars such as Kelleher to understand is that to Ferguson, as to Arnold, there were few if any barriers to taking Welsh literary traits and simply assuming they applied to Celtic literature generally.

Ferguson, essentially a romantic, insists that

> sentiment is the soul of song, and sentiment is one imprescriptible property of the common blood of all Irishmen. . . .
>
> Heaven help us! what a key to the whole melancholy mystery is here. It is the first part of the Song of Sorrow, and mournfully true to its name it is. . . . Desire, despair, and the horrible reality of actual famine—these are the three dread prompters of song. Whoever first sung the Song of Sorrow had felt them all; but desire was his paramount inspirer, and the concluding stanzas rise into such a fervid frenzy of undisguised desire that we shrink from exhibiting them in their literal English. Yet there is

nothing impure, nothing licentious in their languishing but savage sincerity. This is the one great characteristic of all the amatory poetry of the country; and in its association with the despondency of conscious degradation, and the recklessness of desperate content, is partly to be found the origin of that wild, mournful, incondite, yet not uncouth, sentiment which distinguishes the national songs of Ireland from those perhaps of any other nation in the world.[16]

Ferguson, remember, is fighting the British image of the stage Irishman, and so he argues that no one should "imagine that humour is the characteristic of the Irish. Their sentiment is pathetic. . . . We know no Irish song addressed to the judgment: if an Irish song fails to go to the heart at once, it fails outright. Even in the most whimsical there is some touch of the sentiment, some appeal to the pathetic principle." Ferguson notes that the Irishman has a "natural piety." When in love, however, the Irishman is "consumed, dissolved, lapped in a lambent glow of tenderness—intense, delicious, deadly-sweet. . . . His passion communicates this tenderness of sentiment to all the ordinary scenes of his coarse life." These coarse lives, in the medieval past at least, have been remarkable for the defeats. Ferguson finds, in the stories of the Irish clans, a willingness to go on and fight despite a prophecy and certainty of defeat. On go "the doomed Clan Brian Roe, and find their fated destroyers." Ferguson tells his readers that he "could give such a scene after the battle, as we defy the annals of any other country to equal for sanguinary horror and savage interest." But to Ferguson, the main ingredient of the great lyric is pathos. All of these Celtic qualities Ferguson defines, including the willingness to go to certain defeat, are to be found in Arnold's essay; they are not to be found in Hardiman, the subject of Ferguson's articles. Hardiman's book misrepresents what are to Ferguson the essential Celtic qualities. Their translations are mere "perversions" and "lamentably bad."[17]

More than this, Ferguson believes the interpretive notes betray Hardiman's "sectarian hatred" and "religious fanaticism"; he does not recognize his own anti-Catholicism when he comments on, for example, Hardiman's note to "Roiseen

Dubh," later famous in James Clarence Mangan's version as "Dark Rosaleen." The conventional reading of the poem is to see it as a political allegory, and this is how Hardiman saw it in 1831. But Ferguson says that the poem, according to Hardiman, "is an allegorical political ballad—it seems to us to be the song of a priest in love, of a priest in love, too, who had broken his vow . . . and why, in the name of divine reason, do the Roman Catholic priesthood of the present day submit to a prohibition so unnatural, monstrous, anti-scripture?"[18] He goes on to speak for a column against priestly celibacy.

The point of this destruction of Hardiman's effort is to clear the ground for his own translations, prepared with the assistance of Celtic scholars such as O'Curry. Ferguson offers an Appendix containing "Versions from the Original Irish" to demonstrate to his readers how Irish poetry should be translated into English without being unduly "Saxonized." Ferguson's selection of poetry, and his versions, are all in accord with Arnold's Celtic literature essays.

Ferguson notes that in one "the hopelessness of passion rises to such a paramount excess of anguish as overbears and obliterates all other griefs." Many of the poems ("Torna's Lament," "O'Bryne's Bard to the Clans of Wicklow," "Agnew's Lamentation," and "Timoleague") are about defeat in battle, with the Irish watching the invaders taking over their ruined and oppressed lands. The "love poems" are all about lost or unsuccessful love, lamenting the absence of a lover or pleading with a lover to flee with the speaker. The women in "uileancan Dubh O!" and "Nora of the Amber Hair" refuse to marry the speaker until he becomes prosperous, and the speaker in "Kitty Tyrrel" hopes that with the help of God he will be able to soften Kitty's will in his favor before he dies at her door in anguish.

What is interesting from an Arnoldian point of view is that Ferguson felt perfectly free to take tremendous liberties with his translations, even though they appear as the demonstration at the end of this long attack on Hardiman for his inaccuracies. Ferguson dropped stanzas he thought unnecessary or incidents and repetitions he found tedious; he added refrains when he liked the effect. These changes were perfectly all right because, he reasoned, he was in keeping with the Celtic spirit, whereas

Hardiman and his collaborators were writing "Saxonized" verse. Making this point was tremendously important for Ferguson believed "that this literature would not only be the means of realizing the destiny which he considered rightfully Ireland's but would also provide a link between people of diverse convictions: it would, he argued, minimize and ultimately remove the antipathies between Orange and Green, Protestant and Catholic, aristocrat and peasant."[19] Ferguson had the same faith as Arnold in the power of literature as a healing tool.

Other writers of Ferguson's time could be mentioned who follow a similar theory of translation of Celtic materials: Robert O'Driscoll and B. G. MacCarthy both mention J. J. Callanan as someone, probably not influenced directly by Ferguson, who freely translated in the same manner. Both Callanan and Ferguson translated "The Lament of O'Gnive." According to MacCarthy, "The original Gaelic poem is a lament for the ruin of the Gael, interwoven with writhing scorn at their submission. Neither Callanan nor Ferguson retains these two ideas. Callanan takes the motif of scorn, which he exploits to the full. Ferguson takes the idea of tragedy, but very little of the wild scorn. Callanan's poem is like a battle-cry—a fiery incitement. Ferguson's is melancholy, meditative and personal. In this it is more like the original."[20] The same freedom may be found in the numerous popular translations by James Clarence Mangan, a favorite poet of Joyce and Yeats, who also published in the *Dublin University Magazine* in the same period as Ferguson. Ferguson, Mangan, Callanan, and others felt free to add, change, embellish, combine, abbreviate, or simply be "inspired by" literal translations of Gaelic poetry in writing their own versions. These versions were often quite distant from the originals, especially by the middle of the century. For the most part, the Protestant Ascendant poets who did such translations after 1850 did not know any Gaelic. And where Ferguson worked with literal translations prepared with the assistance of such renowned Celtic scholars as O'Donovan, later poets simply "repoeticized" the poetic translations of the poets of the 1830s and 1840s.

In 1849, Ferguson began his Celtic epic *Congal,* which, according to O'Driscoll, was completed by 1861 but not published until 1872 because Ferguson feared "the reception the poem would be given by a public antipathetic to Ireland and to Irish publications, and for the most part ignorant, or at least sceptical, of the value of Irish legend as subject matter for poetry."[21] To prepare the way for *Congal,* he published in 1865 a group of shorter poems, *Lays of the Western Gael,* using major Irish legends. I cannot prove it, but I assume that Arnold was familiar with this book, published only a year before he wrote *On the Study of Celtic Literature;* the negative reviews the book received in the English press (such as the *Saturday Review,* which would also dislike Arnold's Celtic lectures) would certainly add to Arnold's list of English "asperities." Said the *Saturday Review,* "There is perhaps no class of matters, historical or legendary, in which it is so hard to get up an interest as in matters purely Celtic. . . . No one cares for any Welsh hero except Arthur, and people care for Arthur only because they do not realize he was Welsh."[22] In addition, Hersart de la Villemarque, Arnold's major French source for Celticism, published in 1864, with a very warm preface, a poem by Samuel Ferguson, noting that Ferguson "combines poetic skill with an archaeologist's learning that has placed him in the forefront of the Royal Society of Ireland." Ferguson also is represented in the Chevalier de Chatelain's five-volume anthology *Beautes de la poesie anglaise* (1860–72, published in London in French).[23] It is difficult to think that these publications would have escaped Arnold's attention. Interestingly, Ferguson's poems in French translation often betray the same Celtic traits Renan and Villemarque, and later Arnold, were to find. And they indicate Ferguson's Pancelticism, which was certainly shared by Arnold. As with Arnold, a negative review did not cause Ferguson to lose his faith in the powers of literature to draw people together; he published *Congal* in 1872 and *Conary* in 1880. Besides, Ferguson did not expect his work to be taken seriously by English reviewers; his real audience was the Irish intellectuals, especially the moneyed Protestants he expected to maintain a leadership role as Ireland moved toward home rule.

Brown and O'Driscoll have noted that Ferguson's three

Celtic books have features associated with the Celtic Twilight poets: "The twilight colouring and supernatural atmosphere generated by wayward unemphatic rhythms and subdued assonantal music and imagery; the mood of heavy enchantment during which a mortal is spirited away from the mundane world; the fascinated terror of the victim and the blighting terror of those who remain."[24] Ferguson's three books, along with his series *Hibernian Night's Entertainments* (begun in the *Dublin University Magazine* in 1834), contained many of the episodes from Irish (and even Welsh) medieval materials that were later used by Yeats and the Celtic Twilight and Renaissance writers (such as the Deirdre legend, which Ferguson retold in *Conary*). Yeats fully acknowledged the debt of the Celtic Renaissance movement to Ferguson. Ferguson, he declared, with his usual restraint,

> is the greatest poet Ireland has produced, because the most central and most Celtic. Whatever the future may bring forth in the way of a truly great and national literature ... will find its morning in these three volumes of one who was made by the purifying flames of National sentiment the one man of his time who wrote heroic poetry—one who, among the somewhat sybaritic singers of his day, was like some aged sea-king sitting among the inland wheat and poppies—the savour of the sea about him, and its strength.[25]

Kelleher chooses to reject Yeats's statements about Ferguson and insists that the movement Yeats was involved in came directly from Arnold, despite Yeats's specific denial of this origin. Kelleher's reason for this argument is that the Celtic Revival writers were ignorant of real Celtic literature, and so was Arnold, so they must be connected.[26] This argument, often repeated by others, seems to be blissfully unaware of the social and political factors of nineteenth-century Irish literature, well described by Malcolm Brown.[27] Yeats was using literature as a political tool to draw the Irish people together toward a self-created national consciousness. Arnold was using literature as a political and social tool in his Celtic essays, hoping to gain some measure of respect for the Irish by showing the British establishment, which was his audience, the mass, variety, beauty, and antiquity of Celtic literature. Ferguson was using literature as a political and social tool in all his post-1833 writings for exactly the same reasons as Arnold and to create a claim, for the first time, of the "Irishness" of the Protestant Ascendancy. For Ferguson, the Protestant establishment could in this way avoid being shut out of the power in Ireland in the continuing home rule controversies. In the third part of his review of Hardiman, Ferguson pleads with the Protestant "wealth and intelligence of the country" to assist efforts to "introduce the Saxon and the Scottish Protestant to an acquaintance with the poetical genius of a people hitherto unknown to them" and for the Irish Protestants to read and research this material so as to understand their "Catholic fellow-citizens."[28]

Bromwich notes that Arnold invites criticism for failing to consult or mention the many sources in translation that were available to him; his use of O'Curry is very selective, and he mentions just one of the many works of John O'Donovan. Arnold does not refer to the texts about Fionn mac Umhail published by the Irish Ossianic Society in the 1850s and 1860s but sticks to secondary sources. According to Bromwich, "His use of actual texts is limited to Lady Guest's *Mabinogion*, a few Irish extracts translated by O'Curry and Whitley Stokes, Villemarque's second-hand renderings of Old Welsh poetry, Macpherson's *Ossian*, and Villemarque's collection of Breton ballads, whose sources are no less equivocal than those of Macpherson."[29] Kelleher has argued that, at least until his own article in 1950, no one had seriously criticized Arnold's comments and perceptions in the Celtic essays, that Arnold's remarks were uncritically assumed to be true both by the ignorant Celtic Revivalists, who accepted them for political reasons, and by the ignorant British audience of the time, and then by everyone else. Kelleher claims that "there are many reasons for this hands-off attitude," the most obvious being "that those competent to criticize the essay at the time it appeared were not impressed by it or thought it too wide of the mark to discuss. Afterwards, it would be thought of as out of date and forgotten." Until the Celtic Renaissance was in full swing, according to Kelleher, that is, "until 1892 or after, nobody in Ireland paid any serious attention to what Arnold had

to say on any Celtic or Irish subject."[30] None of these statements is accurate.

Frederic Faverty noted that Kelleher's belief that Arnold's
commentary in the Celtic literature essays "has gone virtually
uncontradicted since it was made, in 1866" is "strangely at
variance with the facts." He points out the immediate attacks,
to which Arnold responded, in the *Times,* the *Daily Telegraph,*
and the *Saturday Review,* the later scholarly attacks by Andrew
Lang, Alfred Nutt, George Saintsbury, and E. D. Snyder, and
numerous unscholarly, splenetic attacks, such as the famous
one by Swinburne. According to Faverty, Arnold's *Celtic Literature* was severely criticized by each "of the three early reviews
of the work," those in the *Pall Mall Gazette,* the *Fortnightly Review,* and the *Contemporary Review.* In short, all of the English
sources disliked Arnold's essay, for both scholarly and political
reasons, from the outset.[31] Arnold's *Celtic Literature* was very
popular in Wales, however, and received a warm reception in
Ireland, especially among the Protestant Ascendancy there,
again exemplified by the *Dublin University Magazine.*

In October 1867, an anonymous essayist noted,

> The average, tolerant, liberal English editor can see that the
> Germans, Spanish, Italians, and French have produced some
> literature "worthy to be mentioned in the same breath with our
> Anglo-Norman masterpieces." But while his mind is in this un-
> ruffled and tolerant state, mention but an unfortunate bard or
> historian of either Celtic branch, and no bull ever found his
> wits so thrown off their balance by the appearance of a scarlet
> mantle, as our hard-headed English scholar and critic by the
> mere sounds which embody the names of Tiernach, or Oisin, or
> Taliesin, or any work imputed by them.

In contrast to this typical "hard-headed" attitude in the "average, tolerant, liberal English editor," the essay goes on to recommend "Mr. Arnold's thoughtful and candid essay on a
germain subject." Arnold's *On the Study of Celtic Literature* is
"one of the most delightful volumes which it has been our
good fortune to make acquaintance with." The same essay
makes an interesting connection in a footnote to the readers:
"For a beautiful and weird version of the recovery of the *Tain,*

thoroughly Gaelic in its turns of thought and poetic expression, see 'Lays of the Western Gael,' by Samuel Ferguson, LL.D., M.R.I.A."[32] The Irish intellectuals, at least of the *Dublin University Magazine,* clearly found their own beliefs in Celticism reflected in Arnold's essay and in Ferguson's poetry. Ferguson's book is not recommended for its scholarship and accuracy but because it contains a "beautiful and weird" version of the *Tain* and because it is "thoroughly Gaelic in its turns of thought and poetic expression." The writer shares with Arnold the same Celtic-race theories.

This returns us to Macpherson's *Ossian,* which I mentioned earlier. Many of the attacks on Arnold's essay center on his injudicious decision to cite Macpherson at the beginning of his essay. Kelleher is a spokesman for this argument:

> Indeed, after an examination of the *Study,* it seems fairly reasonable to conclude that Arnold had made up his mind about Celtic literature before he consulted his material on it. How else can one explain his bland insistence that Macpherson's *Ossian,* for all that it was a fraud, still had "a residue with the very soul of Celtic genius in it"? Alfred Nutt pointed out that if Arnold had known any of the genuine Gaelic poems attributed to Oisin he would have noticed—and presumably have admitted—the utter difference in tone. Oisin, as Nutt has truly said, does not weep about going forth interminably to battle and as consistently failing; rather, he does the knocking down and he enjoys it very much.[33]

This interpretation misses the point about Arnold completely. Arnold undoubtedly did make up his mind about Celticism before he studied any of the authentic materials that became available after the 1830s; but Arnold's view of the Celtic "race" was formed by Macpherson. As Bromwich points out, "The whole controversy surrounding Macpherson's work was to [Arnold] irrelevant. Believing as he did that innate national characteristics revealed themselves in literature, it was sufficient for his purpose that Macpherson was of Scottish nationality."[34] In addition, for political and social reasons, Arnold wanted to present the best image—noble and romantic, long-suffering, brave although fated to fail—of the Irish that he could. It is certainly significant that fifteen years after writing his Celtic literature essays, after hearing all of the attacks upon him, Arnold did not budge from his position. In one of his last essays, "The Incompatibles" (1881), Arnold quotes again the statement about the Irish being "always ready to react against the despotism of fact." To their detractors, seeing the unwilling-ness of the Irish to become fully assimilated to English control and culture, it may seem that the Irish are giving themselves a miserable future. Arnold writes, "It seems as if this poor Celtic people were bent on making what one of its own poets has said of its heroes hold good for ever: 'They went forth to war, *but they always fell'*" (*CPW,* 9:245). Further, at a time when En-gland was witnessing Fenian bombing attacks, the doomed hero was more likely to receive English sympathy than a more authentic Ossian who "does the knocking down and enjoys it very much."

The 1867 *Dublin University Magazine* essayist understood and respected Arnold's political viewpoint:

> In the presence of so many literary censors who would prob-ably sleep the sounder after hearing that all the Celtic books, both MS. and print, that existed two days ago . . . were since destroyed by fire, and that at the same hour its dialects had completely dropped out of the minds of all human beings who formerly spoke or understood it—in the presence of these men of bilious and cast-iron natures we repeat, the Oxford professor of poetry exhibits no small amount of moral courage by making the declaration which follows: [quotes for more than a column from *On the Study of Celtic Literature,* from the passage beginning with the Celtic "chord of penetrating passion and melancholy" and including the passages about the "despotism of fact," "Ti-tanism in poetry," and Macpherson's *Ossian*]. . . .
>
> We must express our gratitude to the distinguished poet and critic who with the tide of English feeling against him, has undertaken to assert the claims of the unfashionable literature of a portion of the peoples of Ireland, of the Highlands, and of Wales to respect and consideration. Let us rejoice that the task so kindly and genially done has fallen into the hands of a true poet as well as a sound critic, and thus the better fitted to adju-

dicate on a subject so compact of imagination and its prod-
ucts.[35]

It is interesting here that the essayist does not contradict any of
Arnold's notions about Celtic passion, melancholy, or sensuousness, his understanding of Celticism generally, or his use
of Macpherson.

Macpherson's *Ossian* was, of course, discredited in England as early as 1761 and in France in 1763. From the beginning, to the Irish, French, Germans, and others, it seemed
unimportant that *Ossian* was a fraud. Goethe was a lifelong fan
of the work, Napoleon carried it with him on the battlefield.
Patrick Rafroidi has written an interesting survey of a genre he
calls "sub-Macphersonism." Basically, the sub-Macphersonists
recognized that *Ossian* was not based on the translations of any
particular manuscripts, but they felt, rather like the Society for
Creative Anachronism of today, that if such manuscripts did
not exist, they ought to have. So Edmond Baron de Harold
published *Poems of Ossian Lately Discovered* in Dusseldorf in
1787 and admitted in his preface that the poems were all his
own, although "founded on tradition." Rafroidi was unable to
locate any remotely similar originals and believes the baron's
tradition was simply Macpherson's *Ossian*.[36] Macpherson influenced almost all of Arnold's Irish and French sources, including Renan, Vallancey, Charlotte Brooke, and others. The Gaelic
Society, the Scottish Highland Society, the Hiberno-Celtic Society, the Royal Irish Academy, the *Revue Celtique*, and, in the
1850s, the Irish Ossianic Society were all founded in response
to the enthusiasm created for Celtic medieval literature and
history by Macpherson. In the *Dublin University Magazine* in
1867, the same year Arnold's *On the Study of Celtic Literature*
was published as a book, the anonymous reviewer of *West
Highland Folklore* admitted that Macpherson's poems were not
authentic in the sense of being accurate translations of specific
texts. The reviewer notes, however, that Macpherson must
have done some research, had used some authentic Gaelic materials, and had probably incorporated oral versions of the tales
in his poetry (the reviewer testifies that he had once heard a
beggar recite for half an hour one of the Ossianic poems, "The

Chase of Sliabh Guillinn"). The reviewer notes that on his first visit to Dublin "in his boyhood," Macpherson's *Ossian* was the first book he purchased.

> That volume was our dearest literary treasure for many a year, and we are not ashamed of enjoying the phraseology of the Poet of Badenoch to this day. However, since assurance became certain that his translations, as to substance and garb were not reliable, we have learned to prefer the less tasteful, and occasionally the more turgid but more than truthful tales made from the old Gaelic bards. [He quotes from *West Highland Folk Lore* for a column and a half.] . . . Admirers of the English Ossian, unaccustomed to the *bona fide* translations from the bardic relics, will pronounce the above much inferior to the dignified march of the language of Fingal and Temora.[37]

Like the Irish Protestant Ascendancy, Arnold did not wish to see Ireland break completely with English culture, traditions, language, trade, industry, and so on. He did not favor Welshmen or Irishmen or Scots studying Celtic languages instead of English or using modern forms of these languages. This practice, he felt, reflected a confused nationalism that would function mainly to isolate and further impoverish these countries. Like the Irish intellectuals, Arnold could see that a painful and violent break between Ireland and England would result unless the English showed far greater respect for the Irish culture and traditions and showed that England represented, in fact, a higher civilization, and not merely a country with a powerful military and economic presence.[38] England had to demonstrate to Ireland its sincerity. With regard to English concessions to the Irish Catholics in the nineteenth century, such as the Land Act of 1870, Arnold, backed by the authority of Edmund Burke, notes that the concessions "were given too late to produce the effect which they might have produced earlier, and they seemed to be given not from a desire to do justice, but from the apprehension of danger (*CPW*, 9:250). Arnold's Celtic literature essays were written with these goals and ambitions in mind. It was only the beginning, as Arnold gave up literary criticism for ten years, but he continued to write about

Ireland's problems, and England's lack of understanding of Ireland, for the next twenty-one years.

NOTES

1. Park Honan, *Matthew Arnold: A Life* (New York: McGraw-Hill, 1981), p. 117.

2. See the references in the following: Rachel Bromwich, *Matthew Arnold and Celtic Literature: A Retrospect, 1865–1965* (Oxford: Clarendon Press, 1965); Frederic E. Faverty, *Matthew Arnold the Ethnologist* (Evanston: Northwestern University Press, 1951); John V. Kelleher, "Matthew Arnold and the Celtic Revival," in *Perspectives of Criticism,* ed. Harry Levin (Cambridge, Mass.: Harvard University Press, 1950), pp. 197–221.

3. On Thomas Arnold the younger, see the entry in the *Dictionary of National Biography.* Arnold's comments on O'Curry appear in *CPW,* 3:305; "Obscure Scaliger of a despised literature, he deserves some weightier voice to praise him than the voice of an unlearned belletristic trifler like me; he belongs to the race of giants in literary research and industry,—a race now almost extinct."

4. Honan, *Arnold,* p. 333.

5. R. H. Super, "Arnold and Literary Criticism: (ii) Critical Practice," in *Matthew Arnold,* ed. Kenneth Allott (Athens, Ohio: Ohio University Press, 1976), pp. 150–51.

6. James Simpson, "Arnold and Goethe," in *Arnold,* ed. Allott, pp. 314–15.

7. Faverty, *Arnold the Ethnologist,* pp. 112, 114, cites these remarks.

8. Kelleher, "Arnold and the Celtic Revival."

9. Bromwich, *Arnold and Celtic Literature.*

10. For an excellent introduction to Ferguson's life and work, see Malcolm Brown, *Sir Samuel Ferguson* (Lewisburg, Pa.: Bucknell University Press, 1973).

11. See, for example, J.S., "On the Learning of the Ancient Irish," *Dublin University Magazine* 5 (May 1834):541.

12. See James Hardiman, ed., *Irish Minstrelsy; or, Bardic Remains of Ireland, with English Poetical Translations; Collected and Edited, with Notes and Illustrations,* 2 vols. (London: Joseph Robins, 1831).

13. Brown, *Sir Samuel Ferguson,* p. 46.

14. [Samuel Ferguson,] "Hardiman's Irish Minstrelsy," *Dublin*

University Magazine 4 (August 1834): 153. Ferguson's "review," ran through several issues of the journal: vol. 3 (Apr. 1834):465 [typographical error in the magazine; read 456 for 465]–78; 4 (Aug. 1834):152–67; 4 (Oct. 1834):447–67; 4 (Nov. 1834):514–42.

15. Bromwich, *Arnold and Celtic Literature*, pp. 17, 18, 19, 29–30.

16. Ferguson, "Hardiman's Irish Minstrelsy" 4 (Aug. 1834):154.

17. Ibid., p. 155; 4 (Oct. 1834):448; 4 (Aug. 1834):159; 4 (Oct. 1834):462; 4 (Aug. 1834):155; 4 (Oct. 1834):455n. Ferguson praises the translators for donating their efforts to Hardiman's edition, but "we must equivocally condemn the execution. . . . We are sorry to be obliged to add, that the majority of these attempts are spurious, puerile, unclassical—lamentably bad." D'Alton's "goose-quills flutter with Icarian feebleness over the dead sea of literature," only occasionally rising above "the spurious pretensions and bombastic feebleness of the great majority of his more ambitious attempts." D'Alton's "perversions are, however, mere petty-larceny travesties compared with the epic grandeur of Mr. Curran's open war against the original," doing whatever he thinks necessary to achieve the "creditable Saxonization" of a poem. Furlong's "mawkish poverty" is relieved by "the genuine flow of sentiment." Only Drummond is praised for "legitimate achievement" because of "the absence of anything like political hatred or sectarian malignity in his contributions."

18. Ibid. 4 (Aug. 1834):158.

19. Robert O'Driscoll, "Ferguson and the Idea of an Irish National Literature," *Eire-Ireland* 6 (1971): 85.

20. B. G. MacCarthy, "Jeremiah J. Callanan: Part II: His Poetry," *Studies: An Irish Quarterly Review* 35 (1971): 391.

21. O'Driscoll, "Ferguson," p. 89.

22. *Saturday Review* 29 (Jan. 1865): 116–17, cited by O'Driscoll, "Ferguson," p. 91.

23. Patrick Rafroidi, *Irish Literature in English: The Romantic Period (1789–1850)*, 2 vols. (Atlantic Highlands, N.J.: Humanities Press, 1980), 1:239–41.

24. O'Driscoll, "Ferguson," p. 90 n. 17.

25. W. B. Yeats, "The Poetry of Sir Samuel Ferguson," in W. B. Yeats and Thomas Kinsella, *Davis, Mangan, Ferguson: Tradition and the Irish Writer* (Dublin: Dolmen Press, 1970), pp. 46–47. Yeats's essay was originally published in the *Irish Fireside*, Oct. 9, 1886.

26. Kelleher, "Arnold and the Celtic Revival," pp. 204–5. Despite Yeats's denial in "The Celtic Element in Literature" (1897) of the influence of Arnold's essay on the Celtic Revival, Kelleher is sus-

picious: "Of course, it may have been entirely accidental that the Celtic Revival reproduced, element for element, Arnold's picture of Celtic literature, with the difference that every weakness Arnold deplored in the Celt has now become a strength. Or it may be that the Revival did revive the true qualities of Celtic literature, and that Arnold has been uncannily right in his estimate of those qualities. Neither is very likely. . . . Celtic Revival literature does not resemble Celtic literature very much at all; and Arnold's knowledge of the subject was neither wide nor trustworthy. For that matter . . . Yeats and his followers did not know much about Celtic literature, either. And there is the real connection."

27. Malcolm Brown, *The Politics of Irish Literature: From Thomas Davis to W. B. Yeats* (Seattle: University of Washington Press, 1972).

28. Ferguson, "Hardiman's Irish Minstrelsy" 3 (Apr. 1834):457: "We address in these pages the Protestant wealth and intelligence of the country, an interest acknowledged on all hands to be the depository of Ireland's fate for good or evil. The Protestants of Ireland are wealthy and intelligent beyond most classes, of their numbers, in the world: but their wealth has hitherto been insecure, because their intelligence has not embraced a thorough knowledge of the genius and disposition of their Catholic fellow-citizens. The genius of a people at large is not to be learned by the notes of Sunday tourists. The history of centuries must be gathered, published, studied and digested, before the Irish people can be known to the world, and to each other, as they ought to be."

29. Bromwich, *Arnold and Celtic Literature*, p. 10.

30. Kelleher, "Arnold and the Celtic Revival," pp. 198–99, 200.

31. Faverty, *Arnold the Ethnologist*, pp. 112–13, 223–24 n. 138.

32. Anon., "Celtic Manuscripts and Their Contents," *Dublin University Magazine* 70 (Oct. 1867):400, 418, 403n.

33. Kelleher, "Arnold and the Celtic Revival," p. 207.

34. Bromwich, *Arnold and Celtic Literature*, p. 18.

35. Anon., "Celtic Manuscripts and Their Contents," pp. 418–19.

36. See Rafroidi, *Irish Literature in English*, 1:156–59.

37. Anon., "West Highland Folk Lore," *Dublin University Magazine* 70 (Feb. 1867):190.

38. Compare Arnold's statements about whether England offered a higher civilization to Ireland in his essay "The Incompatibles," (*CPW,* 9:270–71) to the remarks of the anonymous *Dublin University Magazine* ("Celtic Manuscripts and Their Contents," p. 399) about the

oppression that results when "an empire includes within itself two distinct peoples" and "the dispossessed or conquered race must resign itself to see its ancient literature disliked, or despised, or, under the most favorable circumstances, neglected by the dominant one."

SAUNDRA SEGAN WHEELER

TWELVE

On the Study of Celtic Literature and the Young Writer: A Place in Arnold's Poetics

At the end of his essay on Maurice de Guérin, Matthew Arnold translates a piece of writing by Guérin called "The Centaur" (*CPW,* 3:36–39). This brief story describes an old, sad centaur, who leaves the dark cave in which he was born after he is weaned to roam the hillside forest but returns to the place of his birth each night and sits there with his hind parts in the cave and his head staring outward. In placing this work by Guérin at the end of an essay about him, Arnold creates both a method for turning back to another writer and a trope for its author's limitations and his own. Like the centaur, Guérin's love for the primeval cave and forest, for the youngest part of himself, traps rather than frees him. The centaur struggles between the conflicting desires to reexperience his early world and to return to a still point of origin. Through Guérin's tale, Arnold implies that human growth depends on separation from that point of origin, for the centaur's return defeats him. To translate this condition into imaginative terms, Arnold seems to suggest that any attempt to return to a point of origin for imaginative regeneration is hopeless. Paralysis rather than discourse accompanies the centaur's attempted repossession of his place of origin.

Nonetheless, in his writings Arnold seems to recommend a return, but it is a return other than that of the centaur; it is a return to beginnings. Arnold urges the recovery of early experience rather than of a moment of origin to advance imaginative life, and he makes his recommendations repeatedly, in both his poetry and prose, through the same persona—the young writer. Unlike the unborn and the newborn, the young writer can seek out imaginative uses of language. He can find ways and means to return to early linguistic experience close to his point of origin and therefore to that which is most pure. Moments of origin, where purity exists in everything, including the word, cannot be experienced directly, but early samples of discourse can be, and these, in turn, can be related by the young writer to his developmental self. To distinguish beginnings in linguistic structures of the past is to engender them in the present and future. In the famous Preface of 1853, Arnold says:

> The confusion of the present times is great, the multitude of voices counselling different things bewildering, the number of works capable of attracting a young writer's attention and of becoming his models, immense. What he wants is a hand to guide him through the confusion, a voice to prescribe to him the aim which he must keep in view, and to explain to him that the value of the literary works which offer themselves to his attention is relative to their power of helping him forward on his road towards this aim. Such a guide the English writer at the present day will nowhere find. Failing this, all that can be looked for, all indeed that can be desired, is, that his attention should be fixed on excellent models; that he may reproduce, at any rate, something of their excellence, by penetrating himself with their works and by catching their spirit, if he cannot be taught to produce what is excellent independently.
>
> (*CPW,* 1:8)

The young writer directed "to penetrate" himself with excellent models and catch "their spirit" appeared in all of Arnold's poetry and prose up until 1867, the year of publication of both the Celtic essays and his last volume of poetry.[1] Such figures as the Strayed Reveller, Sohrab, Balder, Callicles, the Tyrian trader, the Guérins, even Spinoza all represent beginnings, for each is aware of a past that is different from the moment into which he is being borne. The transference of poetic responsibility to the future writer and of poetic authority to the past both verified and temporarily resolved Arnold's own struggle to assess the value of the conflicting voices of his experience and inheritance. In this way his aesthetics and psychology merged. The influence of figures out of his immediate past, such as Burke, Wordsworth, Coleridge, Carlyle, his father, and even his mother, was profound, for they all equated imaginative and full human development. Thus Arnold needed to gain distance from himself, which he did by creating the figure of some future other potentially trapped by the confusion of a present lacking authority. Arnold's poet-personae struggle toward the past to find an authority to guide their future course—the Strayed Reveller reaches for Ulysses, Tristram for Iseult, Empedocles for Etna, Sohrab for Rustum, and so on— and the future writers addressed in his prose are also directed to return to the past for self-definition. Arnold's attention to the young writer, which suffused his poetry and prose, was one of the ways he transformed his personal house divided into a structural whole. Through direct and oblique focus on the figure of the young writer, Arnold sought recovery from what he saw as the great loss of his life and times: imaginative energy.

In *On the Study of Celtic Literature*, Arnold tries to lead the English back along the path to what Walter Benjamin would later refer to as "the many nameless storytellers,"[2] and he connects them to Celtic storytellers first through a landscape metaphor. Alluding to the collection of Celtic tales known as the *Mabinogion* in the second section of his essays, Arnold says, "The very first thing that strikes one, in reading the *Mabinogion*, is how evidently the medieval story-teller is pillaging an antiquity of which he does not fully possess the secret; he is like a peasant building his hut on the site of Halicarnassus or Ephesus; he builds, but what he builds is full of materials of which he knows not the history, or knows by a glimmering tradition merely;—stones 'not of this building,' but of an older architecture, greater, more cunning, more majestical" (*CPW,* 3:322). Here Arnold separates the literary layers so as to reveal not only the existence of artifacts of a linguistic archaeology but also so that its identified strata will advance imaginative reintegration. Arnold's peasant building his hut is a different writer from the noble architect of Halicarnassus and Ephesus, just as Arnold's series of Celtic scholars—David William Nash, Owen Jones, Eugene O'Curry, John O'Donovan, Edward Davies—are different from the poet Taliesin or the author of "The Panegyric of Llud the Great." By exposing the difference, Arnold confronts the Englishman with both how and why his indifference to the early Celt, whose geographic site was the same as that of his heirs, is making him fast become more like the peasant than the architect. In the interest of restoring to nobility both the future English storyteller and his audience, Arnold directs his countrymen to make the most genuine contact possible with the noble, imaginative lives inscribed in the record of the early peoples who lived on his own soil. The strands discovered thereby—the Celtic penchant for style, natural magic, and melancholy (*CPW,* 3:361)—can then function as sources of pride and regeneration in the imaginative lives of young English writers.

Style, natural magic, and melancholy have been central to English literature since Shakespeare, says Arnold in the last of his Celtic essays. "The turn for style is perceptible all through English poetry . . . proving the genuine poetical gift of the race" (*CPW,* 3:363). Of style he says, "Style, in my sense of the word, is a peculiar recasting and heightening, under a certain condition of spiritual excitement of what a man has to say, in such a manner as to add dignity and distinction to it" (*CPW,* 3:364). In Celtic literature, Arnold locates the Halicarnassus and Ephesus, reaches for "a condition of spiritual excitement," and attempts to "recast" and "heighten" the words of the Celts as a means of adding "dignity and distinction" to them. He does so by suggesting that only through many ways of looking back at an early artifact can its distinction be delineated. Just as Strabo, Caesar, and Lucan reveal something of the "profound spiritual discipline" in the character of the Druids, who left no records, Arnold uncovers the essence of the Celt by finding various ways to see him. Using his own penchant for style, natural magic, and melancholy, he finally reveals these as distinctive Celtic qualities in the last of the essays.

At the beginning of *On the Study of Celtic Literature*, Arnold alludes to his personal experience with and response to Wales, and through this encounter, which includes mention of his Saxon father's antipathy to things Celtic (*CPW,* 3:300) and ignores mention of his mother's Cornish origins, he reveals that not only does a complex underlying autobiographical element energize his work but also that a romantic return to landscape is part of his method of imaginative renewal. In the opening section of the essay, Arnold responds very personally to the northern Welsh coastline during a holiday there. Through the landscape, he expresses a sense of kinship with the powerlessness of a people proud of an ancient culture of which it has limited understanding. As a persona in his narrative, he records the following impressions: "The summer before last I spent some weeks at Llandudno, on the Welsh coast. The best lodging-houses at Llandudno look eastward, towards Liverpool; and from that Saxon hive swarms are incessantly issuing, crossing the bay, and taking possession of the beach and the lodging-houses"(*CPW,* 3:291). Narrating this account of his personal experience at an Englishman's vacation spot in the Welsh countryside, Arnold creates and interacts in a scene with which anyone in his English audience might identify. As sympathy is mobilized for the Celt and antipathy for the Saxon invader, the story is begun, and, like early bardic storytellers, Arnold invites the audience to share his emotional and analytic, his immediate and historical observations and responses to the scenes and events in Wales that he witnesses. In addition to picturing the visiting descendants of the historic Saxon conqueror as they occupy the beach and lodging houses in the eastern bay, Arnold expresses impatience with the complacency of these conquerors about their surroundings. The Saxon evokes a sense of nothing but his own presence; he cares for nothing else. The result is an arid, austere landscape whose "horizon wants mystery . . . sea wants beauty . . . and coast wants verdure." Turning westward immediately after this perception, Arnold tells us, "Everything is changed." The rich offerings of a new perspective lie to the west. In a long sentence, he telescopes a gentle, serene, poetic picture of horizon, river, island, mountain—all with exotic names, magic, and mystery. Arnold's brief sensory lyrical response to the Welsh landscape evokes admiring thought and memory of the Welsh people with pride in their past history and poetic tradition. Another image intrudes, however, reminding him of "the prosperous Saxon" (*CPW,* 3:291) whose swarms from their Liverpool hives invade the other side. Thus perception moves backward to the east and forward to the west, making of Arnold's epiphany-like experience with physical Wales at the beginning of the Celtic essays a profound engagement with the rich, romantic Welsh countryside and its people. In "recasting and heightening" his sympathetic responses, which are, in fact, "a certain condition of spiritual excitement," he uncovers "dignity and distinction" in the Celt in contrast to complacency and smugness in the Saxon conquerors. In using Celtic style to trace Celtic dignity and distinction, Arnold reveals means and ends that are the same.

By touching the land where it happened, Arnold attempts to tap Celtic history and spirit, and by exploring the voluminousness of its earliest literary records and the limitations in the perceptions of each translator-scholar, Arnold tries to do the same. In also turning to a science of linguistic beginnings with its capacity to disclose experience both distinctive and common to early branches of English peoples, Arnold introduces another device for looking at the Celt which not only provides another perception but also adds incrementally to the affective response to landscape and to the revelations about the limits of scholarly bias already explored. Thus he shows that there exist "thirteen ways of looking at a blackbird," and such ways may be the only means of contact with the purity in origins. Science, particularly the science of philology to which Vico was devoted, offers an instrument useful not only to Arnold's exploration of his country's and his own literary beginnings but also to a further understanding of the distinction and the unity behind all language. He says, "Philology . . . that science which in our time has had so many successes, has not been abandoned by her good fortune in touching the Celt;

philology has brought almost for the first time in their lives, the Celt and sound criticism together" (328). In presenting science as useful, through its study of origin and development and its system of separation as a means to reintegration, Arnold looks back to Vico. According to Edward Said, Vico's *New Science*[3] explains that to bridle his own savagery, man needs to imagine a force anterior to himself (*B*, 349). When early man abstracted the idea of a divine order to be feared, claims Vico, he arrived at his sense of himself (*B*, 350). By expressing his feelings about man and God in signs, or language, early man placed the abstract and concrete in adjacent positions in his life and arrived at an imagined sense of his own beginning. Eventually, Arnold's Celtic ancestors, like many other peoples, began to create documents that transcribed into words a primitive awe at the mystery of the universe. From the oral record that preceded it, Celtic literature retained what C. M. Bowra identified as heroic and shamanistic elements, or what Arnold called "moral profundity" and "natural magic" (*CPW*, 3:361), and these elements of morality, and particularly of awe, could still convey an emotional intensity powerful enough to generate new imaginative life very directly. Language synthesized early community, history, and spirit and then recorded its achievements. Awareness of this primary linguistic and literary world could connect culture to culture, human to human, and human to divine, thereby revitalizing the divine nature of the word. Science, or seeing things as they are, becomes another of Arnold's intensified ways, another "condition of spiritual excitement," for "recasting and heightening" the experience of the preliterate Celtic world (*CPW*, 3:364).

Vico's philological system informs Arnold's devotion, in the Celtic essays, to the idea of the connectedness of all life and therefore of all elements related to its creation or gestation, as when he says:

> Affinity between races still, so to speak, in their mother's womb, counts for something, indeed, but cannot count for very much. So long as Celt and Teuton are in their embryo, rudimentary state, or, at least, no such great while out of their cradle, still engaged in their wanderings, changes of place and struggle for

development, so long as they have not yet crystallised into solid nations, they may touch and mix in passing, and yet very little come of it. It is when the embryo has grown and solidified into a distinct nation, into the Gaul or German of history, when it has finally acquired the character which makes the Gaul of history what he is, the German of history what he is, that contact and mixture are important, and may leave a long train of effects; for Celt and Teuton by this time have their formed, marked, national, ineffaceable qualities to oppose or to communicate.   (*B*, 336)

All human beings are initially a mixture of two progenitors and then of all the multiples behind them. Thus everyone is a wanderer from his origins and within everyone lies a wanderer-poet. The wanderer can uncover his poetic strand only through full consciousness that he is of mixed blood. Many of Arnold's wanderer-poets—Sohrab, Rustum, Merope, Balder, Guérin, Heine, Spinoza, Marcus Aurelius—are mixtures of strands who yearn for the new through return to their beginnings. By returning to a strand of origin capable of revealing human and divine links, long-buried feelings of abandonment can be dissolved, and the aesthetic and the psychological can merge. In the Celtic essays, Arnold encourages his young English wanderer-poet, an abandoned poet-child of God, to reclaim his birthright and thus experience imaginative recovery.

To Arnold, Celtic identity can best be realized by recognizing the mixture of elements of which it is a part, distinguishing them, and examining them in relation to one another. Since the Saxons invaded an already mixed race among the Celts and conquered them, the cultural identity of the Celt was easily subsumed, and its reemergence came so gradually that "the contempt of the conqueror and the shame of the conquered [were allowed] to become fixed feelings." Now, recognition of the Saxon contempt and the Celtic shame must advance acknowledgment by the English that they are a mixed race whose most easily traceable and pure linguistic origins, now a repressed element in the mixture, are vital to imaginative renewal. Arnold says, "All tendencies of human nature are in themselves vital and profitable; when they are blamed, they are only to be blamed relatively, not absolutely" (*CPW,* 3:348). In an effort to uncover hidden tendencies potentially generative to imaginative life, the Saxon-Celtic Arnold selects a moment in the early history of the Celt and characterizes him from the record. The early Celt, he tells us in an epigraph (*CPW,* 3:291), and later on as well, "went forth to war, but . . . always fell" (*CPW,* 3:346). The Saxon-Celtic Arnold identifies the ineffectual in the Celt by assessing both strands. From the Germanic, the Englishman has inherited "steadiness with honesty." In the German this has produced a national spirit capable of "patient fidelity to Nature, in a word, science" (*CPW,* 3:341). In the Englishman, such "steadiness" functions as a corrective by virtue of its capacity to examine itself scrupulously. Thus the Celtic character, so "quick to feel impressions" and "always ready to react against the despotism of fact" (*CPW,* 3:342) can be guided by the Germanic in the English nature. Arnold says, "This colossal, impetuous, adventurous wanderer, the Titan of the early world, who in primitive times fills so large a place on earth's scene, dwindles and dwindles as history goes on, and at last is shrunk to what we now see him." Despite a sensibility "full of reverence and enthusiasm for genius, learning, and things of the mind" (*CPW,* 3:346), the Celts have always been overrun. Also, the Celt has suffered from "nervous exaltation," which has something feminine about it: the Celt, says Arnold, "is thus peculiarly disposed to feel the spell of the feminine idiosyncrasy; he has an affinity to it; he is not far from its secret" (*CPW,* 3:347). These qualities, not only unacceptable to most Saxons but also easily conquered by them, reaffirm how heavily Germanic the English are. Nonetheless, neither English rhetorical power nor its particular variety of strength in what Arnold calls the "plastic arts" comes from the German, for the Germans have power of language without power of rhetoric, and Sharon Turner's impulse "to express the inexpressible" is hardly a Germanic acquisition. Thus a weakness of each strand becomes a strength in a balanced mixture of elements.

To Arnold, imaginative renewal for the Englishman demands a reawakening of all strands with emphasis on the Celt, and identification through tracing of the unique qualities of each element becomes an apt point from which the Englishman can begin. Arnold yields to some conquest of his own Celtism, but he directs others, the young in particular, not to yield to theirs. Although it appears to be too late for Arnold as a poet after 1867, it is not too late for him as a critic to suggest that true confrontation of a true self through acknowledgment of true beginnings can reformulate the experience of creation. Such experience does not necessitate a return to residency in the mother's womb, but it does require methods to identify beginning strands and then trace their separate development. The tracking is itself the creative experience, and a chosen point of beginning is an opportunity to reexperience the making power. Vico saw the creative process as beginning with God's perception or creation, which made the world (B, 353), and Arnold forged his model for imaginative renewal out of the Viconian premise that God made human perception possible and compelled it to create. Human imagination does best when it retains awareness of its creations as part of a finite world possessed of a creative force greater than its finiteness. Impelled to create perpetually and at times to record its creations in language because of an urgent sense of its own mortality, the human imagination continually relinquishes its old perceptions and embraces others in an experience of death and rebirth. Compelled to efface a previous creative act through the formation of a new one, the imagination is in a perpetual and essential state of loss and recovery. Arnold seems to suggest that by connecting to early manifestations of its imaginative nature, the pressure of change, of loss and recovery, can be made tolerable and thereby useful. Arnold's directions appear to say: go back, delineate the strands of the self, trace them, connect to an awe-inspiring moment in the language and literature of human beginnings, and then move forward.

For Arnold to confront limitation in his Anglo-Saxon self, a side of his nature that he had been taught to value absolutely and to advise others to approach the same way, was for him to experience ritual death, burial, and rebirth and to suggest the same to others. To bury part of the Saxon in him by acknowledging the value of his Celtic side impelled a possible dying into life for Arnold and his fellow Saxons. It meant recognizing repeatedly that it was the Celtic ardor for nature's magic and beauty that had made him a poet by allowing him to get as close to nature's spirit as only poets can get, and repeated contact with beginnings would inspire new creations. Arnold, then, made the will to create determinable by the will to look at one's past and thus to know oneself. This process demands heroic efforts, but only a willed effort toward self-knowledge, with its concomitants of loss and recovery, can serve the poet's imaginative life, can provide the young writer with the chance to achieve unity or integration. Arnold believed like the early Celts that "to be a bard, frees a man" (*CPW,* 3:347); that is, continuing experience of loss and recovery frees the poet, and the poet in everyone, from constant concern with his own mortality. The Celtic bard, who had committed to memory the tales of many mortals out of the past and present, had a sense of both eternity and human finiteness. His storytelling art demanded a capacity to see death as part of life, as part of the history of man and nature. The Celt's "undisciplinable, anarchical and turbulent" (*CPW,* 3:347) nature, then, was not only misdirected good but was also his way of confronting this difficult truth of nature's ways.

To make poetry in the future, Arnold advises the Englishman that he must not only acknowledge his Celtism but also revere it. The poet must avoid his Germanic goodness, docility, and fidelity to nature in his writing and replace it with Celtic Titanism. Despite its faults, this Celtic quality is more useful to English poetry than anything Germanic in him. Besides, the Celts have other qualities that have served poetry well. Arnold tells us, "The Celt's quick feeling for what is noble and distinguished gave his poetry style; his indomitable personality gave it pride and passion; his sensibility and nervous exaltation gave it a better gift still, the gift of rendering with wonderful felicity the magical charm of nature" (*CPW,* 3:374) Also, devices of the early Celtic storyteller are recoverable generative models in both manner and matter. Just one lengthy citation of a Celtic tale, in which Arthur's messengers, embarking on a search for someone called Mabon, ask many—from ousel to stag to owl to eagle to salmon (*CPW,* 3:319–20)—for his whereabouts, illustrates how dense are the strategies through which first the early bard and then Arnold gets his story told. Arnold reinforces his own method of building evidence by piling up real connections with samples of early Celtic imaginative strategies that do exactly the same thing.

In these essays, Arnold ultimately advises that one must confront that in oneself which is destructive and bury it, for only in that willed death is there life. The moment of true endings is the same as the moment of true beginnings. It was Vico who pointed out that the word *human* comes from the root *to bury* (B, 373), and it was Arnold who closed the introduction to these essays with the passage from Matthew 8:22 that reads, "But let us leave the dead to bury the dead, and let us who are alive go on to perfection" (*CPW,* 3:395) Although it can never be reached, perfection can be approached in shadow, and that is an act of creativity. To train the elements that make up the Englishman instead of riding each to death will reduce the blur and confusion of one-sidedness that continues to be apparent in his "eccentric, unattractive, and unharmonious" (*CPW,* 3:384) nature. Having confronted the most shameful things about himself as well as the most distinguished, the young English writer will find that new energy has been released to propel his imaginative life and new habits developed to shape it.

The early storyteller who addressed life and death from within the community of man never allowed his audience to forget his humanness, particularly his relationship to others. The writer faces the constant and repetitious task of trying to retrieve this knowledge, and that task will keep him perpetually young. Yet Arnold, despite his lyrical response to the Welsh landscape, can no longer use the Celtic power he is trying to revive to create his own poetry. He still, in part, remains in his mother's Celtic womb. Since his own lyrical response connects through an element other than language, it does not return to some identifiable beginning in literature, to a place where utterance, emotion, and idea are so close to one another that they can be experienced as one pure expression of language. Vico had noted that early man engaged both human and divine elements through the purity of his belief that it was possible to do so (B, 352). Purity of language, then, included purity of the motives of one man committed to another as manifestation of divinity, but Arnold's personal beginnings were a mixture of

Saxon and Celt that were still at odds in him. Since he could not balance the elements for himself, he resolved to create the groundwork for the future writer. This young writer might then emerge not as a double of the conflicted Arnold but as someone capable of advancing beyond the forces of time, place, personality, and inheritance that impeded Arnold's own poetic progress. Whatever resolution of personal issues Arnold could experience through the Celtic essays by giving greater assent to a side of himself kept down for much of his poetic life, he could no longer write much poetry. Arnold ultimately confronted psychological issues in himself by displacing them on to his countrymen in the hope that this paradigmatic confrontation might allow the future poet to go forth to the war of imaginative struggle and not fall. In these essays, Matthew Arnold tells his own story in the interests of another, and as Walter Benjamin concludes at the end of his essay on the subject, "The storyteller is the figure in which the righteous man encounters himself."[4] In *Culture and Anarchy,* his next work, Arnold was to move further away from issues of personal poetic aspiration and thus avoid any confusion created in the Celtic essays by his attention to himself, the young English writer, and the English citizen; however, he was to continue to address the young writer obliquely as he used his strategies of separation, confrontation, and reintegration to give direct attention to a society devoted to the development of cultivated men.

NOTES

1. According to R. H. Super, in the "Explanatory Notes" for *On the Study of Celtic Literature,* in *CPW,* 3:492–93, Arnold delivered two Oxford lectures, "The Study of Celtic Literature," on December 6 and 7, 1865, the third on February 24, 1866, and the fourth, entitled "The Celtic Element in English Poetry," on May 26, 1866. In the same year, the essays appeared in the *Cornhill* for March, April, May, and July and in New York's *Eclectic Magazine* for June, August, September, and October. The Preface took a long time for Arnold to compose, and the essays did not appear in book form under the title *On the Study of*

Celtic Literature until June 4, 1867. His *New Poems* (London: Macmillan, 1867) was published in July, according to *The Poems of Matthew Arnold,* ed. Kenneth Allott, 2d ed. Miriam Allott (London: Longman, 1979). This edition reprinted "Empedocles on Etna" at Browning's request. Allott says, "From this time forward [Arnold] writes very little verse but is increasingly widely known for his controversial social and religious writings" (p. xxiii).

2. In his essay "The Storyteller," in *Illuminations,* trans. Harry Zohn (New York: Schocken, 1969), Walter Benjamin recaptures Arnold's purpose when he says, "Experience which is passed on from mouth to mouth is the source from which all storytellers have drawn. And among those who have written down the tales, it is the great ones whose written versions differ least from the speech of the many nameless storytellers" (pp. 83–109).

3. In *Beginnings: Intention and Method* (1975; rpt. New York: Columbia University Press, 1983), Edward Said begins the section on Vico, which concludes his book, by quoting the following axiom from Vico's *New Science:* "Doctrines must take their beginning from that of the matters of which they treat" (p. 347). He goes on to explain that Vico viewed the human mind as possessed of an indefinite nature, and by looking back at origins from a mature state, the nature of things, which is to be found only in beginnings, can be determined. Further references to this work will be given in the text as *B* with page numbers.

4. Benjamin, *Illustrations,* p. 109.

Park Honan

THIRTEEN

Arnold, Eliot,
and Trilling

T. S. Eliot and Lionel Trilling became major critics with Arnold's help, and I want to use a biographer's privilege to show, as briefly as possible, why they found him useful and what it means when we say that one *makes oneself over* as a critic. When, in 1970, I began to write the first detailed life of Matthew Arnold and had access to his mother's early household journals—and I recall driving down the M-1 motorway from Ripon to Birmingham cautiously, with the manuscript evidence of Arnold's childhood on the seat beside me—I found two surprises. The first was that Dr. and Mrs. Arnold were oddly playful parents, who loved comic acting, funny poems, nicknames, jokes, horseplay, and (in Dr. Arnold's case) running and leaping. I had expected them to be graver (even after I had read the three useful biographies by A. P. Stanley, Arnold Whitridge, and Norman Wymer on Dr. Arnold). My second surprise was that the Arnolds, at Laleham and Rugby, kept their children in a bath of feeling; Matthew Arnold was brought up in a very sentimental atmosphere, extreme even in the Victorian sense. Dr. Arnold wept when admitting new boys to Rugby, wept over his sons, hugged his children, swept them up, kissed them on the lips, talked to them while holding their heads. He once told Matthew and Tom he would rather they die than that they become "hard" or hardhearted (at which Tom, at least, burst into tears). Mrs. Arnold was addicted to newspaper reports about hangings, murders, bloodshed, war, and multiple crimes; the sight of anyone sitting still bored her;

she admired violent seas, vibrant colors, pathos, and drama; she wore bright dresses, kept a tricolor sewing bag, and visited London's diorama and panorama exhibits about which she wrote verses. But again, what is truly extreme is her feeling. Death was her friend, she said, for death gives reality to the dream of life. But her enemy was time; she had a passionate Celtic yearning for the past, for last year, last summer, last month, yesterday, and, as cheerful as she was, she could hardly reconcile herself to the loss of sights, faces, and places, or to the loss of relatives whom her friend death took away. She had the elegiac temper.

It is not surprising to find young Matthew Arnold weeping on a sofa as he reads Mrs. Gaskell, nor is it surprising to find his sister Jane laughing at him with amused approval because he is weeping. Arnold's wit, dandyism, jokes, and fondness for variants on the Chaucerian word *shit*—"Golly, what a !!!Shite's!!! oracle," "those Lombard republicans were shits, if ever such they were," and other phrases shocking to Balliol and Oriel friends and dons, "I am . . . a very whoreson Bull-rush," so-and-so is "an hass," "the natural functions of a man [are] to eat and copulate"—were really screens for an emotional and even sentimental temperament.[1] The relation between poetry and the poet's emotions is a topic of debate from Wordsworth's prefaces to T. S. Eliot's *The Sacred Wood*. But it is likely that one cannot make a good poem unless one has a personality, a *bedeutendes Individuum,* and some emotions to escape from. "Poetry," wrote T. S. Eliot, is "an escape from emotion; it is not an expression of personality, but an escape from personality. But, of course, only those who have personality and emotions know what it means to want to escape from those things." Arnold knew what it was to indulge emotions: he was immobilized by his father's death in 1842. He avoided friends at Oxford and met a small "Clougho-Matthean set" whose tears for Dr. Arnold he shared. He read books until weary and then became a disciple of European sentimentalists such as Foscolo, Novalis, Jean Paul, and Senancour, who believed that feeling is the only guide to truth. In "Memorial Verses," he praised Wordsworth as the poet who made us feel:

"He found us," he wrote of a friend and neighbor at Rydal Mount whom he had known for seventeen years,

> when the age had bound
> Our souls in its benumbing round;
> He spoke, and loosed our hearts in tears.
> He laid us as we lay at birth
> On the cool flowery lap of earth. . . .
> Others will teach us how to dare,
> And against fear our breast to steel;
> Others will strengthen us to bear—
> But who, ah! who, will make us feel? (ll. 45–49, 64–67)

But paradoxically in other poems he rejects the subjective emotiveness of Wordsworth and Senancour. His critical career begins in poetry; he sorts writers useful to him, rejects most of them, and uses poetry to explore a dividedness between thought and feeling in the modern mind, and then at last explores the bane of contemporary feeling. In "The Strayed Reveller" Arnold's painterly Olympian gods are childish spirits of feeling with no penetrating insight into human life. In "Empedocles on Etna," modern thought has overwhelmed the hero's capacity to feel anything but a self-pitying despair. In "The Scholar-Gipsy," controlled feeling is possible only for a timeless figure who lives outside the modern era with its debilitating nostalgia, complaint, and sentimentality, and the speaker is infected by that typical nostalgic complaint. "O born," he tells the Gipsy-Scholar self-pityingly,

> in days when wits were fresh and clear,
> And life ran gaily as the sparkling Thames;
> Before this strange disease of modern life,
> With its sick hurry, its divided aims,
> Its heads o'ertaxed, its palsied hearts, was rife—
> Fly hence, our contact fear!   (ll. 201–6)

A difficult period for Arnold began after this poem appeared in 1853; it was not so much that his first child, Tommy, was born unhealthy, or that in time he knew that three of his boys would die (Victorian parents knew grief), but that having renounced subjective feeling in the Preface of 1853, he wrote poorly and became demoralized with himself. When we think of Samuel Johnson walking between Lichfield and Birmingham to stave off suicide, we may conclude that suffering helps a critic. When, after failing to finish essays or to write well in verse for four or five years, Arnold emerged as a critic in the lectures *On Translating Homer,* he referred to the need to be "purged seven times in the fire" (*CPW,* 1:157). The critic must be purged of emotion, he believed, because the critic's primary task is perceptual: he must *see* the object. To see "the object as in itself it really is" is to come to it without any prior emotions, not even with the emotion of respect, which Shakespeare's reputation seductively incites. It is even a small matter that the critic of literature happens to be ignorant. "Mr. Newman," Arnold says of a Homer translator, Francis Newman the Latinist of University College in London, and to the delight of Oxford students who heard this lecture in the Sheldonian Theatre,

> ends by saying that my ignorance is great. Alas! that is very true. Much as Mr. Newman was mistaken when he talked of my rancour, he is entirely right when he talks of my ignorance. And yet, perverse as it seems to say so, I sometimes find myself wishing, when dealing with these matters of poetical criticism, that my ignorance were even greater than it is. To handle these matters properly there is needed a poise so perfect that the least overweight in any direction tends to destroy the balance. Temper destroys it, a crotchet destroys it, even erudition may destroy it. To press to the sense of the thing itself with which one is dealing, not to go off on some collateral issue about the thing, is the hardest matter in the world. The "thing itself" with which one is here dealing,—the critical perception of poetic truth,—is of all things the most volatile, elusive, and evanescent; by even pressing too impetuously after it, one runs the risk of losing it. The critic of poetry should have the finest tact, the nicest moderation, the most free, flexible, and elastic spirit imaginable.
>
> (*CPW,* 1:174)

Although in this lover of Oxford there is nothing really anti-academic, one finds in that reply to a University College professor a warning against academic literalism. More than anything else perhaps that Arnold wrote, the passage explains why two adequate critics, T. S. Eliot and Lionel Trilling, later were able to make themselves over with his aid. For Arnold the watchwords of good criticism include *poise, balance, perception, flexible, free,* and even *ignorance.* Their harmful opposites are terms of emotion and even of learning: *erudition, crotchet, temper.* Yet erudition harms in making the mind less flexible, not when it brings fresh light to keep one from intellectually hardening. Trilling, in 1950, was to comment in an Arnoldian vein on critics who simply believed anything whatever "can be discovered through hard intellectual work and concentration," and Trilling's complaint about the academic critic is that he treats influences too simply and imagines that ideas "have a life independent of the thinker and the situation."[2]

When in 1920 T. S. Eliot tried to improve taste by countering the effects of Edwardian dilettantism and impressionism, he produced in *The Sacred Wood* one of the most delightful volumes of criticism in our century. Eliot's essays illustrate the Arnoldian message that style, tact, and even beauty of expression are critical tools. He uses Arnold as a foil almost throughout *The Sacred Wood* and offers essays in the Arnoldian way as being specimens or examples of the critical act. He comments on emotion: "A literary critic should have no emotions except those immediately provoked by the work of art."[3] Thus Eliot begins a strategic attack on emotive critics, and, as we might expect, on Shakespeare's failures as an artist. For again the eminence of Shakespeare corrupts seeing, so that if we see or read a tragedy with prior respect or reverence, we neither see nor read the play as it is. We should bring no emotions to Shakespeare and keep his faults in mind; his worst fault is a "vice of style," which is "a tortured perverse ingenuity of images which dissipates instead of concentrating the imagination, and which may be due in part to influences by which Marlowe was untouched."[4] That interesting complaint was inspired by Eliot's reading of Johnson's "Life of Cowley," but later he is more original. The tragedy of *Hamlet* is "most certainly an artistic failure" because Shakespeare lacked the art to delineate Hamlet's "emotion," and Eliot supports that comment with his famous idea of the "objective correlative." He introduces it in an off-hand way when he says that the only way the artist can express emotion is by finding "a set of objects, a situation, a chain of events which shall be the formula of that *particular* emotion" so that when the sensory facts or events are given the desired emotion is evoked.[5]

Arnold and Eliot do not think emotion is foreign to art. What I have been saying is that they agree on a severe dietetics for the critic, who is adequate when purged of emotion. Arnold as a poet learned to purge or control his emotions, the last and most subtle of which was the respect he felt for writers he most admired. Today a criticism of Arnold that intends to account for his development must take his emotional history, his dalliance with the sentimentalists, and his entire commentary on "feeling" into account.

Lionel Trilling in the 1930s and 1940s made himself over by reacting to Arnold and Eliot, and indeed as a critic he shares with Arnold a perceptual emphasis, a concern with the critic's needful beauty of style, a sense of the unparaphraseable nature of art, a belief that the critic exists to hand on the instrument of criticism, a sense of foreign literature as a part of English and American, a desire to bring in light from other fields (such as Freudian psychoanalysis), and a conviction that a literary comment impinges on politics, religion, philosophy, and other aspects of a contemporary society. Since Trilling excels in four essay collections we need to know his essay "The Sense of the Past" and the rest of *The Liberal Imagination* (1950), all of his *Beyond Culture* (1965), at least the essays on Flaubert, Dickens, and Jane Austen in *The Opposing Self* (1955), and the pieces on American topics—on Edmund Wilson, David Riesman, the academic vice of a lack of manners in the essay "On Not Talking," and the fine revelatory comments on America in the essay on Santayana at Harvard—in the collection called *A Gathering of Fugitives* (1956); these are the minimum, but I would add his last book, *Sincerity and Authenticity,* and even his unfinished report of a Jane Austen seminar at Columbia (first printed in the *Times Literary Supplement*). To know these and Arnold's Preface of 1853, his *On Translating Homer,* two volumes of *Essays in Criticism,* and the *Discourses in America,* as well as Eliot's *The Sacred Wood* and *Collected Essays* and a handful of Eliot's later pieces such as "The Music of Poetry" and "The Frontiers of Criticism," is to know the best criticism in English from the 1850s to the 1970s and therefore to have a sense of how the Victorian sensibility relates to ours. Trilling's first book, *Matthew Arnold* (1939), is the venue through which he comes to terms with his chief mentor. As a "biography of a mind," it is weak on Arnold's poetry and religion, based on a poor edition of his letters, and filled with inaccuracies (such as that Arnold died when leaping over a low fence). Even so it is valuable because it is the book in which Trilling purged his debilitating emotions about Arnold himself.

But why do Trilling and Eliot cite Arnold so often, when his reputation after World War I and on into the 1930s and 1940s was in general not very high—though I. A. Richards was virtually his disciple and F. R. Leavis devoted a perceptive essay to him in *Scrutiny* in 1938? Eliot's tireless concern with Arnold reminds one of the behavior of articulate lovers when they are apart; in its verbal phases love is an endlessly pleasurable exercise in epistemology, it seems, in which John can never quite find the best images or phrases he needs to say what he feels about Mary, and, clearly, neither John nor Mary wants to get over the process of knowing the self and the other. What is it in Arnold's writing that Eliot and Trilling do not wish to get over learning about? Part of Arnold's lasting value to them is that he does not assume that art or criticism matters; hence he must implicitly justify art and the act of criticism in each essay, and in no other respect does he better merit his place in the company of Sidney, Dryden, Johnson, and Coleridge, the major critics before him who can still refresh us. Since he does not take it for granted that Heine, Keats, or Wordsworth matters, he must show in each essay why the artist is relevant to life and how art is involved in society. His implicit topic is the relation between art and society, and this is essentially Eliot's and Trilling's topic.

Understandably, Eliot, to define his position and to challenge the view that poetry can substitute for religion (though that is not quite Arnold's view), is often severe with Arnold. The most interesting of his attacks on Arnold are in the two early essays "The Perfect Critic" and "Imperfect Critics"

(1920), then in "The Function of Criticism" (1923), the essay on F. H. Bradley (1927), "Arnold and Pater" (1930), the essay concerning Matthew Arnold in *The Use of Poetry and The Use of Criticism* (1933), and in the two books *After Strange Gods* (1933) and *Notes toward a Definition of Culture* (1944), all of which show a useful Arnold.[6] The test of a critic's worth is not that he cannot be refuted, because critics thrive on being damned, but whether he can be usefully cited and reread. Though Eliot can lower Arnold to the status of a "propagandist" and quarrel with his use of words, he views him as a master critic who kept a delicate balance between the rival claims of society and aesthetics; and, indeed, Arnold's essays helped Eliot to correct his own initially restricted aestheticism. Trilling from the start was almost too distracted by society's needs and likely to forget art's claims; he is far less censorious of the socially minded Arnold and more able to adapt Arnold's positions profitably than Eliot can. Trilling is also a more concealed and subtle adapter since the most Arnoldian of his essays do not casually reveal their Victorian sources.

Eliot's praise of Arnold tends to be stylized, smart, and vaguely evasive. "Matthew Arnold was intelligent," Eliot stated in *The Sacred Wood*, "and by so much difference as the presence of one intelligent man makes, our age is inferior of Arnold's."[7] This is reasonable, if it is rather unfair to the intelligent Eliot himself; but it is vague. Eliot implies that Arnold wrote without the vices of sentiment or impressionism and that in the general imprecision of feeling and during an explosion of new information from science, he brought a cleared sensibility to the essay—that was his intelligence. As Eliot recognized, at historical times when science tells us too much, the mind resists a surfeit of facts so that most of the "thinking" we do is only to consult our emotions. Scientists themselves are too frequently sentimentalists. Recoiling from emotion, the sentimentalist may insist on rigid and overrefined definitions of "culture," "criticism," or anything else that is necessarily ambiguous in human life. Arnold resisted that oddly sentimental and academic temptation to be hard and literal with terms, and he could be valuable to Eliot and Trilling because he had cleared himself of the emotionality of his own temperament, family, and sentimental era and thus could write with a clarity they found in no other critic since Coleridge's time.

No other word Arnold used has had a deeper influence on twentieth-century English and American thought than *culture.* Arnold's propagation of his concept of culture, or of the attitude of seeking the best that has been thought and said so as to turn "a stream of fresh and free thought upon our stock notions and habits," is usually involved in Eliot's and Trilling's responses. In 1920, Eliot could accuse Arnold of having wasted his time by writing *Culture and Anarchy* and of misdirected efforts in social criticism. Art, for Eliot, makes demands of its own; Arnold should have saved his critical strength for poetry. But by 1928 Eliot could admit that poetry has "something" to do with morals, religion, and politics;[8] and in editing his journal *Criterion* between 1922 and 1939, Eliot gradually undertook a more and more Arnoldian program. His aim was to reform English provincialism by bringing to bear the mind of Europe on current thinking about literature, and Eliot published essays on history, politics, and a large number of social topics as well as on literature. By 1930, in "Arnold and Pater," however, he makes clear his chief objection to his mentor when he says, "The total effect of Arnold's philosophy is to set up Culture in the place of Religion, and to leave Religion to be laid waste by the anarchy of feeling."[9] Unfortunately, by then the objection hardened him too often against Arnold, and Eliot, whose classicism was out of key with the political issues of the 1930s, became less effective as an essayist.

In contrast, Lionel Trilling, maturing in a politically conscious decade, felt more comfortable with Arnold's social essays. He studies them well in his book on Arnold in 1939. Starting with *The Liberal Imagination* (1950), he is subtle and capable in adapting Arnold's social insights. It is true that the preface to *The Liberal Imagination* is naive and dated, as when Trilling equates the liberal tradition with "ideas" and the American conservative tradition with "irritable mental gestures which seek to resemble ideas." (In its political enthusiasm that remark neglects the Hamiltonian tradition of intellectual conservatism.) But Trilling elsewhere is humane and balanced; to take one delightful example of his use of Arnoldian tactics against literalism and mere quantification, in his essay "The Kinsey Report" he criticizes Professors A. C. Kinsey, W. B. Pomeroy, and C. E. Martin for taking an absurd quantitative view of sex in their book *Sexual Behavior in the Human Male.* Kinsey in his interviews had found a man, "clearly the hero of the Report," says Trilling, who had "an orgasmic frequency of thirty times a week." (Some other men had about half an orgasm per week, to the alarm of Kinsey, who believed that good robust sex means nothing but frequent orgasms.) "Masturbation in children," Trilling mildly comments, "often is the expression not of sexuality only but of anxiety. In the same way, adult intercourse may be the expression of anxiety; its frequency may not be so much robust as compulsive." [10] Trilling thus exploded a minor instance of the modern faith in quantity and helped us to see that by confusing love and sex with ejaculation, forgetting anxiety, and taking Americans as the only "human males," *Sexual Behavior in the Human Male* is nearly as naive as a Salem discourse on witchcraft; Kinsey's faults, of course, echoed those of Robert Lowe and others who confused quantity with quality in schools and whom Arnold had attacked in his *Fraser's* piece "The Twice-Revised Code." Yet when his faith in Arnoldian humanism is challenged, Trilling excels, we may say, on his own, and I know of no better instance than his criticism of "culture." In *The Opposing Self* he met Eliot's objection to the frigidity of Arnold's calling poetry a "criticism of life" by saying that Arnold had meant to shock us, or to show that poetry is a criticism of life in the same way that "The Scholar-Gipsy" is a criticism of the life of an inspector of schools and that the "despair" in that poem is the despair of those who, having committed themselves to culture, have thus given up the life of surprise, elevation, impulse, pleasure, and imagination. There is something in our habitual life of culture to make us dissatisfied, and the objection (one of the main insights of Trilling's last years) is developed in *Beyond Culture* of 1965 and especially in "On the Teaching of Modern Literature" in which Trilling finds much of modern literature under the influence of Sir James Frazer's *The Golden Bough* (with its antirationalism and belief in the primal blood-urges) and indeed opposed to civilization itself. Trilling suggests that art dangerously purges itself, that in praising savage energies and endangering the rational society upon which art depends, the artist at least ensures that the life of culture rids itself of what is hostile to surprise, impulse, pleasure, and imagination. The critic, however, must point to the danger as well as to the release; there can be no comforting answer either to the restrictions of culture or to the problems posed by an antirational, antidemocratic art, if we admit that democracy depends on restraint and rationality and is undermined by primal, nonethical energies.

In his comments on the paradoxes of culture, Trilling best reveals his clarity and restraint, his sense that what the critic is always dealing with, once he has purged his own emotions, is the emotional basis of most of our thinking, most of our "answers" and enthusiasms. It is a paradox that Trilling, like Arnold and Eliot, placed the highest value on feeling and spontaneity. They are concerned as Jane Austen was almost uniquely in her time for the survival of the capacity for deep feeling, and it is not coincidental that Trilling's greatest essays on the novel concern Jane Austen. What he, and Arnold and Eliot before him, locate as the cause of grief in modern society is our confusion of rationality and impulse, scientific objectivity and emotionalism, which now and then is a contributing factor in the killing of 6 million Jews, a Vietnam war, or the murder of a Polish priest. Whether Arnold and Trilling misused their talents in showing that the same mistakes that result in false judgments of Shakespeare or Keats may be seen in British education reports or in analyses of sexual behavior is, perhaps, debatable. But an emotional problem is at the root of the human dilemma and may always be expected to be, and those whom we call the great critics from Sidney, Dryden, and Johnson to Arnold, Eliot, and Trilling continually refresh us because they manage to penetrate it.

NOTES

1. See Park Honan, *Matthew Arnold: A Life* (New York: McGraw-Hill, 1981), p. 59.

2. Lionel Trilling, *The Liberal Imagination* (London: Secker and Warburg, 1955), pp. 183, 194.

3. T. S. Eliot, "The Perfect Critic," in *The Sacred Wood* (London: Methuen, 1972), p. 12.

4. Eliot, "The Blank Verse of Marlowe," in ibid., p. 88.

5. Eliot, "Hamlet and His Problems," in ibid., pp. 98, 100.

6. His treatment of Arnold has been touched on by many critics of Eliot's essays, but see especially the remarks in John D. Margolis, *T. S. Eliot's Intellectual Development, 1922–1939* (Chicago: University of Chicago Press, 1972); C. K. Stead, "Eliot, Arnold, and the English Poetic Tradition," in *The Literary Criticism of T. S. Eliot,* ed. David Newton-De Molina (London: Athlone, 1977), pp. 184–206; and Ian Gregor, "Eliot and Matthew Arnold," in *Eliot in Perspective: A Symposium,* ed. Graham Martin (London: Macmillan, 1970), pp. 267–78.

7. See T. S. Eliot's section "The French Intelligence" in *The Sacred Wood,* p. 45.

8. Eliot, "Preface to the 1928 Edition," in *The Sacred Wood,* p. x.

9. By 1930 Eliot's religious objection affected even his view of the clarity of Arnold, who produced only "a kind of illusion of precision and clarity; that is, maintained these qualities as ideals of style," although the essay on F. H. Bradley had implied as much in 1927; see T. S. Eliot, *Selected Essays* (London: Faber, 1951), pp. 433, 436.

10. Trilling, *Liberal Imagination,* p. 231.

Robert H. Super

FOURTEEN

Sweetness and Lightness: Matthew Arnold's Comic Muse

There is a well-known caricature by Max Beerbohm in which a baggy-trousered, carpet-slippered Matthew Arnold leans upon a mantelpiece, guffawing, while a little girl in crinolines, hands properly clasped behind her back, looks up at him severely. The little girl is his niece Mary Augusta (later Mrs. Humphry Ward), and she is saying: "Why, Uncle Matthew, Oh why, will not you be always wholly serious?" Mary Augusta's daddy could have told her that Uncle Matthew as a young man had never been wholly serious. There was the time when he slipped up behind his father's desk while the doctor was teaching and made faces at the class, putting them on their mettle to keep their own faces straight so that the sacrilege would not be betrayed. There was the time, a few years later, when Arnold and a friend were traveling in a stagecoach, and Matthew quietly let it be known to the other passengers that he was an attendant at an insane asylum, escorting his companion from one madhouse to another.

Indeed, it was Mary Augusta's father who, in an obituary notice of his older brother, laid great stress on Matthew's "bright playfulness" and "humorous masterfulness." And the thought led him to recall a conversation in which Matthew had offended Arthur Clough by his high praise of Voltaire.[1] It may come as a surprise that Voltaire's name appears again and again in Arnold's prose: it occurs in every one of the eleven volumes of his *Complete Prose Works*, and there are twenty-five jottings from Voltaire in Arnold's pocket diaries and notebooks. (This is far fewer than the number of quotations from Goethe or the *Imitation*, but it is still a substantial number.) Only a little more than two years before his death, Arnold wrote in the *Encyclopaedia Britannica:*

> Certain spirits are of an excellence almost ideal in certain lines; the human race might willingly adopt them as its spokesmen, recognizing that on these lines their style and utterance may stand as those, not of bounded individuals, but of the human race. So Homer speaks for the human race, and with an excellence which is ideal, in epic narration; Plato in the treatment at once beautiful and profound of philosophical questions; Shakespeare in the presentation of human character; Voltaire in light verse and ironical discussion. A list of perfect ones, indeed, each in his own line! (*CPW,* 11:119)

A dozen years earlier, in *Literature and Dogma*, Arnold named Shakespeare, Voltaire, Cicero, and Plato as "the great men of other nations whom alone one can cite as [Goethe's] literary compeers" (*CPW,* 6:158). He amazingly calls Voltaire "the French Luther of the eighteenth century," "a splendid professor and propagator of" logic and lucidity (*CPW,* 8:363). Praising Joubert in a lecture as professor of poetry at Oxford for his sound evaluation of Voltaire, he speaks of the author of *Candide* as "a charmer of the literary sense": "Perhaps we English are not very liable to catch Voltaire's vices, while of some of his merits we have signal need" (*CPW,* 3:205). He did "a big spell of work in this world," Arnold commented on the centenary of Voltaire's death (*CPW,* 8:363).

Arnold's most obvious acknowledgment of Voltaire came when, in the summer of 1866, he embarked on a series of witty letters to the editor of the *Pall Mall Gazette* on various idiosyncrasies of English society and politics and adopted as a nom de plume "Arminius von Thunder-ten-Tronckh," a descendant of the Baron von Thunder-ten-Tronckh in *Candide* (the Christian name, "Arminius," comes from the German national hero who led the resistance to the Roman emperor Augustus). The few quotations from *Candide* in Arnold's works are, to be sure, commonplace: dissenting clergymen must marry within the forbidden degrees (their deceased wives' sisters) for the same reason that Voltaire gave for the execution of Admiral Byng, "to encourage the others" (*CPW,* 5:318), and a political economist is ridiculed for telling us that "all is for the best"—by implication, in this best of all possible worlds, in which the more competition, the more prosperity (*CPW,* 10:250).

An English ironist of the eighteenth century, a generation older than Voltaire, was perhaps less admired by Arnold (presumably because he was a less elegant stylist than Voltaire), but to a phrase of Swift's—the phrase I have desecrated in my title—Arnold gave a currency that led many of his contemporaries to identify the expression with Arnold himself and with his concept of "culture," rather than with the source Arnold acknowledged. Culture, Arnold remarked in his last lecture as professor of poetry, conceived of "perfection" as "a harmonious perfection, a perfection in which the characters of beauty and intelligence are both present, which unites 'the two noblest of things,'—as Swift, who of one of the two, at any rate, had himself all too little, most happily calls them in his *Battle of the Books,*—'the two noblest of things, *sweetness and light'"* (*CPW,* 5:99).

The identification of this language with Arnold was such that when Lord Salisbury bestowed on him the Oxford degree of D.C.L. in 1870, the marquis remarked that he should have addressed him as "Vir dulcissime et lucidissime"—the sweetest and most lucid of men. And if Arnold mentioned Swift much less frequently than he mentioned Voltaire (only this one quotation from Swift appears in his pocket diaries), he made a very telling gesture when in 1880 he prepared his selected *Passages from the Prose Writings of Matthew Arnold.* Sixteen years earlier, in "The Literary Influence of Academies," he had remarked, "When a literature has produced Shakespeare and Milton, when it has even produced Barrow and Burke, it cannot well abandon its traditions." Now, in 1880, he crossed out the name of Barrow and substituted that of Swift (*CPW,* 3:257, 529). The eighteenth-century temper was more important to Arnold than we are likely to think.

Modern critics tend to take Arnold seriously. A few have perceived his wit—Professor Sidney Coulling, in his lively and tightly packed book *Matthew Arnold and His Critics,* Professor William Robbins in his superb monograph *The Arnoldian Principle of Flexibility.* Among Arnold's contemporaries also, many indeed were "wholly serious," but some of the quickest minds then too were likely to recognize his talent as a witty controversialist. When the twenty-six-year-old Henry James made his first sojourn in London as an adult, he found "thrilling" the "opportunity to sit one morning, beside [his hostess's] tea-urn . . . opposite to Frederic Harrison, eminent to me at the moment as one of the subjects of Matthew Arnold's early fine banter. . . . Has any gilding ray since that happy season rested here and there with the sovereign charm of interest, of drollery, of felicity and infelicity taken on by scattered selected objects in that writer's [i.e., Arnold's] bright critical dawn?—an element in which we had the sense of sitting gratefully bathed, so that we fairly took out our young minds and dabbled and soaked them in it as we were to do again in no other."[2] One has the sense that for James, Frederic Harrison was almost a creation of Matthew Arnold's genius.

That, of course, he was not. He was a young Comtist, one of the leaders of the positivist movement in England, nine years younger than Arnold, who might be said to have begotten *Culture and Anarchy* by remarking publicly that "perhaps the very silliest cant of the day is the cant about culture" (*CPW,* 5:87). Harrison was one of the few writers who could give Arnold as good as he got, for when Arnold responded to this remark in his final lecture at Oxford, Harrison made a *riposte* that was "so amusing that I laughed till I cried," Arnold said. This *riposte* was an imaginary dialogue between Arminius and Harrison, in which the latter, now ostensibly converted to the Arnoldian doctrine of culture, had to explain that doctrine to the logical mind of the German.

"How do you describe the basis of your social philosophy?" [Arminius demanded of the new disciple of culture]. "Remember, my friend," I rejoined, with a confident smile, "culture knows nothing so finite as a system." "No!" he answered; "not any system, but you have principles? These principles are of course coherent; they are interdependent, subordinate, and derivative, I presume?" . . . "My friend," I replied, laughing aloud, though, I trust, always within the limits of the courteous and the graceful . . . "Learn how culture—with that flexibility which sweetness and light give, with that exquisite sensibility to truth which is its note—has no need of these leading-strings and finger-posts. . . . It is eternally passing onwards and seeking—seeking and passing onwards eternally. Where the bee sucks, there suck I," I murmured cheerily.   (*CPW*, 5:424)

Thereafter the expression "principles coherent, interdependent, subordinate, and derivative" appeared frequently in Arnold's ironic descriptions of himself. Some years later, it is said, when Harrison was asked if Arnold believed in a God, he replied, "No, but he keeps one in his back-yard to fly at people he doesn't like."[3]

It seldom happened, however, that Arnold met a controversialist who could respond with the liveliness of Frederic Harrison. "Seriousness" was generally the tone, and seriousness is harder to deal with than one might suppose. At best, it seems a bit ungenerous to ridicule someone who takes himself seriously; in all fairness, one should respond to his tone, not his mind. When a pair of right reverend prelates, the bishops of Winchester (Samuel Wilberforce) and Gloucester (C. J. Ellicott), in their admirable zeal for the religion they served, moved in Convocation to bar Unitarians from taking communion in the Church of England, "for the honour of our Lord's Godhead" (a godhead which the Unitarians of course denied, thereby separating themselves from Christians "for time and for eternity"), the author of *Literature and Dogma* found his risibilities stirred and could not avoid ridicule. But the ridicule offended many good people, who concluded, in Arnold's words, that "the order of bishops has upon [me] the effect of a red rag upon a bull" and filled him "with rage and hatred" (*CPW*, 6:466; 7:151–52). When one is seriously advancing an important and revolutionary truth, as Arnold was doing in *Literature and Dogma*, one dare not offend one's readers and send them away before they have given their attention to one's argument. And so Arnold was obliged to explain himself. The bishop of Winchester (himself a debater of some talent, who notably tangled with Huxley on the descent of man) died before Arnold wrote in self-defense:

> He was a man with the temperament of genius; and to his energy, his presence, his speech, this temperament could often lend charm and power. But those words of his which we quoted, and his public deliverances far too frequently, had a fault in which men of station and authority who address a society like ours, deserve at all times as severe a check as either blame or ridicule can inflict upon them. . . . A man of Bishop Wilberforce's power of mind must know, if he is sincere with himself, that when he talks of "doing something for the honour of Our Lord's Godhead," or of "that infinite separation for time and for eternity which is involved in rejecting the Godhead of the Eternal Son,"—he must know that by this singular sort of mixture of unction and metaphysics he is solemnly giving a semblance of conceivability, fixity, and certainty to notions which do not possibly admit of them. He must know this, and yet he gives it, because it suits his purpose, or because the public, or a large body of the public, desire it; and this is clap-trap.
>
> (*CPW,* 7:153)

Earnestness, in other words, is not enough; an intelligent person has a moral obligation to keep his public utterances up to the level of his intelligence. People are too likely, when they read, to submit themselves to the writer, to accept his (or her) premises; wit, however, requires that we stand far enough off to perceive the implications of what we read.

Then there is always the danger of having subsequently to face someone to whom one has given offense; it is probably better to ridicule a good friend, as Arnold did with Huxley in "Literature and Science," than a stranger. He did not know Frederic Harrison and learned, only in the nick of time, that a fanciful description he had written of Harrison's appearance hit too close to home. He came to know the bishop of Gloucester and to have a personal regard for him, and was obliged in courtesy to praise him for his scholarliness, his serious intellectual achievement, more than once after thus coupling his name with that of the bishop of Winchester in *Literature and Dogma*.

In his controversy, Arnold had a rule that came from Voltaire (Arnold jotted it in his memorandum book): "The great art of literary warfare is never to appear to defend one's terrain, and only to ravage that of the enemy, to demolish it gaily."[4] Arnold was not quite forty when John William Colenso, Anglican bishop of Natal in South Africa (another bishop!), took the religious liberals by storm with the first part of his *The Pentateuch and Book of Joshua Critically Examined* (1862). Colenso had been a mathematics teacher at Harrow and was the author of textbooks in arithmetic and algebra (a Victorian bishop was much more likely to have risen from a mastership in a public school or a fellowship in one of the universities than from the parish clergy). When Colenso went to Africa as a missionary bishop, he with commendable zeal learned the Zulu language and translated the Bible into that tongue. But as he worked, he could not help checking his sums, and he found that the figures given by Moses were impossible. Since God clearly could not have got his addition wrong, the first five or six books of the Bible obviously were not written under divine inspiration. And so Colenso wrote at great length to prove his point. His book was entirely negative, did not face the question of precisely what "inspiration" might mean, and did not so much as consider the value of the Bible to the human spirit. It was, indeed, like the very worst of the contemporary German "higher criticism" and was hailed by the English partly, at least, because it gave them an English rival to the Germans. Arnold took the Scripture and Christianity too seriously to be content with such stupidity, and he demolished it gaily by the simple device of framing Colenso's propositions as a series of what we used to call "thought problems" in an arithmetic textbook.

> The Bishop of Natal's arithmetical demonstrations . . . are a series of problems, the solution of each of which is meant to be the *reductio ad absurdum* of that Book of the Pentateuch which supplied its terms. This being so, it must be said that the Bishop of Natal gives us a great deal too many of them. For his purpose a smaller number of problems and a more stringent method of

stating them would have sufficed. It would then have been possible within the compass of a single page to put all the information which the Bishop's book aspires to convey to the mind of Europe. For example: if we take the Book of Genesis, and the account of the family of Judah there related—*"Allowing 20 as the marriageable age, how many years are required for the production of 3 generations?"* The answer to that sum disposes (on the Bishop's plan) of the Book of Genesis. [The allusion is to the curious story of Judah's having twin sons by his twice-widowed daughter-in-law, and being still alive, as was his father, when these twins had children.] Again, as to the account in the Book of Exodus of the Israelites dwelling in tents—*"Allowing 10 persons for each tent (and a Zulu hut in Natal contains on an average only 3½), how many tents would 2,000,000 persons require?"* The parenthesis in that problem is hardly worthy of such a master of arithmetical statement as Dr. Colenso [since you can't have three and a half Zúlus in a hut]; but, with or without the parenthesis, the problem, when answered, disposes of the Book of Exodus. Again, as to the account in Leviticus of the provision made for the priests: *"If three priests have to eat 264 pigeons a day, how many must each priest eat?"* That disposes of Leviticus. Take Numbers, and the total of first-borns there given, as compared with the number of male adults: *"If, of 900,000 males, 22,273 are first-borns, how many boys must there be in each family?"* That disposes of Numbers. For Deuteronomy, take the number of lambs slain at the Sanctuary, as compared with the space for slaying them. *"In an area of 1,692 square yards, how many lambs per minute can 150,000 persons kill in two hours?"* Certainly not 1,250, the number required; and the Book of Deuteronomy, therefore, shares the fate of its predecessors. . . . Even a giant need not waste his strength.

(*CPW,* 3:48)

The newspapers and the parliamentary debates furnished Arnold with his easiest prey. All too often one is tempted to suppose that he simply made up those choice quotations he sprinkled through his works, just as Huxley assumed that he had invented the Bishop Wilson he quoted so often (*CPW,* 5:231). But he didn't; the remarks were there where he said they were. In Arnold's view, the preeminent ambitions of the middle-class, Nonconformist businessman were wealth and salvation. No doubt he could hardly believe his eyes when he read, buried in the back pages of the *Times* for March 4, 1868, an account of the coroner's inquest into the suicide of a London insurance man named Smith; he had shot himself, it was testified, because "he laboured under the apprehension that he would come to poverty, and that he was eternally lost." How desperately sad, Arnold thought, when the "two grand objects of concern . . . of all the strongest, most respectable, and most representative part of the nation" were "the concern for making money, and the concern for saving our souls!" (*CPW,* 5:186). Four months later the newspaper's remark about Smith appeared in *Culture and Anarchy.* In mid-June 1867, one William Murphy held anti-Catholic revival meetings in the industrial city of Birmingham, which had a large population of Irish laborers, and he induced a number of Nonconformist Protestant clergymen to sit on the platform with him, including a Methodist minister with the regrettable name of William Cattle. Murphy, a former Catholic who had seen the light, warned his audience of the evils that lurked; after attacking the institution of nunneries, he proclaimed that "his object was to protect their wives and daughters. If Mayors and magistrates [who had refused to allow him to speak in the town hall] did not care for their wives and daughters, he did. He cared for his wife, and therefore she should not go to the confessional." "What I wish to say to you as Protestant husbands is, *Take care of your wives!*" "Away with the Mass! It is from the bottomless pit; and in the bottomless pit shall all liars have their part, in the lake that burneth with fire and brimstone" (*CPW,* 5:131, 427). Six months later, Arnold was quoting this newspaper report also in *Culture and Anarchy.* And the issue in this case was not mere harmless stupidity; Murphy's impassioned speeches led to serious anti-Catholic, anti-Irish riots in Birmingham.

One of the more trivial pursuits of the Nonconformists was the attempt to legalize marriage between a man and his deceased wife's sister, which was forbidden not only by canon law in the Church of England but also by civil law framed under the influence of the church. The Liberal Quaker statesman John Bright, supporting in Parliament a bill that would remove the prohibition, thundered:

> The Church of England permits the marriage of first cousins. . . . Is there any man of common-sense who will not say that on every natural ground the marriage of first cousins is more objectionable than the marriage of a man with his deceased wife's sister? . . . [Moreover,] it is notorious beyond dispute that there are many cases . . . in which the dying mother hopes that her sister may become in a closer sense than that of aunt the protector of her children. . . . I appeal to . . . all . . . opponents of the Bill, as to whether they themselves deem the man who marries his deceased wife's sister a profligate man? ("No") . . . Is there any man that regards a woman married to her deceased sister's husband as an immoral person who is not to be admitted to his house, and who he thinks will be likely to taint the society of his wife and daughters? (Hear, hear.) No such feeling exists. (Hear, hear.) And if there are children of those marriages there is no man in the House or out of it cruel enough—I have nearly used a harsher word—to point to those children by the almost odious name of bastard. (Cheers.)
>
> (*CPW,* 5:468–69)

Seven weeks later, in one of his letters to the *Pall Mall Gazette,* Arnold imagines the Young Lion of the *Daily Telegraph* standing with his Paris correspondent, Nick, by the deathbed of Mrs. Bottles and speculating on the future of her daughters and of Mr. Bottles (the prototypical middle-class Nonconformist businessman). Young Leo has just come from the debate in the House of Commons, and as he sees Mrs. Bottles's homely sister and her lovely niece standing by the bedside, he is moved by "a shower of ideas, full of import for the Liberal party and for the future": why should not Bottles marry, not his deceased wife's homely sister, but her lovely niece?

> "Let us apply John Bright's crucial tests. Is she his first cousin? Could there be a more natural companion for Selina and the other Bottles girls? Or,—to take the moral ground so touchingly and irresistibly chosen by our great popular tribune,—if

legislation on this subject were impeded by the party of bigotry, if they chose not to wait for it, if they got married without it, and if you were to meet them on the boulevard at Paris during their wedding tour, should you go up to Bottles and say: "Mr. Bottles, you are a profligate man?" "Oh dear, no," said Nick; "I should never dream of it." "And if you met them a year later on the same spot," I continued, "with a Normandy nurse behind them carrying a baby, should you cry out to the poor little thing: Bastard?" "Nothing of the kind," he answered.

(CPW, 5:315)

In arguing for the greater utility of modern languages than of Latin and Greek, the Liberal Utilitarian Robert Lowe (incidentally Arnold's superior in the Education Department) once remarked (with what was intended as humor): "The advantage of knowing French would be that when [an Englishman] goes to Paris he would be able to order his dinner at the café, and to squabble over his bill without making himself a laughingstock to every one present" (*CPW,* 5:429). Two months later Arnold in *Culture and Anarchy* spoke of the new trend "of preparing ourselves by the study of modern languages,—as after Mr. Lowe's great speech at Edinburgh we shall do,—to fight the battle of life with the waiters in foreign hotels" (*CPW,* 5:126). I have myself been present at faculty debates on the foreign language requirement that were very reminiscent of Lowe's principles.

Arnold's descriptions of the American newspapers he read on his first lecture tour here are hilarious—the more amusing because they are quite literal, without the least bit of exaggeration. I remember thinking, as I watched Arnold at work with the daily newspapers and the periodical press, that he was extraordinarily lucky to find precisely the statement he wanted just when he needed it. And then I recalled what Emerson said of Thoreau, that this was the luck that happens only to good players. When a stranger inquired where Indian arrowheads might be found, Thoreau replied, "Everywhere," and stooping on the spot picked one up at his feet. On another occasion, Thoreau fell and sprained his foot; as he painfully struggled to get up, he saw that he had fallen in a patch of arnica, an herb from which he could immediately make an anti-inflammatory poultice.

Arnold's genius was the ability to bring the critical mind— the wit—to bear upon the events and (especially) the speeches, review articles, and news reports of everyday life and to show how they might be viewed *sub specie aeternitatis*—in the light of eternal truths. It is not the least of his virtues that he shows us, a hundred years after his death, how to read our newspapers, how to listen to our politicians. There is the same topicality about much of his writing that there is in the poetry of Pope and Dryden. One is, indeed, inclined to turn upside down Arnold's statement about those authors, his contention that they "are not classics of our poetry, they are classics of our prose" (*CPW,* 9:181) (a verdict T. S. Eliot echoed when he said of Johnson's *Vanity of Human Wishes,* "Such poetry, it can be said without prejudice, has the virtue of good prose"). One might, I say, speak of Arnold's prose as having, in preeminent degree, the imaginative grasp of the finest poetry. Arnold never, in other words, lost his talent for poetry; he changed its sphere.

But no man can, by wit alone, shake off the impact of his culture, with its local and temporal prejudices. If Arnold is so much more satisfying than John Stuart Mill, it is because Mill totally lacked the ability to view himself and his world from a distance; and for this failing Arnold had fun with Mill too. But Arnold also had temporal biases that sometimes seem to have blinded him. There is the firm conviction (for which our generation habitually sneers at him) that the French were defeated by the Germans in 1871 because of their too great devotion to the goddess Aselgeia, or Lubricity (*CPW,* 7:44; 10:155, for example). However much one may share Arnold's admiration for "conduct," a nation's success in warfare probably has very little relation to its morality.

And in his high concept of poetry and art, even Arnold is perhaps too much afflicted with seriousness. He began his reading of poetry as a boy with Pope and Byron, we are told.[5] Curiously, however, he seems to have undervalued the very work of Byron we might have expected him to seize on—the wonderful comedy of *Don Juan.* When he was a little fellow his father used to stand him on the living room table to recite the death speech of Marino Faliero; at the age of fourteen, as a Winchester schoolboy, he won a competition in elocution by delivering that same melodramatic speech. His Byron was the author of *Childe Harold* and *Manfred,* the poet of "inborn force and fire," of "Titanism" (*CPW,* 3:132, 370), who displayed to all the world "the pageant of his bleeding heart."[6] In the volume of selections from Byron that Arnold published late in his life, there is a section headed "satire," but it is a short and unimpressive group. Arnold did not even include the superb characterizations of Voltaire and Gibbon from *Childe Harold.* The real Byronic wit of Arnold's generation is, ironically, to be found in the work of the author of "Amours de Voyage" and "Dipsychus"—Arthur Clough.

Arnold's expectations sometimes led him to overlook the obvious. "Wordsworth calls Voltaire dull," Arnold tells us (*CPW,* 9:50), and properly rebukes him for so doing. Yet there is a passage of Arnold's on Wordsworth that tears my soul whenever I read it (as I do frequently, since it is in one of Arnold's best critical essays, "A French Critic on Milton"): "What leagues of lumbering movement! what desperate endeavours, as in Wordsworth's

'And at the "Hoop" alighted, famous inn,'

to render a platitude endurable by making it pompous!" (*CPW,* 8:183). The line is from *The Prelude,* the passage in which Wordsworth describes his own country-boy excitement at his first journey to take up residence at Cambridge, the university in which he would soon come to know a friend who occupied Milton's rooms at Christ's, in which he would see, through the window of his own room, the statue of Newton in the antechapel of Trinity. As the stagecoach drew close to Cambridge, his excitement mounted; he saw an undergraduate in cap and gown and leaned far out of his carriage window to follow the phenomenon with his eye. Then came the river Cam, of which he had heard so much. And finally he arrived at his destination, the principal hotel of Cambridge, the Hoop. All of us who have come from the provincial town to the big university have had the experience. Arnold knew Wordsworth personally for well over a decade and indeed reported some of the gentle fun of his conversation, yet Wordsworth's sympathetic humor here, as he looked back in his mind to the excitement of that first day in Cambridge, entirely escaped Arnold.

And yet Arnold could often stand off and look at himself with that same humor. One of Arnold's liveliest bits of satire is his Preface to the first series of *Essays in Criticism,* a collection made up largely of his lectures as professor of poetry. In that Preface he good-humoredly remarks that he has always been "shy of assuming the honorable style of Professor," partly because he could not actually claim to speak for the university, partly because it was a title customarily assumed by stage magicians performing in the popular theaters, "who adorn it, I feel, much more than I do" (*CPW,* 3:288). What must have been his thoughts when his publishers advertised that very book as written by (in heavy black type) PROFESSOR AR-NOLD?[7] Before one dismisses anything of his as silly (and some modern critics do so with a good deal of regularity), one must be certain that one has not missed a neat twist of irony. Arnold's value for us often lies not in his being always wholly right so much as in his being not always wholly serious.

NOTES

1. [Thomas Arnold, Jr.], "Matthew Arnold (By one who knew him well)," *Manchester Guardian,* May 18, 1888, p. 8.

2. Henry James, *The Middle Years* (London: W. Collins Sons, 1917), p. 35.

3. M. D. Conway, *Autobiography,* 2 vols. (Boston, 1905), 2:399.

4. Matthew Arnold, *Note-Books,* ed. H. F. Lowry, K. Young, and W. H. Dunn (London: Oxford University Press, 1952), p. 521. This volume has been the source of all references to Arnold's pocket diaries.

5. In Thomas Arnold's obituary notice.

6. "Stanzas from the Grande Chartreuse," l. 136.

7. *Athenaeum,* Dec. 1, 1866, p. 703.

WILLIAM B. THESING

Afterword

The fourteen essays in this collection began as papers delivered as part of a symposium held at Texas A&M University, February 28 and March 1, 1985. The announced purpose of the conference was to study the "multitudinous" areas of Matthew Arnold's influence and importance, not only in his own time but also in ours. This attempt to identify discernible categories or centers of Arnoldian influence and importance is not a new one. It is, however, appropriate that such categories be freshly reevaluated as we approach the centenary of Arnold's death. G. Robert Stange in his *Matthew Arnold: The Poet as Humanist* (1967) employed such a method for ordering Arnold's poems, arranging them by theme or the "organizing centers" of the verse, which deals with the four "ideas" of poetry, nature, self, and love. Frederic E. Faverty in *The Victorian Poets: A Guide to Research* (1968) offered more than fifteen categories of Arnoldian studies; David J. DeLaura in *Victorian Prose: A Guide to Research* (1973) offered as many; and several more areas can be found in Sidney Coulling's "Matthew Arnold, 1945–1974: A Review of Criticism and Research," in *British Studies Monitor* (1978). The primary organizing centers of Arnold's influence and importance according to the present essays are Arnold and religion, Arnold and criticism, Arnold and America, and Arnold and education. Secondary centers of attention are Arnold and poetry, Arnold and philosophy, and Arnold and humor. With the larger picture of Arnoldian scholarship in mind, a few well-tempered reactions to some of the essays in the categories covered might be useful.

As Jerold Savory has pointed out, recent attempts to

understand and encompass the entire range of Arnold's career have focused on two key words: *culture* and *religion*. For example, Joseph Carroll's *The Cultural Theory of Matthew Arnold* (1982) analyzes Arnold's "successful effort to use conflicting ideas in creating a unified theory of culture." More to the point of the present collection, Ruth apRoberts's *Arnold and God* (1983) demonstrates "the clear centrality of Arnold's religious ideas to all his work." In defining the special terms of Arnold's religious outlook—piety, devotion, or whatever—apRoberts creates a new harmony that joins the poetry and prose phases of the writer's career. Arnold's *Note-Books* are extensively referred to in apRoberts's book. In Chapter 5, she quotes the editors of the *Note-Books*, who "mark Arnold's consecration to a life larger than that of the poet and essayist. Whatever one thinks of his studies in religious subjects, few men have tried harder to attend to the great language of faith and to make it the word of their daily lives. The note-books can rightly take their place, we feel, among the best of the books of devotion. . . . The piety is there." Several interesting directions emerge from this quotation. One direction, of course, is the attention to a literary life that transcends the old critical arguments that narrowly focused on Arnold as poet versus Arnold as essayist. Beyond that are some of the many questions and answers that apRoberts poses and elucidates: "In what sense can we call him religious? . . . In what, then, can piety consist? . . . What is the phenomenon called religion? How are we to understand the term *God?*" Arnold's meditations on these questions nurtured his own self-development; our consideration of Arnold and religion enhances our appreciation of the unity of his career. It points us to a new center stage of Arnoldian scholarship. It also shows us the sidelight of his influence on twentieth-century scholars' approach to and interpretation of both secular and religious texts. Through her central chapter on metaphoric language, in which she shows how Arnold perceived the basic similarity between literary and religious texts, apRoberts has forever revealed the simplicity of the notion that Arnold merely sought to substitute literature for religion.

Inevitably, there will be reservations concerning any study. Some trenchant points are raised in James C. Livingston's essay and in his earlier review in the Spring 1984 issue of *The Arnol-dian*. His conservative position concerning the need to restrain our modernizing tendency is especially worth reiterating here: "It is wrong . . . to conjoin Arnold's God with Wallace Stevens' notion of the 'Supreme Fiction.' Arnold scholars generally have, I fear, failed to make some important distinctions and continue to see the likes of Richards and Stevens as 'perpetu-ating' the Arnold line. There are affinities, yes, but there are also crucial differences." In an extended review essay in *Review* (1985), David DeLaura voices various concerns about ap-Roberts's approach in her book. Essentially he calls for less ho-mogenizing unity: "We now have some fairly distinct versions of Arnold's career to choose among—ranging from the 'total-izing' views of apRoberts and Madden, across a spectrum, to-ward the more disjunctive and dialectical Arnold I have been arguing for."

More than twenty years ago, Stephen Spender in *The Struggle of the Modern* designated Arnold the "unacknowledged legislator of twentieth-century criticism." Park Honan in his excellent biography seconds the nomination by saying: that "no other English critic has so influenced the nation [that is, the United States]." In *Matthew Arnold's Prose: Three Essays in Literary Enlargement* (1983), William E. Buckler offers a simi-larly high assessment of Arnold's ongoing critical importance: "He was, quite simply, the founder of the main line of modern criticism in English. During the 1860s and 1870s, he gave crit-icism an identity, a broad-based cultural complexity and in-tellectual respectability, and a social mission that was both modern and indispensable." In another book published in 1983—*The Social Mission of English Criticism, 1848–1932*—Chris Baldick uses a series of enlivening adjectives to describe the early vision of Matthew Arnold, the "bold," vigorous founder of modern English literary criticism: Arnold fostered a "new sense and status" for English literary criticism. In the essays by Linda Pratt and Park Honan we see an endorsement of Arnold's forward-looking influence upon such modernist critics as Ste-phen Spender, T. S. Eliot, and Lionel Trilling. But in John P. Farrell's use of Raymond Williams, a cultural critic who came into prominence after 1950, we begin to see some of Arnold's eroding influences on twentieth-century outlooks. We are reminded here of the development that Baldick traces so carefully in his book. Baldick argues that although Arnold was an "expansionist" in assigning wider social and cultural responsibilities to English critical writing, he also demonstrated elitist tendencies in insisting on its "special guardianship." It is from this lofty point that Baldick's searching analysis of the deficiencies of the Arnoldian "line" of modern critical development begins.

The clashing armies of twentieth-century criticism are threatening our cultural legacy, according to Allan C. Dooley's essay. Dooley offers all august Arnoldians a mild Jeremiad. He is part of a growing movement of reaction against new schools of theoretical criticism. In a recent review, Wendell V. Harris spoke of critical writing wherein "the very structure of argument produces the sense that one is clinging to the crumbling edge of meaning." He notes that Elizabeth W. Bruss in her book *Beautiful Theories: The Spectacle of Discourse in Contemporary Criticism* (1982) described the cumulative effect of such writing as "producing a 'porous' text 'full of minute fissures through which concepts seep in and leak out, impossible either to claim or entirely disclaim.'" Several years ago, Joseph Epstein in his article "Matthew Arnold and the Resistance" imagined "Matthew Arnold reeling at an MLA meeting, in his hand a program announcing one goofy paper after another, while in the room the graduate students come and go, talking of Michel Foucault." Like Dooley, Epstein nominates Arnold to stand as the leading figure in today's "resistance" against such rising systems as "structuralism, semiology, deconstructionism." Dooley votes for Arnold because of his emphasis on clarity and understanding in criticism as well as his emphasis on pleasure in reading texts. Epstein backs Arnold because of his "superior perspective and large-mindedness" that made him skeptical of systems. But if Arnold's vitality as a critic is to be sustained, he must be related more clearly than he is in this collection of essays to the modern critical approaches, especially as found in the writings of Roland Barthes, Jacques Lacan, Michel Foucault, Claude Lévi-Strauss, Jurgen Habermas, Louis Althusser, and Jacques Derrida. Indeed, just as Arnold appreciated the interrelatedness of other disciplines, so too it is important not to reject out of hand what various other disciplines—anthropology, sociology, linguistics, and philosophy—have to offer the study of literature. If the critical debate is to go on effectively, the writings of Arnold cannot serve merely as a censorious roadblock to the new critical approaches.

Before leaving the category of Arnold and criticism, however, I would remark briefly on some new signs of progressive interpretations. Based partly on reader-response criticism and on the social-historical criticism of Raymond Williams, John P. Farrell's essay speculates on Arnold's effects on audiences and readers. Surely, Farrell's distinction between direct practical and political action versus spiritual action or the telling upon people's minds is of great assistance in expanding our understanding of the nature of Arnold's influence. By drawing on Durkheim's writings on the problem of consciousness and modern techniques of discourse analysis, Farrell reminds us of the value of looking to related disciplines for a fuller appreciation of how Arnold's prose works upon audiences. In a similar spirit of progressive compromise, Patrick Brantlinger's recent essay "Raymond Williams: From 'Culture' to 'Community'" [*Postscript* (1986)] calls for a process of communication that will avoid the extremes of authoritarian narrowness and cultural relativism and move toward an ideal of democratic community. He sees both drawbacks and possibilities in Arnold's outlook, but at least he attempts to relate him to such figures as Habermas and Lévi-Strauss.

Three essays in this collection deal with Arnold and America and extend our knowledge beyond Chapter 17, "Invasions of the United States," in Park Honan's biography. What intrigues me about the findings of Laurence Mazzeno and Allan Lefcowitz is not just the question of who influenced whom but the suggestion of negative influence. When assessing Arnold's influence, we tend to view it as a positive force. But the two Naval Academy professors are speculating on patterns of negative influence: first, that Bryce's influence on Arnold on the topic of winning over Britons for America for political reasons may have been largely negative, and second, whether in *The American Commonwealth* the inspiration Bryce draws from Arnold is negative. I would add one more suggestion of negative influence: the idea that the promotion of Anglo-American friendship itself in the late nineteenth and early twentieth centuries was a bad idea. For as the social critic John A. Hobson has argued in two overlooked books—*The Psychology of Jingoism* (1901) and *Imperialism: A Study* (1902)—between the years 1885 and 1900, England was being led down the self-destructive path of expansive militarism and imperialism. Mary G. McBride's essay examines Andrew Carnegie, one of nineteenth-century America's industrial capitalists who has approached sainthood because of his generosity and humanity. Fortunately, McBride is fully aware of the "ironies and strange anomalies" inherent in the American Arnoldian tradition. It seems almost an axiom of American history that the money temple and the cultural storehouse are separate and distinct edifices. A symbolic and revealing moment in McBride's discussion is when Carnegie suggests but Arnold refuses to visit the "pig-sticking" scene of the Chicago stockyard. Yet in our own times this separation of industry and culture may be changing: in recent reports on industry relocations, companies often consider both hard economic realities and the nature of a city's "quality of life"—including art museums, concert halls, libraries, and educational facilities. The third essay, by Sidney Coulling, provides us with a valuable and expansive treatment of Arnold and the American South. Here I have only two minor questions to raise. First, although Coulling is reluctant to question Arnold's sincerity in his praise of his southern hosts, I wonder after reading Park Honan's chapter and Farrell's essay on "performative directions" whether Arnold did not sometimes resort to "a little rhetorical excess" in his assessments of various North American stops. After all, besides designating Virginia "the most beautiful state," he also said: "Nowhere did I meet more charming people than in Chicago. I liked Milwaukee and St. Louis better as cities, but I prefer Philadelphia to any American city." And later, "Quebec is the most interesting thing by much that I have seen on this Continent." Second, should we not pay a little more attention to the incident that Honan's chapter mentions whereby Arnold to the dismay of his southern hosts, General and Mrs. Anderson, "asked to see an

all-black school, where he was astonished by 'the line of de-
marcation between the white and the negro in the south
still'"? Coulling's portrait of the "melancholy" Arnold accu-
rately captures a dimension of his personality. R. H. Super's
essay on Arnold's comic side, however, offers balancing evidence for seeing another facet of his complex and lively personality.

My final category, Arnold and education, is one that was
much discussed in the 1940s and 1950s but needs more systematic reevaluation in our times. W. F. Connell's comprehen-
sive study *The Educational Thought and Influence of Matthew
Arnold* appeared in 1950. But before that book, other critics
rendered sometimes contradictory assessments. For example,
in 1934, Everett L. Hunt concluded, "With increased specialization and the disappearance of the general reader, Arnold has
lost his audience. Today he is reduced to the inglorious level of
introducing college freshmen to culture." Of Arnold's influence, Lionel Trilling wrote in 1940 that he "may even be said
to have established the teaching of English as an academic profession." Several essays from this symposium collection begin a
new process of reevaluation of Arnold's influence on education. In comparing Arnold's thoughts on private and public notions of self-development in the 1850s and 1860s, DeLaura
argues that Arnold in an educational context arrived at a more
tamed and public ideal of development. Dooley's essay also
touches upon educational issues. In fact, his was one of the
few papers delivered at the Texas A&M conference that specifically discussed Arnoldian studies in relation to both undergraduate and graduate students. Although he stresses the
Arnoldian principle that the aim and purpose of literature is
the pleasure of the reader, do we not in fact—in our day-to-
day movement from study to classroom—tend to enforce a different dichotomy? As one of my colleagues once put it, in our
study of literature, aren't we all closet Paterians and classroom
Arnoldians? Isn't the received assumption that on campus the
Arnoldian outlook on literature is essentially critical and not
pleasurable? Leonard Orr and Saundra Segan Wheeler credit
Arnold with fostering the "unfashionable" study of ethnic
studies as well as creative expression in various young writers.

All of these essays are part of a new awareness of the relevance of Arnold's experiences as school inspector to current issues in contemporary education, especially in America. Several recent articles could also be mentioned: Patrick G. Scott's "Matthew Arnold and Minimum Competency: The British Experience with Basic Skills Assessment" (*Carolina English Teacher* [1983]), Myron C. Tuman's "Matthew Arnold and Minimal Competency Testing" (*Journal of General Education* [1979]), Mary J. Black's "Matthew Arnold and Proficiency Testing" (*English Journal* [1982]), and William V. Spanos's "The End of Education: 'The Harvard Core Curriculum Report' and the Pedagogy of Reformation" (*Boundary 2* [1982]). It seems that two publications are now called for in this area: a reprinting of Arnold's annual reports to the Privy Council and a collection of essays on Arnold and modern educational issues. Surely part of any such current discussion should focus on one area of the modern American cultural scene in which Arnold's influence appears to be very extensive because of the indomitable presence of William J. Bennett—the National Endowment for the Humanities (NEH) and the Department of Education.

A few observations should be made concerning how Matthew Arnold's importance continues to live in the popular media and federal agencies of twentieth-century America. In November 1984, William J. Bennett, then director of NEH, issued a forty-two-page report entitled *To Reclaim a Legacy*. My attention was first directed to this report because a front-page story in our local paper gave it some attention. At the conclusion of the article stood Matthew Arnold's famous definition of culture, although to be precise, the phrase had been rewritten. The report states: "But to define the humanities by itemizing the academic fields they embrace is to overlook the qualities that make them uniquely important and worth studying. Expanding on a phrase from Matthew Arnold, I would describe the humanities as the best that has been said, thought, written, and otherwise expressed about the human experience." It is no surprise that critics of this conservative report have lamented that Arnold's past-tense verbs have been exactly doubled. Why is it that the Arnoldian critical tradition seems to be constantly linked with an attitude of hostility toward such intellectual disciplines as science and the social sciences and toward such phenomena as mass literacy, advertising, and popular culture? And so the debate goes on in a lively fashion. In a provocative opinion-page essay, Norman Birnbaum (*Chronicle of Higher Education,* January 9, 1985) regrets that Bennett narrows his criticism of American higher education to the point that it excludes more of the subject than it includes. Some feel that to haul Arnold and his narrow views into the fray today is almost comical. But there are other critics on the cultural scene who find potent ammunition in Arnold's writings to fire at those commentators who err in swinging too far to the opposite extreme of cultural or social "relevance." If the status quo is to be attacked in the original spirit of Arnold's writings, then Bennett can be viewed as a new Arnold on the landscape of American education. To defend the status quo—so the argument goes— is to exclude iconoclasm in defense of mediocrity, which is always allied with faddism. Against such an outlook, Bennett's criticisms may have been justified, healthy, and in every way enlivening for education in America.

For a final glimpse into the crystal ball, we might reflect for a moment upon what categories of Arnold's career are not developed in any significant detail in this collection: Arnold and women, Arnold and political/social reform, Arnold and romanticism, Arnold and the classics, Arnold and science, and Arnold's relationship to various modern critics such as Derrida, Lacan, and Foucault. (The link to Foucault, with his perennial concern with relationships between the life of the individual and the power of social institutions, might be an especially worthwhile area of investigation.) Some of these topics have been discussed elsewhere. Perhaps the broadest area that needs to be worked out, however, is the category of Arnold and women. Several of the present essays do touch on this topic: specifically, the influence on creativity by women close to or familiar with Arnold and his works is discussed in the essays by Honan and Wheeler. But there remains the feeling that Nina Auerbach is correct when she writes in *Woman and the Demon: The Life of a Victorian Myth* (1982) that "the most authoritative studies of Victorian England agree [she lists works by Walter E.

Houghton, David J. DeLaura, and Steven Marcus] that the age was pervaded by a buried angst stemming from a manifold spiritual crisis. These students of troubled Victorians relate this atmosphere of impending crisis only superficially to women, if they speak of women at all."

The many dimensions of Arnold's influence and importance both in his time and ours are revealed in this collection of essays. That other areas should also be explored is a testament to his vitality. Part of his legacy is recorded and debated in these essays; we are all enriched by the insights and discoveries worked out at the Texas A&M University symposium.

CONTRIBUTORS

INDEX

Contributors

RUTH apROBERTS is Professor of English and Department Chair at the University of California at Riverside. She has published the books *The Moral Trollope* (1971) and *Arnold and God* (1984), as well as articles on aesthetics, Jane Austen, Flann O'Brien, and the English Bible. She is now writing a book on Carlyle.

SIDNEY COULLING is S. Blount Mason, Jr., Professor of English at Washington and Lee University. He holds an undergraduate degree from Washington and Lee and graduate degrees from the University of North Carolina at Chapel Hill and is the author of *Matthew Arnold and His Critics* as well as various reviews and articles on Victorian literature.

DAVID J. DeLAURA is Avalon Foundation Professor in the Humanities, Professor of English, and Chairman of the Department of English at the University of Pennsylvania. He is the author of *Hebrew and Hellene in Victorian England: Newman, Arnold, and Pater* (1969) and editor of *Victorian Prose: A Guide to Research* (1973). He has published articles on a wide range of nineteenth- and early twentieth-century authors. He is currently working on the influence of German literature, and especially Goethe, on Victorian England.

ALLAN C. DOOLEY is Associate Professor of English at Kent State University. He is Executive Editor of *The Complete Works of Robert Browning,* for which he is editing *Men and Women* and other works. His articles on Browning, Arnold, and nineteenth-century textual problems have appeared in various journals. He is currently writing a book on nineteenth-century printing technology and its impact on authorship.

JOHN P. FARRELL, Professor of English at the University of Texas at

Austin, has written a number of essays on Arnold and is the author of *Revolution as Tragedy: The Dilemma of the Moderate from Scott to Arnold* (1980). He is coediting with Jerold Savory a special double issue of *Victorian Poetry* for the Arnold centenary.

PARK HONAN, who holds the Chair of English and American Literature at the University of Leeds, is coauthor with William Irvine of *The Book, the Ring, and the Poet: A Biography of Robert Browning* (1974) and author of the first detailed biography of Arnold, *Matthew Arnold: A Life,* published by McGraw-Hill and by Weidenfeld in 1981 and by Harvard University Press in 1983. For a number of years he has also carried out research on Jane Austen.

ALLAN B. LEFCOWITZ is Professor of English, U.S. Naval Academy. Author of *The Writer's Handbook* and numerous articles on British and American literature, he is Advisory Editor of *The Arnoldian* and Executive Director of the Writer's Center, a Washington, D.C., organization for the creative arts.

JAMES C. LIVINGSTON is Walter G. Mason Professor of Religion at the College of William and Mary, where he was founding chairman of the Department of Religion in 1968. Livingston is author or editor of six books, including *Modern Christian Thought, The Ethics of Belief,* and *Matthew Arnold and Christianity* (1986). He has held fellowships from the American Council of Learned Societies, the National Endowment for the Humanities, and Clare Hall, Cambridge University.

LAURENCE W. MAZZENO is Chairman of the English Department, U.S. Naval Academy. He has published essays and reviews on British and American authors and is Managing Editor of *The Arnoldian.* He is currently working on a new concordance to Tennyson's poetry.

MARY GORTON McBRIDE is Professor of English and Dean of the College of Liberal Arts at Louisiana State University in Shreveport. She teaches courses in nineteenth-century prose and poetry, the novel, and autobiography. McBride serves as chairman of the Louisiana Endowment for the Humanities. She has recently explored Matthew Arnold's relationship with Louisiana Senator Randall Lee Gibson, one of the founders of Tulane University.

PATRICK McCARTHY, Professor of English at the University of California, Santa Barbara, is the author of *Matthew Arnold and the Three*

Classes (1964) and has written several biographical and critical essays on the poet. He has also published essays and reviews on a range of other Victorian writers, most recently Dickens, on whom he is writing a book-length study.

LEONARD ORR teaches Anglo-Irish literature, history of criticism, and critical theory and methods at the University of Notre Dame. He has edited *De-Structing the Novel: Essays in Applied Postmodern Hermeneutics* (1982); his *Semiotic and Structuralist Analyses of Fiction* was published in 1987. Currently he is completing a dictionary and a handbook of critical theory.

LINDA RAY PRATT is Professor of English at the University of Nebraska–Lincoln, where she teaches Victorian and modern poetry. Her previous work on Arnold includes "Callicles on Etna: The Other Mask," *Victorian Poetry* (Winter 1969) [as Linda Lee Ray]. In recent years her publications include essays on Tennyson, Eliot, Yeats, Frost, and Williams.

R. H. SUPER has edited Arnold's *Complete Prose Works*, has written *The Time-Spirit of Matthew Arnold*, an essay in criticism, and is coeditor (with Miriam Allott) of the *Oxford Arnold*. He is author of a biography of Walter Savage Landor and of an account of Anthony Trollope's career in the British Post Office. He is now completing a life of Trollope.

WILLIAM B. THESING is Associate Chairman and Associate Professor of English at the University of South Carolina in Columbia. He is the author of *The London Muse: Victorian Poetic Responses to the City* (1982), coauthor of *English Prose and Criticism, 1900–1950* (1983), and coauthor of *Conversations with South Carolina Poets* (1986), editor of *Victorian Prose Writers before 1867* (1987), and editor of *Victorian Prose Writers after 1867* (1987). He has published articles on Victorian figures, from Gerard Manley Hopkins to Mrs. Humphry Ward, in several journals. For the past several years, he has written the annual review essay of Matthew Arnold scholarship for *Victorian Poetry.*

SAUNDRA SEGAN WHEELER teaches British literature at Yeshiva University. She is currently at work on two Arnold projects, one of which is a book based on her dissertation, "Matthew Arnold and the Young Writer." She has presented several papers on Arnold's poetry over the last few years.

Index